CW01304623

Copyright © 2018, 2019 by Björn Staschen & Wytse Vellinga
All rights reserved. This book or any portion thereof
may not be reproduced or used in any manner whatsoever
without the express written permission of the publisher
except for the use of brief quotations in a book review.

Printed in Europe.

Second Printing, April 2018

ISBN 9781980620518

www.mobile-storytelling.com

Mobile Storytelling

A journalist´s guide to the smartphone galaxy

written by

Björn Staschen

& Wytse Vellinga

translated from the German textbook

"Mobiler Journalismus" by

Tina Busch

3rd revised and updated edition January 2019

A note before you start

While reading this book, you will find that several paragraphs are written from a personal perspective, indicated by "I" or "my view". The context might explain whether it is Wytse or Björn (see "The Authors" at the back of the book) who is writing – especially, if Dutch or German examples are mentioned. We decided not to use "we" throughout the book as this would have generalized personal experiences and views.

We have tried to make this book as up-to-date as possible. We revised every text translated from the German edition (which was published in 2017), we have have changed pictures and graphics. But the development of mobile journalism gear and software is happening at such a pace that some information might already be out of date. We apologize for this – and we are happy if you tell us about things that have moved forward that we did not notice: bjoern@bjoernsta.de.

Introduction by Glen Mulcahy: "We are all storytellers"

The very first experiment I did with a "smartphone" was in 2007. Nokia had just released the Nokia N93i and it looked like a miniature palmcorder with flip out screen and a tiny Zeiss Lens. I was working in the Irish language news service of RTÉ at the time and my role encompassed managing the technical and people resources in production.

I commissioned one of our camera crews, Cyril O'Regan, to shoot a news story with the N93i and to explore the feasibility of importing the content into our field editing solution Avid Media Composer. The video size was 640x480 and the file type was 3gp / H263 but it was a codec that was not widely supported at the time and as a result the import into Avid took several hours to transcode and the results were…. let's just say underwhelming.

Around the same time I came across a clip online of Ilicco Elia from Reuters speaking at a session at the Frontline Club in London where he was showing the Nokia N95 together with a solar charger and a "hacked" microphone that Reuters had issued to the regional bureaus to facilitate content for online. Instinctively I knew that the mobile data network of the time GPRS / WAP would take time to develop proper support for video but the addition of Wi-Fi connectivity was the breakthrough. Later that same year Steve Jobs introduced the iPhone and the rest, as they say, is history.

In the decade since then I have witnessed the exponential technological evolution of smartphones. Along the way I have been very fortunate to have had the opportunity to research, develop training courses, share my knowledge with people all over the world and to realise my aim of bringing the growing community of mobile content creators together at an annual conference.

Though the ten years have been remarkable from a technology perspective, it is only when you consider how user habits have shifted toward mobile that you truly appreciate what a monumental shift mobile has become. However, what lies ahead is going to increase the dependence and the ubiquity of smartphones in our daily lives…

At the premium end of the smartphone market, where most professional mobile journalists and content creators operate, we are entering a new phase in the evolution of the smartphone. The imminent arrival of the fifth generation of mobile network (5G) brings with it a massive jump in data throughput rates in the range of 10x - 100x greater speed, substantial reduction in latency and also the ability to have dedicated slicing of the network spectrum to enable Quality of Service for specific applications/users.

In the last three years many of the top end premium handset manufacturers have introduced 4k / UHD video recording in their devices. The top of the range smartphones are now capable of shooting 4K/UHD content at 100Mbps, editing the content on the device in full resolution and sharing that content to 4K ready platforms like YouTube and Vimeo. While many broadcasters shun 4K, mainly I believe due to the phenomenal full-system upgrade costs it would incur, the mobile ecosystem has, in effect, leapfrogged the traditional broadcasters and become a complete production and distribution platform in its own right.

The key thing to remember here is that mobile is non-linear and mainly on demand content. Your smartphone also facilitates an immense collection of user information about you, from your location data, browser history, contact and social media profiles and if you wear a paired wearable device like Apple Watch, a huge store of biometric and health data. The time will come, it is arguably already upon us, when your personal data profile, your social profile and all the other key metrics will be used to create hyper personalised content recommendations for you. Facebook, Twitter, Amazon and Google are already leveraging the user data they have on you to deliver tailored results and recommendations but as the data trove expands it is inevitable that your "digital footprint" will lead to profiled content.

The thing is, TV broadcast is a massive hosepipe of general linear content which can be consumed in real-time as broadcast or (mostly) be consumed post broadcast via catch-up services. It is built on the principle of scarcity and premium quality. It costs thousands if not hundreds of thousands to create an hour of broadcast content. Mobile on the other hand is the absolute opposite. It is built on ubiquity and a full range of quality from appalling to exceptional. Note, the quality is not generally dictated by the technology but by the users / creators' skill base and it is here that the mobile journalist has the opportunity to thrive.

We are all storytellers. The desire to share stories is ingrained in our DNA. That said, our storytelling traditions have evolved over time. In the beginning it was visual and verbal. We either drew pictures in caves or on canvas and/or sat around camp fires and listened to stories from tribal elders and bards.

For millennia the written word was the preserve of the scholars and the wealthy. Gutenberg's printing press democratised the technical process of creating and distributing the "written word" but it took centuries to reach the point of ubiquity where any voice could be heard.

Photography is nearly two centuries old (Louis-Jacques-Mandé Daguerre 1839), Cinema is a century and a quarter (William K.L. Dickson 1888) and Television is just shy of a century old (John Logie Baird 1925) – each of these media forms took decades to reach any level of ubiquity. Smartphones have taken ONE decade and they are on track to be the most pervasive form of communication ever invented.

With a connected audience in the billions, it is inevitable that communities and groups will begin to cluster around common ground. In the recent past Wikis, blogs and podcasts have all served those niche audiences' appetite for relevant content. Now mobile will serve those demands in the visual media of the day: video, virtual reality, augmented reality. The smartphone is the gateway and conduit to all of these new platforms. The audience has the devices, billions of them. The role of the mobile journalist going forward is not to comply with the demands of the "churnalism" of TV news but to find a passion, give it a voice and a visual presence and find or build a community to serve. As personalisation grows the smartphone will drive the rainbow coloured spectrum of diverse content to serve niche audiences and to give a voice to the voiceless.

***Glen Mulcahy** has inspired and championed the growth of mobile journalism and more recently 360 across the globe. A former Head of Innovation with RTÉ, Ireland's national public broadcaster, he also founded Mojocon - the 1st international mobile journalism conference which was held on an annual basis from 2015-2017.*

Glen has trained in excess of 1500 journalists in Europe, the Middle East and the U.S., across television, radio, print and online and his specialities are Mobile Journalism, Video Journalism, DSLR FilmMaking and Photography. He is at the forefront of engaging with new technologies and working up solutions for how such technologies can transform the way traditional media organisations work. Glen's currently working on 360 degree immersive storytelling and 360 Degree Drone Cinematography.

He is the founder of Titanium-Media, a media training and consultancy company.

What´s in the book?

Mobile Storytelling..3
    Introduction by Glen Mulcahy: "We are all storytellers"..5

1 Mobile Storytelling: An Overview..11
    1.1. What is "Mobile Journalism"?..12
    1.2. The pros and cons of "smartphone reporting"..16
    1.3. Mobile reporting and news consumption...19
    1.4 Do we get rid of our fellow colleagues?...23
    1.5 Do we eliminate ourselves?..24
    1.6 Mobile journalism gives new freedom of expression..26
    Interview with Philip Bromwell: "Storytelling is no longer the preserve of a small number of people in newsrooms."..29

2 "News Gathering" on the move: Modern news agencies.......................................33
    2.1 Receive: Personal news feeds..37
    2.2 Receive: Real-time seismograph...39
    2.3 Receive: Crowdsourcing..40
    2.4 Send: Distribution of your own news...41
    2.5 Send: Curating news sent by others..44
    2.6 Send: Community building...46
    2.7 Verification of sources..48

3 What's in a reporter's bag? "Mobile Journalism" equipment................................53
    3.1 Networks and Connections..54
    3.2 Too many choices – which phone should you buy?...55
    3.3 External Microphones..58
    3.4 Tripods...65
    3.5 Smartphone Rigs...68
    3.6 Gimbals..70
    3.7 Add-On Lenses..73
    3.8 Light...76
    3.9 Batteries and Charging..78
    3.10 Drones...80
    3.11 Miscellaneous..82
    Interview with Marc Blank-Settle: "May I use your WiFi, please?"................................85

4 Radio broadcasting on the move..90
   4.1 A little bit of theoretical background: audio formats................................91
   4.2 Android: Recording and Editing..93
   4.3 iOs: Recording and Editing...101
   4.4 Windows: Recording and Editing..107
   4.5 Publication..111
   4.6 Live streaming and apps with an input server.......................................112
   Interview with Nicholas Garnett: "A reporter needs to be on the road."........115

5 TV on the go: Filming..121
   5.1 Fundamentals..122
   5.2 Image composition, eye line and handheld tripod.................................123
   5.3 How to divide scenes: The Five Shot Rule...127
   5.4 Video Camera Apps: Filmic Pro..132
   5.5 More Filming Apps..143
   Interview with Richard Lackey: "Nothing I am doing is rocket science. It is the combination of it all and the process which is most difficult to learn.".........153

6 TV on the move: Editing..160
   6.1 Fundamentals..160
   6.2 Editing with an iPhone..162
   6.3 Editing for iPhone and Android...173
   6.4 Editing with Android phones...174
   6.5 Editing with Windows phones...186
   Interview Mike Castellucci: Phoning it it: "Professionals still need to be able to tell a good story."..190

7 TV on the move: Live Streaming..193
   7.1 Not only an eyewitness: live streaming asks for responsibility.............195
   7.2 The legal aspects of live streaming..199
   7.3 Content-related live streaming tips and tricks..201
   7.4 It's not just the content that matters...204
   7.5 Live streaming apps: Periscope...206
   7.6 Live streaming apps: The rise and fall of Meerkat..................................209
   7.7 Live streaming apps: Facebook Live..210
   7.8 Live streaming apps: Instagram..213
   7.9 Live streaming apps: YouTube..214
   7.10 Additional live streaming apps for professional users.........................216
   7.11 Non-journalistic live streaming apps..220
   7.12 Live streaming with several image sources..222

7.13 Professional solutions with separate hardware..225
Interview with Philipp Weber: Livestreaming: "Thorough preparation is everything." 228

8 Digital Storytelling on the Move...233
    8.1 Post-processing of photos..236
    8.2 Bringing photos to life..239
    8.3 How to combine audio, image and video...243
    8.4 Snapchat..250
    8.5 Instastories..256
    8.6 Instagram TV (IGTV)...259
    8.7 Digital Storytelling Apps...259
    Interview Sumaiya Omar, Hashtag Our Stories: "Reality is the new quality."...............263

9 360 degrees – Being on the move in all directions...266
    9.1 360 Degree – With an App..269
    9.2 360 Degree – With a Camera..271
    9.3 360 Degree: Filming and Storytelling..273
    9.4 Publishing 360 Degree...276
    Interview with Martin Heller: 360 Degrees - "The viewer gets more autonomy."........279

The Authors..284

1 Mobile Storytelling: An Overview

Summary

A review of the current situation as an introduction – Who uses "mobile journalism" and how? What are the experiences, successes, and failures? Is #Mojo helpful when it comes to producing content for mobile usage on a smartphone? Is #Mojo the answer to cost reduction? How will the job profile of a journalist change?

It was a radical decision. The Swiss regional station "Léman Bleu" based in Geneva changed to smartphone-only production in the summer of 2015. All reporters received iPhones and reporter kits. This is how Editor-in-chief Laurent Keller explained the step in a newspaper interview with "Le Temps": "We have started to look for more ease and a faster way to respond. But it's also obvious that this is a way of reducing the costs of news programs."

"Live in 90 seconds" – almost equally extreme is the news philosophy of the British TV station "SkyNews": 90 seconds after a reporter arrives at the location of an event, he is supposed to be live on air. Apart from figuring out how to gather all necessary information needed for his live broadcast in such a short period of time, it's also a technical challenge. At SkyNews (as well as at a few other stations) iPhones have been the solution for a couple of years: the reporters use a special app that bundles several channels of live broadcastings (see chapter 7.1.1.). They also set up their equipment themselves, as did, for example, the Sky reporter Harriet Hadfield during the hijacking of a plane at the airport in Geneva (fig. 01-01).

Figure 01-01 "Live in 90 seconds": for years SkyNews has been broadcasting with iPhones. Harriet Hadfield has been pioneering in this field.

More ease, a faster ability to respond and the potential for cost reduction– are these the main arguments for "Mobile Journalism"? In recent decades a key characteristic of video journalism has been that its production was extremely cost- and time-consuming. Video and television were generally not a one-man or one-woman-show (at least until the first VJs started doing their job). In addition, technology was expensive and a real investment – even for VJs. Only a few freelance journalists could afford to buy their own personal equipment. Video production was (almost) always organized as a work sharing project.

A paradigm shift has started with smartphones becoming increasingly powerful and phone cameras that are always improving,: some phones already film in 4K resolution while the majority of TV stations still produce with a resolution of 1920 x 1080 pixels (or even less). Television technology is becoming affordable and controllable. The multitude of experts sharing their work (camera, sound, edit, reporter) is going to be replaced – at least within news journalism – by smaller teams that are mobile, can work on location and are proficient in each step of the production process. This won't affect every single topic or context, but it's going to happen more frequently.

1.1. What is "Mobile Journalism"?

The term "Mobile Journalism" goes back to #MoJo founding fathers such as the Australian journalist Ivo Burum (see 1.6.), author of the book "The Mobile Journalism

Handbook", or Glen B. Mulcahy. Glen has been working at the Irish public station RTÉ as a technology innovator and who founded the "Mobile Journalism Conference" in Dublin in 2015. For years Mulcahy has been training journalists in the context of the European Association of Public Service "Circom" and has pioneered in this area. The expression "Mobile Journalism", however, is somehow misleading: it goes without saying that all journalists are mobile. Quality and committed journalism have always been "mobile" according to the international use of the professional term. Journalistic work means to directly follow an event on location after thorough research, to move with the event and to stay "mobile". However, video and TV journalists in particular often reach their limits within the traditional production process.

If someone plans to follow a long protest march and also wants to report at the same time – may it be live or with edited reports – he is dealing with big logistic challenges: where can we position the OB van for the live broadcast when the protest march is moving? An OB van cannot transmit anything while it is moving since its satellite dish needs to be precisely angled. And this stands in opposition to work safety and traffic regulations. It gets even more complicated: where and, more importantly when can a reporter edit his report for the hourly newscast when a protest march is still moving? The answer is often a complex, expensive logistic process of producers, messengers, camera and editing positions. And since current events tend to go off script, the result is often unsatisfactory because in the end a reporter will still be in the wrong place at the wrong time.

First and foremost "mobile journalism" is "mobile reporting" and as such it applies to the entire production process. Up until now journalists usually had to go "back to base", i.e. back to the newsroom or the OB van to produce content. In "mobile reporting" they carry the production equipment themselves and work on the go. This makes a new form of mobility and new forms of content possible. The NDR has not yet changed its production process for linear television (as per autumn 2016) – in contrast to Léman Bleu in Switzerland. Yet we have already made positive experiences with multimedia projects for which we relied on "mobile reporting".

An example is the "#politag" project (fig. 01-02): six teams of reporters, made up of two colleagues each, followed six politicians for a whole day and reported about their daily work routines before a city parliament meeting that generally takes place in the late afternoon and evening hours – an "after work parliament". It was the reporters' assignment to produce several TV reports on the move and to also use social media, mainly Twitter, Periscope, and Snapchat.

This was an assignment that could not have been managed with traditional means of production: on the one hand the implementation would have become astronomically expensive. On the other hand it could not have been solved logistically: six reporter teams who are on the move in the city, edit reports, do voice-overs and also report live while the protagonists who they follow are already on their way to their next appointment. What could have been the location of the OB van, mobile edit car etc.? The decision to produce with smartphones only was therefore the only one possible. In other words: it would not have been possible to realize this project if we had not been able to film with smartphones.

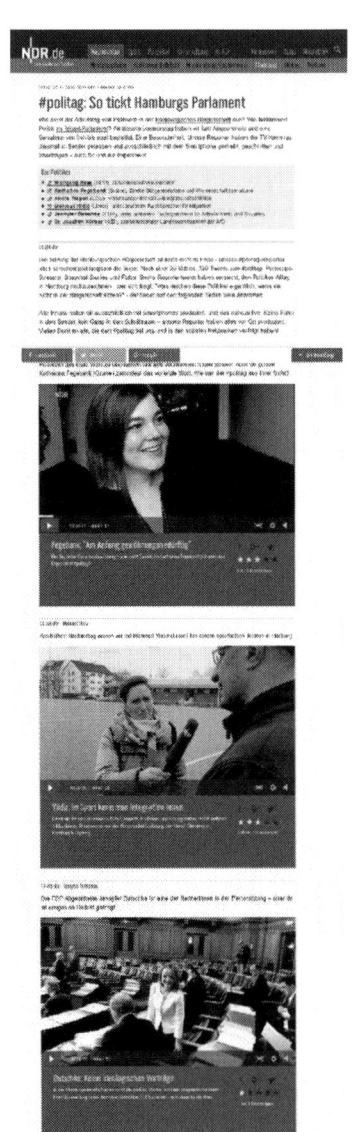

The result tells its own tale: we produced more than 20 video reports, each report was about one to two minutes long. The quality was mostly good enough for airing on linear TV. In addition, we produced several live streams on Periscope and we were also a "trending topic" on Twitter Germany all day – whereas the latter might just be an indication of how small the world of Twitter still is.

The "behind the scenes" learnings are of equal importance: for half a day we taught the basics of "mobile reporting" on an iPhone to twelve editorial and technical colleagues with a background in television. This shows that the basic technological skills can be mastered in a short time period. Due to the low technical hurdle it should be discussed whether mobile reporting training with a smartphone shouldn't be the first step in the camera training of video journalists. Even if smaller VJ-cameras were used, the hurdles would still be incomparably higher.

More insights: during this project we did not only include colleagues working in the TV newsroom but also camera people, members of the OB technical department, entertainment editors as well as a radio journalist. Since job profiles are changing and "mobile reporting" is seen as a piece of the media change puzzle, it is my opinion that future changes, opportunities and risks need to be tested and experienced in a collaborative environment.

Figure 01-02: NDR´s project "#politag", a liveblog focussing on regional politican´s everyday work.

Lowering the cost of production might also be an issue – though this mainly refers to lower hardware expenses. I don't think that the same news content that was produced by a three-man-team can now be expected of smartphone reporters who are working on their own. This is why we worked in duos at the "#politag" whose members frequently took turns with regard to their activities: while one of them was shooting new content, the other one edited footage of the preceding event. It is important to understand and make use of these opportunities of "mobile reportings" to produce different and new content.

"Mobile reporting" is an extension of journalistic possibilities: for me this conclusion lies at the heart of the development and this is what drives my interest. I can't deny that I'm also interested in the technical details. The main advantage though is the content-related opportunities in news journalism. I worked as a radio journalist myself for several years. Since I started working in television, I've envied my radio colleagues for their flexibility to report on location and for the minimal technical effort. If worse came to worse all that would be necessary was to reach for the phone and go "live on air". "Mobile Reporting" with a smartphone now enables television reporters to do almost the same thing. They don't need much more than a smartphone and a few accessories (see chapter 3) to report an event. And a reporter can stay much longer on location if he is producing with a smartphone on the go. People who used to be in radio and are now active as MoJos for video find that their workflow actually is very similar. They don't feel limited by their equipment in the same way they did when they had to do video work with a cameraman or as a VJ.

It is not an "either / or" question: we are not going to sell all existing cameras and we won't film with smartphones only. It's a question of how to integrate these new means of production into our production processes and to identify their usefulness. It might be worthwhile, for example, to use the smartphone in a traditional shoot as a "secondary camera" – for a wide shot with a bird's eyes perspective or a time-lapse recording. And if a reporter and his team produce a report for the daily evening news, he will now be able to use his smartphone to deliver photo material that can be used on the website or Facebook.

Up until now online colleagues were the ones that usually had to wait; reports could only be published online after they had been broadcast on linear TV. As bad as it may sound: even though many newsrooms have declared "online first" as their strategy, our production processes are often still designed for having content ready for a specific air date on linear TV. Thus, the smartphone may also help to publish material online right after it was taken on location – in a secondary, parallel production process that complements the traditional one: this may be an additional sound bite that adds to a previously recorded TV interview, a short piece to camera by the reporter that explains the situation on location, or an additional interview with the protagonist that is streamed live.

Another example of MoJo reporting is Omrop Fryslân's coverage of the general elections for the Dutch parliament in 2017. It used to be pretty hard to get voters of the Freedom Party (PVV) to talk about their political beliefs in front of the camera. They mistrusted the journalists because they saw them as 'part of the system'. The idea was to try and get them to talk to us, to be more low-profile and more casual in our way to approach these voters. We just went out into the streets as a 'one-man-show and without doing any research beforehand. We randomly spoke to people and because all we carried was a small bag and a phone, it was easier to talk to people.

After first talking to the people without the camera, we then could convince them to talk to us 'on the record'. By doing this we made about 50 small TV segments of about one minute. In these segments a voter would talk about what he or she thought about current politics and the future of the country. It was used in the news programmes on TV as well as online. A three minutes version of the same conversation was used for radio. The people that were interviewed told us that they found it easier to talk to us because we used the mobile phone. We were less intimidating because we did not bring a big camera but used technology that was familiar to them.

A single reporter could go out with his mobile phone and produce three of these multimedia stories in one day without any help of an editor, cameraman or researcher. We could not have done that with any other technology but MoJo.

1.2. The pros and cons of "smartphone reporting"

When we talk about "mobile reporting", colleagues sometimes make fun of us. In their eyes we are just some guys who go on and on about future production processes that they don't really believe in. That's why we've started to talk about how we actually produced a specific report only after it had been aired. Our explanation always comes as a surprise and often leads to astonishment – the quality of the images and editing differ from the traditional production process, and a camera person or an editor can easily identify these differences right away. But they usually don't see any significant differences that may prevent the report from being aired.

1 Mobile Storytelling: An Overview

What would have happened if Steve Jobs had launched his iPhone and had not defined it as a product for the masses but as a highly specialized hybrid product for image, sound and broadcast that only camera people were allowed to use? A hypothetical question, for sure, that still contributes a little bit to this explanation: many smartphones have hidden talents. The most obvious features are often easily missed: a TV camera records images. The most recent models are able to transfer them via Wi-Fi or via LTE with additional equipment – but even this is not the norm. A smartphone, however, can record images, and at the same time it functions as a computer that allows me to edit them. It also functions as a radio tower that enables me to transfer them. It even allows us to have direct contact with our audiences while we are in the field.

The smartphone works like a Swiss Army knife: this metaphor was once put forward by Mark Egan, a British #MoJo-trainer and reporter, and, in my opinion, it hits the nail on the head. It's not the best tool for every use, but it is the best combination of tools for journalism in the digital age.

Images taken by a smartphone have a wide angle due to camera specifications. They have a wider angle than images taken with many VJ or photo cameras which has two consequences: one the one hand it is difficult to shoot press conferences, statements of politicians that draw a big crowd or football games because the smartphone should be positioned as close as possible to the protagonist. This is often impossible when, for example, camera teams get assigned to stand in the far back of a room. Additionally, smartphones have bigger problems when dealing with challenging light situations – whether it´s darkness or considerable differences between glaring light and shadows. This applies to both the smartphone camera itself as well as its display: it is difficult to adjust image composition and setting on the display in extreme light situations.

Figure 01-03, 04 iPhone material in a Tagesthemen report.

17

On the other hand, smartphones have a big advantage: they are already part of daily life. Many people talk on their phones; they take selfies and make videos of themselves, their friends and family members. And this is what they do for journalists, too: the phone is a device that follows and records people. This moves a big obstacle out of the way – an experience shared by many #MoJo-journalists. A smartphone reporter may get much closer to a "normal" person who lacks media experience because he intimidates his counterpart much less than a large camera team. Sometimes it even inspires your interviewee to try for themselves. When the Minister of the Interior of The Netherlands was interviewed for TV with an iPhone, he grabbed his notebook and started asking questions about the tech. "Which app are you using? What kind of tripod is that?"

Reporters can also use the smartphone to their advantage in difficult filming situations: when for example the Department of the Interior in Hamburg permanently banned filming in the reception centres for refugees, we decided that the public interest in the coverage was more important, especially after an outbreak of scabies had occurred in several centres. This is why we filmed with an iPhone when we visited refugees on location (fig. 01-03) – only after consulting the legal department of the NDR, of course.

Figure 01-04 A live-stream from the European Football Championship in France by BBC reporter Nick Garnett.

A smartphone reporter attracts less attention: he delivers images in best television quality, but often looks more like a tourist, a curious onlooker or visitor. When the BBC reporter Nick Garnett (see the interview after chapter 4) reported on the fan riots in Lille during the 2016 European Football Championship in France, his mobile, almost invisible equipment was a big help. This is what he later wrote on Facebook:

> *"Sums up mojo for me – I was able to get really close to what was happening (so close we got hit by the shockwaves of some of the CS canisters exploding) and yet – to all intents and purposes – I looked like everyone else with a mobile phone. Camera crews were set upon and attacked, reporters punched, equipment wrecked." (fig. 01-04)*

A smartphone reporter doesn't get recognized right away. This has other consequences, too, as, for example, with regard to his personal safety. When members of the police need to distinguish between demonstrators and journalists during demonstrations, the advantage may quickly turn into a disadvantage. A smartphone reporter needs to be aware of privacy and copyright issues that apply to people that he films. In contrast to a big camera team he might not get recognized while filming. So he should never ever assume that the people who he films "implicitly agree" to being recorded.

The smartphone is small and handy: in comparison to bigger cameras it invites filming from different perspectives. It may be placed in containers that can be filled. Smartphones may be positioned on shelves or they can surprise with an unusual perspective if a magnetic tripod is used – the sky is the limit. Nevertheless, the smartphone is still only a mass product: battery life and storage space are limited. Limits that a conventional camera team that usually has numerous batteries and empty storage devices available in the OB van does not have to deal with. But smartphone technology is constantly improving which also means that battery life is being extended and storage space even more so.

1.3. Mobile reporting and news consumption

"Mobile reporting" doesn't take place in a vacuum: #MoJo is not just an additional means of production that enters a market that isn't about to change in any other aspect. On the contrary: the media market is experiencing a radical change process – a process that might have similar consequences as the invention of the printing press. It would be easy to write an entire book about it: news will no longer be distributed by using traditional infrastructure (radio tower, cable, satellite) but via IP protocols ("IP news"). Networks are owned by commercial corporations, and the biggest platforms of distribution (such as Twitter, Instagram, Google or Facebook) are also (US) corporations. They follow (almost) exclusively economical laws and widely withdraw themselves from traditional and established media regulators, such as the broadcasting board or state media authorities. Will these corporations always offer open access to their platforms? Won't they discriminate content at some point? It seems to be fair to say that doubts are justified.

IP-News also means: it is now possible to produce news from a pop-up-office within a few hours. This has an effect on the content as well. At times images might get to the newsroom and to the audience before the actual facts do. Well-established standards, the organisation of editorial responsibility as well as operating processes in general are challenged. New news providers pop up on the market: the US-portal "Vice News", for example, recently collected 500 million Euro worth of investments to expand its services. It also offers unusual news content on the German market. What is of particular interest for this book, though, is a different perspective, namely the role of the smartphone in the hands of the consumer of content.

News consumption is becoming mobile. Current research studies prove this development though numbers deviate slightly. In a research study carried out by the Reuters Institute more than 50,000 people from 26 countries who are using online news were interviewed. More than half of the informants (53%) say they predominantly consume news on the smartphone. With 40% mobile consumption Germany is slightly lagging behind this development, but the trend is still obvious: since 2013 news consumption on mobile phones has almost doubled from 22%to 40% today. The audience does no longer wait for the evening news, but consumes news on the go: in the subway, during a meeting. News is becoming omnipresent and the need to update it constantly, even video content, is increasing. 25% of users also watch videos on a regular basis. Mark Zuckerberg, the founder of Facebook, describes video as "the new text" – in his opinion videos are going to become the driving force of social media.

This results in the following consequences: I have to admit that it annoys me that I have to turn my phone to watch videos. And this apparently applies to many other users, too. A trend report issued by the investment company Mary Meeker shows that in 2015 users in the United States spent about one third of their time using web content vertically without turning their mobile phone.

Figure 01-05 A vertical picture might tell a different story compared to its horizontal version.

There are many good arguments for horizontal videos – the most important one: the natural arrangement of our eyes. In addition, we (still) mainly produce for traditional TV – and televisions are still attached horizontally to the walls. That's just how it is. I'm pretty sure though that there are topics that are more suited to be realized vertically. The literal meanings of English expressions describing these formats are quite revealing: "Portrait" mode refers to an image that was taken vertically – does this mean that the vertical position may primarily be used to portrait people in the broadest sense? On a horizontal screen people often get lost in irrelevant surroundings. "Landscape" mode, however, refers to an image that was taken horizontally – does this mean that this format is more adequate to show the complete picture and to give an overview?

A second trend is unmistakably evolving: more and more users are turning to social media to find news. Almost half of the users (46%) use Facebook and the like as a news source. Facebook supports news and video content and its range of content is increasingly becoming broader. In contrast to that websites of news sources are becoming less important.

What does this mean for the content that we produce? What should news look like that people consume online? "Al Jazeera plus", the recent spin-off of the Arabic news channel, experimented a great deal with videos that were produced with mobile phones for mobile phone usage in the United States. AJ+, for example, extensively covered the riots in Ferguson after the death of Michael Brown in 2014. This is how AJ+-producer Shadi Rahimi summarized the principles of her job in Ferguson for a presentation given at the Mobile Journalism Conference 2015 in Dublin:

„We directly and exclusively produced for social media and an audience following us on the smartphones. We exclusively filmed and edited on iPhones. Speed was more important than quality, very dynamic. And we worked a lot with subtitles, not overvoice commentary."

A couple of her principles are mentioned again in the section on videos in social media in chapter 8.

Figure 01-06 A screenshot of AJ+ coverage during the Ferguson protests.

The Ferguson videos create a rushed atmosphere: they are very unsteady, often have a bad sound quality, are sometimes blurred, sometimes under- or overexposed. I presented these videos to a group of students in a class at the University of Hamburg and asked them for an evaluation. Their answer came as a surprise: the videos were well received, mainly because they gave the impression of being authentic. In a world in which people increasingly turn to their mobile phones to produce their own videos, viewing habits are changing. And it seems that in the field of news, too, at least in parts, viewers value videos that allow them to make their own judgement: videos that use unedited material or that only have a few comments. This goes along with the second statement made by the students: what they especially liked about the material is the absence of an "omniscient reporter" who explains everything. In short: smartphones make it possible to produce videos with minimal effort. They might work better in social media than traditional news material that was produced for linear television. But even those can be professionally produced with a smartphone.

It's not a coincidence that mobile phones are becoming more important for both news production as well as consumption. With the introduction of 5G, the mobile standard that will succeed LTE, this trend is going to gain momentum. It is worthwhile to see "mobile reporting" as an opportunity – an opportunity to produce content not only faster but that also differs from anything that we have produced before. It might be worthwhile to pay attention to the smartphone for a while and to also pay attention to news production. Both might offer pieces of wisdom regarding the type of content that works well in mobile usage.

1.4   Do we get rid of our fellow colleagues?

The debate around the consequences of "mobile journalism" eventually repeats the grim discussion that came up when the first journalists started using VJ- or SLR-cameras: many camera people were right to worry about this development – on the one hand it threatened their own workplace. On the other hand, it initially provided results that were of lesser quality. "Should we be happy now with such content?" was a question that was asked many times. "Oh, it's you again with your Mickey Mouse camera" – a comment, meant mainly jokingly, that I'm still getting today when I walk the NDR halls with my VJ-camera.

A corporation can only face these worries if it shapes the change – the keyword here is "change management". It's impossible to stop or slow down this change just because we don't like it. In 10 years we won't produce traditional TV news any longer, while everybody else is producing similar results much faster on mobile phones. This is one aspect. Another aspect, however, is equally important: we have to pay attention to not losing talent, knowledge, and skills along the way. At the NDR we are trying to include all departments and to take our colleagues along when we test "mobile journalism". On the "#politag" project day (see 1.1) both editorial as well as production staff were participating. And we are profiting from each other: the cameraman can explain to the journalist much better how he composes an image or how he deals with a difficult light situation. Likewise, the journalist can advise the cameraman on how to do an interview. For this is also going to happen: we are moving towards each other, at least within the news business. As the editorial department will have colleagues who are reaching out to technical equipment, there will be colleagues in production who will turn towards journalistic areas. In the end all job profiles are going to change.

Do we need fewer people? There will always be Directors Generals or programme managers who will answer this question in the affirmative. If production is less time- and cost-consuming and if job profiles are converging, there is also more space. We desperately need this space to further develop our content. For today we are producing many minutes of linear television with high work intensification. If we want to maintain our quality in "traditional television", but also want to play a role in social media, we need new space.

"Al Jazeera Plus", for example, produced its Ferguson reports exclusively with smartphones for smartphones. Other reporters adopted this style for the traditional TV news channel Al Jazeera. This division does certainly not have a future. I'm predicting that in the future teams of reporters (camera people, technicians) will work on the ground. They will use different platforms in close cooperation and will meet the requirements of these different playout channels. If we want to tell stories vertically on Snapchat (see chapter 8.4.), it's impossible to simultaneously produce a live stream and our own horizontal film for linear TV. Payment-related questions also need to be discussed again: it's no longer possible to reward a reporter for "a single film" that he delivers. As a "mobile reporter" he is going to deliver more than one and very different reports of a single event or topic.

The spectrum of forms and platforms will expand – and the audience will split up, too. We will have to produce more content to be able to reach the same number of viewers, listeners, or readers. This is why it would be careless to see "mobile journalism" as well as further new forms of production as a means of reducing expenses and personnel. First and foremost it is an opportunity to report differently, which opens up new possibilities and therefore requires additional resources.

1.5 Do we eliminate ourselves?

Since many smartphone producers and internet providers see video as becoming more important, cameras are always improving. But there's more: apps that allow content and video editing as well as online publishing are becoming easier to use for everyone. Smartphones are mass products, affordable for everyone. In "mobile journalism" we rely on means of production that everyone can purchase and operate. Which means that we are giving up a significant advantage: professional television (and to some extent radio) equipment was not meant for the masses. This is why television production relied on TV stations that were financed by public service funds at the beginning; commercially funded stations were added later on. Television was an investment technology. This is now history, at least in parts.

Can anyone now make television? Michael Rosenblum, one of the first teachers of the worldwide VJ-movement, agrees. He is deeply convinced that "Mojos" have not yet realized that they are the beginning of the end:

"We make it, you watch it – it's the dumbest thing you can do to believe that will work in the future."

It's Michael Rosenblum's opinion that the smartphone boom is creating a "world full of camera lenses". He made the following shout-out to the participants of the Mobile Journalism Conference in Dublin 2015: "Listen to technology – soon there will be more than 3 billion content producers."

Journalists are turning into curators. Rosenblum is convinced that the journalists' main job will mainly be restricted to curating the content of these "3 billion smartphone producers". We have our doubts: We agree with Rosenblum that the technology is going to be accessible to everyone. Journalistic skills, however, are so much more than just technology. Investigating, structuring a report, telling the "meaningful story" – this is so much more than the bare possibility of recording or streaming videos.

Competition, however, is constantly growing. Journalists are expensive; non-professionals who deliver content are cheap or completely free of charge. Internet services such as Google, Facebook or YouTube rely on curating the content of their users and making them available to others. With services such as Google's "YouTube Newswire" they even offer curated portals with videos of newsworthy events. Their content may then be licensed for further use. In this respect "mobile journalism" is of particular interest to those institutions that are yet to produce video content. The competition in the video market will grow significantly.

Many publishing houses recognize these opportunities, too: though video is important for the success of a website, its production is expensive. For the first time ever smartphones put newspaper or magazine reporters in a position to include videos without having to make a large investment. By now all bigger print media institutions in Europe produce videos, some of them with more success than others. It is noteworthy that it is the publishing houses in particular – and not the traditional providers of video content such as TV stations – that are pioneering in "mobile reporting". In this book we are going to talk about stern.de and BILD-reporters who produce successful live-streams. BILD, for example, successfully experimented with vertical video magazines. Smartphone journalism has set many things in motion – new competitors in the video market that challenge the traditional producers of video content.

1.6 Mobile journalism gives new freedom of expression

In developed countries Mojo primarily represents a new form of competition as well as an expansion of opportunities. It offers more flexibility and might be a way to cut down on expenses. In other countries though smartphone journalism might have a much higher relevance, maybe even with an explosive touch: to actively participate in transforming a country.

Let us have a look at Myanmar as an example; a country that was subject to a fascinating transformational process. After a decades-long military regime the country democratized and the power is now slowly (for some people too slowly) coming back to the people. This has an influence on the media, too. For years the public TV station MRTV was the only voice of the Burmese. Very early on media development charities such as BBC Media Action started to train journalists who independently produce radio and television in addition to public broadcasting services. The problem: in Myanmar independent journalists don't have the financial resources to purchase VJ-cameras, not to mention television technology. In 2014 the former program director of BBC Media Action in Myanmar, Clare Lyons, started a "Moeljo"-program: "Mobile Election Journalism" (fig. 01-05).

Android smartphones have been widely used in Myanmar, and they have been good enough to produce TV reports for a while now. In Myanmar "mobile journalism" enables journalists (among them are many bloggers) for the first time to be a free, independent voice that exists next to public broadcasting. I had the opportunity to work along the BBC Media Action team in Yangon for several days and to advise them on their Moeljo-project. Other #Mojos worked in African countries (Kenya) with journalists and made similar experiences: smartphone journalism makes a huge difference in these countries. It puts the theoretical freedom of expression into actual practice.

Ivo Burum, a so-called "veteran" of the #MoJo-movement, took the first steps of this media development work in Australia after working for the Australian station ABC for several years: In the project "NT Mojo" he taught "mobile journalism" to nine members of the indigenous community and gave them the opportunity to share their topics and interests with a bigger audience. Apart from that Burum educated members of minority groups in other parts of Australia and in Indonesian Timor. It was the smartphone that finally put the participants of his projects in the position to report with images and sound. His #MoJo-projects are not only aimed at trained journalists: Burum also sees "citizen journalism" as a promising approach.

"Mobile journalism" is more than iPhone journalism: this statement is of particular importance with regard to developing countries. In recent years the iPhone has pressed ahead with the development. Now it Android phones, which are much more common in developing countries, need to measure up to this development. They are often the only device that allows journalists to produce video content.

Figure 01-05 Reporter Phyo Wailin films a coconut vendor with his smartphone in Yangon. Photo: Björn Staschen

Additional resources
Books

Burum, Ivo (2016). Democratizing Journalism through Mobile Media: The Mojo Revolution. London: Routledge.

Burum, Ivo & Quinn, Stephen (2015). MOJO: The Mobile Journalism Handbook: How to Make Broadcast Videos with an iPhone or iPad. London: Focal Press.

Goldstein, Taz (2012). Hand Held Hollywood's Filmmaking with the iPad & iPhone. Berkeley: Peachpit.

Links

NDR-Projekt "#politag – So tickt Hamburgs Parlament". Accessed 19 June 2016.http://www.ndr.de/nachrichten/hamburg/So-tickt-Hamburgs-Parlament,politag100.html

Reuters Institute. "Reuters Institute Digital News Report 2016." Accessed 19 June 2016.http://reutersinstitute.politics.ox.ac.uk/sites/default/files/Digital-News-Report-2016.pdf

Rosenblum, Michael. Blog "The VJ". „Most journalists don't get it – yet." Accessed 19 June 2016.https://www.thevj.com/vjworld/most-journalists-dont-get-ityet/

Interview with Philip Bromwell: "Storytelling is no longer the preserve of a small number of people in newsrooms."

Philip Bromwell is a reporter, VJ and mobile journalist with RTÉ, Ireland's national public service broadcaster. Philip has produced dozens of reports with his smartphone. The Englishman has been living in Ireland for 12 years. Prior to his move, he reported for the BBC in the north west of England. RTÉ has sent him on multiple assignments abroad, including trips to the Middle East, the Olympics and the Oscars.

Twitter:@philipbromwell

When did you discover "mobile journalism" for yourself?

That must have been in 2013. At that stage, I had been a video journalist for around 12 years with RTÉ and the BBC. I was used to being out and about with my VJ camera to shoot news stories. Even at that time this form of content production wasn't that common – the traditional way was still the norm: a reporter shoots with a camera operator at his or her side. But I began to talk at length with my colleague Glen Mulcahy (editor's note: innovation manager with RTÉ and founder of the "Mobile Journalism Conference) about the changing media landscape. Glen was exploring how mobile devices and platforms were going to be key players in that evolution. He convinced me that the device in my pocket could do so much more than phone calls, emails and Facebook updates!

When you learned about "mobile journalism" – did you think that it could work?

I thought that I should at least give it a try! I was intrigued by the challenge of trying to create television on my phone. Also remember that as a VJ, I was already used to taking the road less travelled!

What was your first story as a "mobile journalist"?

It was a story about a huge tapestry that was being made to commemorate one of the most significant strikes in Irish history, the 1913 Lockout. To tell you the truth: it worked pretty well. Maybe because I was used to shooting on my own: in sequences, with many close-ups. I simply saw the phone as just another camera. It was a new camera for me, but TV journalism wasn't. There were a couple of small technical problems with variable frame rates in the video, but we were able to get around them. All in all the film could be broadcasted.

How do people who you want to interview react when they see you showing with a smartphone only and not with the usual entourage of a TV team?

They are curious, but given that most people have never been interviewed, they don't usually need that much convincing. I might explain to them that some topics really suit mojo: perhaps it is a very personal story, or a story that is difficult to get to with a lot of gear. I might also point out that nowadays I am not just providing content for television. I could be gathering material for radio, online or social as well. Therefore my iPhone is the broadcasting/publishing equivalent of a "Swiss Army Knife" - a multi-faceted tool which is connected to the audience at all times. All that said, I think it is important that you arrive at a mojo shoot feeling really confident. You don't want to give anyone the feeling that you doubt yourself or the technology. That's what we teach journalists in our #Mojo-classes.

But what about those people that expect the crowds – politicians, for example?

I think nowadays most politicians are used to having multiple smartphones thrust their way when they speak to the press, so why shouldn't they expect to be filmed for television in this way too? In the end, politicians want is to get their message across, so it would be stupid to say no to a journalist with a smartphone, wouldn't it? Nowadays I also see many politicians creating their own content with smartphones, so some will even ask for a few tips!

Are there any topics that work better with #Mojo than others?

I think the "ideal" mojo story for television is probably about one person who is doing something visual which they are passionate about. Those stories are very do-able. But in this multi-platform age, people are really pushing the boundaries of the kind of stories you can do with a smartphone. Over the past couple of years, for example, I've seen many compelling mojo stories about the refugee crisis. The reporters used mojo to get really close to the refugees and their stories. This is where the smartphone comes in handy: the journalist doesn't have a lot of baggage; he almost blends into his surroundings, doesn't draw any attention to himself and can also carry his equipment over long distances. They are also able to broadcast or publish their material from the "front-line" straight away.

Are there any topics that don't work with #Mojo? What about a large media crowd at a press conference or in front of a court?

This is not about #Mojo replacing all other forms of reporting. It's an additional form of reporting that works really well in some situations, but not so much in others. It's important to me that I can still choose the technology that I want to work with, be it the smartphone or the VJ camera. Sometimes it will be better for the newsroom to dispatch a traditional crew – if there are health and safety issues around solo working, for example.

How much does your station RTÉ support your work as a #Mojo?

RTÉ has been very supportive in allowing me to develop my own mojo work. It has also given me extra responsibilities to train and encourage my colleagues. While much of our early mojo efforts concentrated on creating content for television, we are now more focussed on creating better digital content for social and online. As a fairly traditional, "linear" broadcaster, mojo is still just a small part of what we do at RTÉ, but this is growing all of the time.

How do your colleagues support your work?

Many colleagues were sceptical at the start but several years on, I think most people would agree that this technology now offers multiple opportunities. It's just really a question of harnessing that potential better and integrating it more successfully with other workflows.

What are the opportunities of mobile journalism with regard to democratisation?

The ubiquity of quality smartphones means that storytelling or content creation is no longer the preserve of a small number of people in newsrooms. If you have a good smartphone, you have a powerful and affordable newsgathering and publishing tool in your pocket. You just have to know how to get the most from it.

So are we digging our own graves by relying on technology that could be used by everyone?

I don't think so. Lots of people have smartphones, but the vast majority aren't using them to tell good stories. Storytelling is my core strength - not how to use a VJ camera or a smartphone. That said, ratings for "traditional" TV news are falling, while the audience online and on social is growing. The big challenge for all of us in the media is to discover new and better ways of telling stories that people will watch or consume on their smartphones. And I believe one of the solutions – not the only one – is to create those stories on smartphones.

What about your equipment? Which tools do you use?

I am currently using an iPhone 6S Plus but my mojo kit contains various other pieces of equipment including: lightweight tripod; tripod mount for the phone; a couple of extra lenses; handheld and lapel mics; extra battery; headphones; 360 camera; small drone!

What are your favourite apps?

The best app for filming is FiLMiC Pro and the best editing app is LumaFusion. You can use them together to shoot and edit a really high quality news story on your phone.

Philip Bromwell's equipment: iPhone 6S+, tripod "Manfrotto BeFree", Shoulderpod S1 mount and Rig R1-Pro, microphone "iRig Mic HD" and adapter "iRig Pro" for iPhone, AKG lavalier microphone, Gorillapod, iPro-add-on lenses and light "Metz LED mecalight" as well as iblazr.

2 "News Gathering" on the move: Modern news agencies

Summary

How can a reporter stay informed while being on the move? Is it possible to use Twitter, Facebook, Snapchat and other social media platforms as "news agencies"? If you are relying on these sources, you need to follow certain rules: social media is not a one-way street. And the content it provides needs to be verified.

No context, no news (yet). The Pakistani Sohaib Athar describes himself in his Twitter account quite modestly as an "IT-consultant taking a break from the rat-race by hiding in the mountains" of the megacity Lahore. He does consulting work for a couple of IT departments in Pakistan, and if he needs a break, he escapes to the mountains close to Abbottabad. His move to the mountains was also part of a "staying safe strategy", as he describes it – an attempt to escape the dangers of attacks and violence in Pakistan. So this is where he was on the evening of May 1st 2011 using the handle "@ReallyVirtual" on Twitter (fig. 02-01).

> **Sohaib Athar**
> @ReallyVirtual
>
> Helicopter hovering above Abbottabad at 1AM (is a rare event)
>
> 9:58 PM - 1 May 2011
>
> ↩ ⇄ 3,840 ★ 3,332

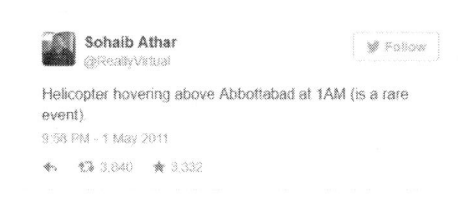

Figure 02-01 Tweet by Sohaib Athar

"Helicopter hovering above Abbottabad at 1 AM (is a rare event)": for several hours Sohaib Athar was the first person to describe an event that was going to dominate the headlines all over the world in the upcoming days. The helicopters above Sohaib Athar were American military helicopters. Their target was a large walled property in Abbottabad – the hiding place of the most wanted man in the world: Osama Bin Laden. The information

33

that Sohaib Athar shared was about to become part of highly relevant news – only did Athar know nothing about this yet. And none of his readers were aware which event Athar was describing in his tweets. Only after the event was it possible to determine the following: a secret US military mission made its way to the social network "Twitter" only minutes after it had started.

This little anecdote reveals three important features of the news channel and social network "Twitter":

1. Many – if not all – events also take place on Twitter; they often happen on Twitter first. Twitter is fast moving and almost always present.
2. Twitter's messages are restricted to 280 characters (plus links) and often lack context. News gets out into the world and it is almost impossible to accurately evaluate its content, authenticity or relevance.
3. Tweets are often written by non-journalists whose messages don't necessarily follow journalistic rules and regulations. Which – to be clear here – these people don't have to follow.

In this respect the expression "news service" is not very precise: Twitter primarily distributes "messages" and these messages are not always news. On the contrary. Describing Twitter as a "messaging service" is more to the point.

Can Twitter still be a source for journalistic work? Whenever people work while traveling, they often have to rely on Twitter and other services that are easily available on the smartphone (Facebook, Instagram, Snapchat, WhatsApp and many more). Athar's tweets, for one, prompted a wave of speculation: what was happening in the Pakistani mountains? It wasn't until several hours later that the first few people in Washington made correct assumptions: rumour had it that the United States had discovered Osama bin Laden's hiding place and killed the leader of Al-Qaida. But this wasn't confirmed until Keith Urbahn came forward (fig. 02-02).

Figure 02-02 Keith Urbahn's tweet

A piece of news – but still without a second source: at that time Keith Urbahn was the office manager of Donald Rumsfeld, the former US Secretary of Defence. He tweeted that a reputable source told him that Osama Bin Laden had been killed. "Hot damn" – and now the news was out. Some journalists might have known Urbahn, but they didn't know his source. So there still wasn't any verified information available, but they had a reliable starting point for further investigation.

Nowadays a journalist cannot not follow Twitter. The events of that particular night in May 2011 already prove this. The use of Twitter as the main communication platform by US president Donald Trump is even more proof that you really need to be keeping an eye on what is happening in the Twitter world. More politicians and celebrities are choosing the same tactic because they feel like they can speak directly to their fans and followers without the 'traditional' media interfering. So Twitter is becoming not just a news source but also a news platform in direct competition to our own channels.

The same applies to other news sources, such as Facebook that is of almost equal importance as Twitter as well as to Instagram, Snapchat, WhatsApp or the multifaceted blogs and news sites beyond the big news media. All of these sources often pick up on events that are developing below the radar of traditional news agencies and online news portals. And they often act much faster, almost in real-time, as for example, while a demonstration is just happening. They are crucial for a reporter who is on location, not only because news agencies are often not fast enough.

Yet journalists need to accommodate their use of Twitter and other platforms to the findings mentioned above: sources on Twitter and Facebook cannot always be trusted – in contrast to the majority of news agencies. On top of that these social networking services are not merely spreading gossip. They are a means of communication that allows both ends to send and receive information.

Twitter or Facebook? Twitter and Facebook! And more! The "Social Media and Political Participation"-lab at NYU (New York University) chose one of the bigger news events that happened in recent years to compare Twitter and Facebook. The researchers analysed information on Facebook and Twitter during the protests at the Maidan in Kiev1. The results are interesting:

Facebook was used more actively than Twitter. The official Euromaidan Facebook page had more than 125,000 "likes" within a few weeks after the protests started. As a consequence, an equivalent number of people was regularly receiving updates posted on this page. Yet most of the information was written in Ukrainian – an evidence that the news feed on Facebook was primarily directed at local and regional target groups. Its main goals were to coordinate the protest, to spread organisational details and to mobilise people on location. Many news updates also included logistic information, such as where to get tea at the Maidan or where demonstrators could warm up during the protest.

Although Twitter was used less intensively, it was still used a lot: within a few weeks the hashtag #euromaidan had 120,000 tweets. Only one third of these tweets, however, was written in Ukrainian; an almost equal percentage (28%) was written in English; 24% in Russian. Those tweets that were tagged with geolocation still indicate that tweets not written in Ukrainian were more often than not sent from the area surrounding the Maidan. The authors' interpretation: while Facebook primarily serves logistic purposes and speaks to a local target group, Twitter transports political messages from the Maidan to an international audience.

Nevertheless, it's impossible to generalise this conclusion: it's impossible to say whether Twitter or Facebook might be the better medium. Services such as Snapchat or WhatsApp have become more important. WhatsApp, for example, is used more frequently for direct communication (peer to peer) between participants or organisers during demonstrations, especially if information should not be readily available to police or media. In the following, the use of Twitter in mobile journalism is going to be used as an example. The conclusions can also be transferred to other social media services that might have similar benefits when used in a comparable way. But please keep in mind that each service has its own characteristics and user requirements.

How social media can support mobile journalism on the move is illustrated in this chapter. However, it does not completely or conclusively define the "social media strategy" that journalists should develop.

2.1 Receive: Personal news feeds

All major daily newspapers, news portals such as Reuters and news shows such as Tagesschau and BBC Newsnight tweet every day. Reporters and correspondents at home and abroad send additional messages using their personal Twitter accounts. If you identify those Twitter accounts that are worth following, you will have a comprehensive news agency on your smartphone in no time.

In addition, many politicians and organisations use Twitter and Facebook to communicate. When, for example, the protests at the Maidan reached their peak at the beginning of 2014, President Janukowitsch tried to get the situation under control by suggesting a compromise. He invited several representatives of the opposition to sit down and talk. Twitter users were the first ones to learn that they would not accept: one of the oppositional leaders, Arseniy Yatsenyuk who was going to be his country's next Prime Minister, tweeted "no deal" (fig. 02-03).

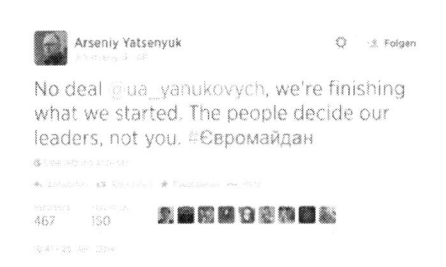

Figure 02-03 Arseniy Yatsenyuk's tweet

Putting together your news sources depending on your area of expertise – Twitter makes it possible. If you are reporting on local politics in Hamburg, for example, you might want to follow the Abendblatt as well as acting politicians and parties. Add a few activist groups, such as groups related to the Rote Flora or groups that campaign for or against refugee housing to the mix and you are good to go. If you are reporting on world economics, you might want to add bigger corporations, economists, major economic news services and one or two colleagues to your portfolio.

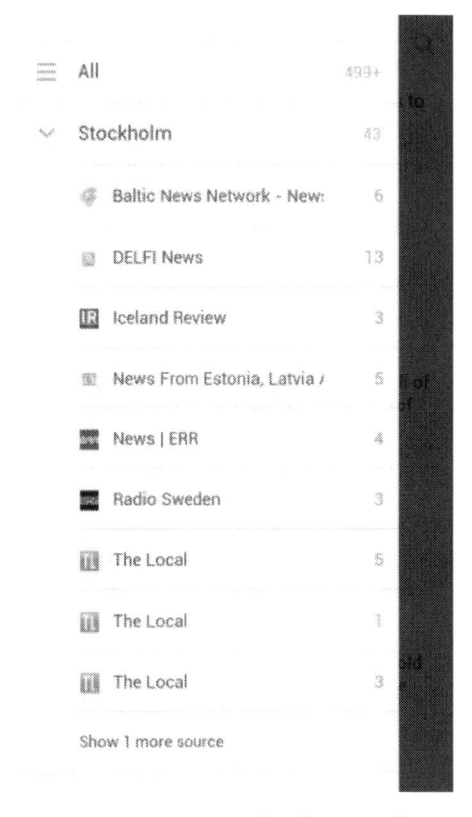

Figure 02-04 An example of a compilation of RSS-feeds in the feed reader "Feedly"

Working with a feed reader is also helpful – in addition to Twitter and checking the Facebook pages of protagonists on a regular basis. Feedly, for example, allows you to subscribe to larger and smaller news portals as well as to blogs on the internet. When I covered for the correspondent of the ARD studio Stockholm at short notice for two weeks, I put together the most important English news sources of the area of reporting – ranging from the Estonian and Swedish broadcasting services to the "Baltic Times" and the Icelandic Department of Civil Protection and Emergency Management. I added the latter because the volcano Bardarbunga was about to erupt. It took me only a couple of clicks to subscribe to the most important news sources. And I was glad to have piece of mind and felt confident enough to go on a shoot in Central Sweden. I knew that I would learn about the eruption of the volcano within minutes. Side note: when this book went to press, the Bardarbunga still hadn't erupted.

2.2 Receive: Real-time seismograph

Beyond the personally chosen news sources, Twitter, Facebook and others may bring topics to the attention of the newsroom that journalists hadn't yet been aware of. Twitter, for example, lists the most relevant Twitter trends ("search") on a regular basis and lets us know what our news sources as well as their sources are up to.

Furthermore, hashtags (#) turn Twitter into a "community for a limited time". An example: when the NDR newsroom frequently reported on the flooding of the river Elbe in North-East Germany in the summer of 2013, @NDRReporter also frequently tweeted about this topic. The NDR turned into a credible source regarding the topic #Hochwasser" (flooding). This is also how reporters in the newsroom learned about topics they would never have heard of if it weren't for Twitter. One Twitter user, for example, directly addressed a question to @NDRReporter (fig. 02-05):

"What's happening in Bleckede? My husband just got a call, EMERGENCY ... all military personnel allowed to go home yesterday now have to go back."

Figure 02-05 Sabrina Mehnert's tweet

The tweet was the starting point for an investigation with a quick result: the flooding forecast for Bleckede had just been revised upwards. The levees were unable to withstand the pressure with the sandbags that had already been put into place to reinforce flood defences. Helpers were needed to fill more sandbags. The media had not been informed yet, but the rescuers knew exactly what was happening since every minute counted. Without Twitter the NDR newsroom would not have been the first news outlet to spread the news.

Some of our traditional sources like the local government, the fire department or the police have also switched to Twitter for providing the latest information. In some cases they don't even officially alert the media that something is going on, so it is important for us as journalists to keep an eye on our Twitter feed. It might even be a good idea to install an alert for new tweets by certain accounts.

2.3 Receive: Crowdsourcing

Social media also qualifies for actively initiating an investigation. This goes far beyond a "Send us your photos of the winter chaos!" shout-out on Facebook as shown by the following example from Great Britain.

The British newspaper seller Ian Tomlinson was on his way back home. It normally took him about half an hour to cross the financial district, the "City" in London. But on April 1st, 2009 he had to pass several police barriers and make detours: the G20 leaders met at the summit in London. There were thousands of demonstrators and reporters from all over the world on the streets. I reported for the NDR from the kettling of protestors by the police in front of the Bank of England. Ian Tomlinson was not involved in the protests, and we, the journalists, wouldn´t hear of him until several days later. At first, we only heard about a man who apparently died without any evidence of third party involvement. This is how the Guardian journalist Paul Lewis initially reported the incident:

Figure 02-06 Tweet by Guardian reporter Paul Lewis

Yet Paul Lewis didn't stop here, but pushed forward to find out more about the tragic death: in subsequent tweets he invited people to send photos, videos and information on Ian Tomlinson's death. For several days, he received material that helped him to reconstruct the events.

Crowdsourcing – Lewis's investigation was supported by eyewitness reports of the G20-protest. Accordingly, he initially twittered using the #g20-hashtag. Bit by bit a scenario evolved that made clear that Tomlinson was first struck by a police baton and then pushed to the ground by a police officer. Lewis actively used Twitter to press ahead with his investigation. In the end, he provided evidence that Tomlinson fell and then died as a consequence of the severe assaults by the police. His Twitter investigation shed light on the events happening on the side-lines of the G20-protests: Ian Tomlinson, who was part of the demonstrations only by accident, became a victim of arbitrary police actions.

2.4 Send: Distribution of your own news

For journalists the distribution of their own news stories is part of daily business. This where they feel safe; they are used to spread news. On Twitter and Facebook many journalists follow their routine without listening or recognizing the relevance of the service for identifying news (see above). But only those who listen and react accordingly will also be taken seriously as a sender of news. This is how Twitter works: give and take, send and listen. As a consequence, only those people will successfully spread their news who also make sure that their own news stories are still relevant or have already been distributed by someone else; people who reply when they are directly addressed.

Under these circumstances, Twitter can successfully be used to show presence on a different channel with your person return address– for individual reporters with personal accounts, for shows, stations or other media with a functional account such as @NDRReporter.

> Björn Staschen @BjoernSta 22. Feb
> Mit dem Fernbus nach Kiew für die @tagesthemen: Abfahrt Hannover ZOB. In 30 Stunden sollen wir da sein. #euromaidan

Figure 02-07 Björn Staschen's tweet

When the protests at the Maidan hit their peak, I took a long-distance coach from Hanover to Kiev on behalf of Tagesthemen (fig. 02-07). Aboard the bus: many Ukrainians living in exile who were on their way back home. It was their opinions, their fears and their hopes that we were interested in.

> Stefan Keilmann @tagesschauder 22. Feb
> Road to Freedom? Was kommt nach #Janukowitsch? Folgt ARD-Reporter @BjoernSta auf seiner Fahrt nach #Kiev. #euromaidan
> pic.twitter.com/KEW28BwJYD

Figure 02-08 Stefan Keilmann's tweet

During that nightlong bus journey, Yulia Tymoshenko was released from prison. At that time the detached and disillusioned perspective of the people on the bus was a small counterpoint to the euphoria (on Twitter) about the apparent success of the #Euromaidan protests. As a mobile reporter I knew about the events in Kiev while my contribution of my protagonists' perspective from the general public completed the overall picture. That night I gained a couple of new followers even though I was forced to take several long Twitter breaks due to bad phone reception in Ukraine. Yet @tagesthemen and @Weltspiegel were still able to pass on several of my tweets and show that one of their reporters was present in the country.

Twitter, Facebook and others work well as additional playout channels of traditional news products: At Omrop Fryslan, we usually tweet a link to the story that is broadcast on TV in the news program Fryslan Hjoed later that same day. But our reporters try to share short videos on their own accounts as well because they want to get people to visit the website or watch the news program on TV. When reporting on the scene of a big gas explosion in Drachten in the North of the Netherlands, I used Twitter to share short video clips, but also to get input from the public. There were some rumours about what caused the explosion that I was not aware of. But because of the response I got on Twitter (and the live streaming app Periscope), I was able to use these insights in my report on the explosion later that evening when I talked about the incident on the late night news show on national TV (NOS).

Sharing your video via Twitter also is a way of reaching a broader audiences. People who usually don't watch your broadcast will now be able to see your footage and might be tempted to start watching your TV show. When news breaks, Twitter might also be the quickest way to get your material on the company website. Just share your video on Twitter and embed the tweet on the website. Upon reaching the scene of the explosion, I immediately shot a ten seconds clip and posted it on Twitter. I did this for two reasons: first, to have some material embedded on the website and second, because people could now see that we were on location.

> **WytseVellinga**
> @WytseVellinga
>
> De buurt is voor een deel geëvacueerd. Er is mogelijk sprake van instortingsgevaar. #omropfryslan #drachten
>
> [video: 0:03, 5.969 keer bekeken]
>
> 27 dec. 15 om 22:57

Figure 02-09 Wytse Vellinga's tweet

2.5 Send: Curating news sent by others

It's impossible for a reporter to always be in the right place at the right time, as for example when he investigates the context of a demonstration. As a consequence, he can only present a fraction of the events on Twitter. If you add retweets of observations made by other participants to your own news tweets, you will give your followers a more complete but yet still not a fully complete picture. In return, you will gain credibility and maybe even more followers. It will be worthwhile to think about the credibility of a source (see verification of sources below). Many Twitter users add a short note to their profile stating that "RT" does not mean "approval" or "endorsement". Which means: an opinion or an evaluation that is retweeted is not simultaneously agreed upon. Retweets may harm a sender or, at the worst, an entire media brand.

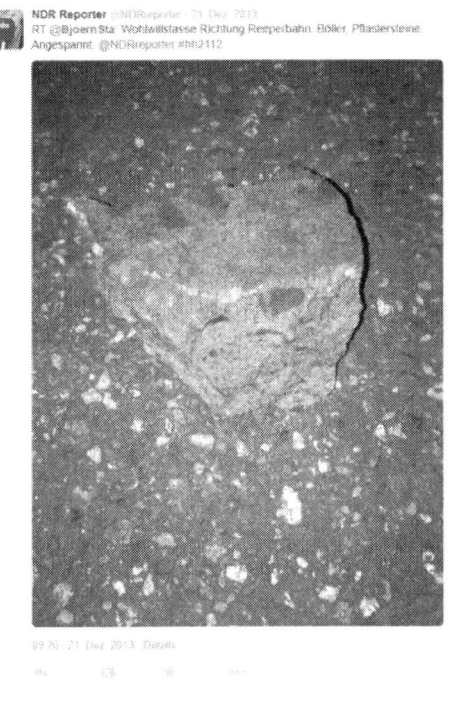

Figure 02-10 "NDR Reporter" retweets

Many media corporations maintain so-called "umbrella accounts". The newsroom of the NDR TV department, for example, uses the account @NDRReporter, mentioned frequently above,. Apart from sending their own tweets, @NDRReporter also tweets news provided by colleagues on location, as for example during the protests in the Schanze neighborhood in Hamburg (fig. 02-10). Authenticity provided by the reporter on location strengthens the entire brand. For me as a reporter the curated umbrella account has the following advantage: while I'm in the middle of the event, I don't have to decide for each Twitter message whether it is of interest to all followers – in this case, for example, also to those followers outside of Hamburg. It is up to the colleague in the newsroom to decide which tweets are retweeted. Those people who are looking for more detailed information that go beyond the Twitter messages know where to go: to the reporter who is regularly retweeted by the umbrella account.

2.6 Send: Community building

If you start sending, you will raise expectations: if you are using a Twitter account, you should be willing to use it in the long term. When @NDRReporter had started to tweet more frequently from the newsroom in Hamburg in autumn 2013, an explosive mix was starting to develop in the Schanze neighbourhood in Hamburg. The squatters of the Rote Flora had mobilised a demonstration throughout Europe that attracted thousands of violent participants – also because at the same time the city of Hamburg argued over the demolition of the iconic "Esso"-buildings on the Reeperbahn and the handling of a group of refugees that had arrived in Hamburg from Africa with a stopover in Lampedusa. The demonstration on December 21st escalated; hundreds of police officers and demonstrators were injured. As a consequence, the police in Hamburg created a "danger zone" that allowed them to examine people without any reason.

Media is "requested" as a protagonist: this happened to us on a regular basis while we were reporting about this danger zone (fig. 02-11):" Are you on location to get an idea of what's going on?" This is a new level of quality in the relationship between audience and medium – a conversation about whether reporting might make sense or not.

Figure 02-11 Conversation with "@forza"

In this respect Twitter also strengthens the media brand – it is communication on a meta level: not about the content itself, but about how reporting is done. The latter happens in our programmes only infrequently but takes up more space on social networks. Providing a look "behind the scenes" and explaining how reports are made on our traditional channels are of great interest – as in this example of "mobile reporting" from the city for our local news (fig. 02-12).

Figure 02-12 Tweet by "NDR Reporter"

The purpose of Facebook, Twitter and other social media

receive:

– personal news feed

– real-time seismograph

– crowdsourcing

send:

– distribute your own news

– curate news sent by others

– community building

2.7 Verification of sources

The strategic meaning of Twitter for international politics has a downside as the authors of "Blogs and Bullets: New Media in Contentious Politics" prove: "information" turns into "influence"2. Not only ISIS-terrorists have been using Twitter, Facebook and YouTube for propaganda purposes. During a demonstration protestors, residents, police and fire brigade alike predominantly use Twitter in accordance with their own interests. During the violent protests in the financial district that accompanied the opening of the new headquarters of the European Central Bank, the police in Frankfurt did not limit their Twitter use to simply sharing information: they asked peaceful demonstrators to stay away from violent offenders – and put the latter in a questionable light (fig. 02-13). According to critics several of these tweets opposed the police's responsibility of neutrality. 3

Figure 02-13 Tweet by Frankfurt police

The police department "Oberbayern Süd" was criticised that their Tweets were not only friendly, but almost cheering for the protests against the G7-summit in Elmau in Bavaria (fig. 02-14). In contrast to that the police head office in Munich used its Twitter account very professionally after the rampage at the Olympia shopping centre in Munich in the summer of 2016: they informed the citizens, asked for help, warned against publishing photos of police operations – all of this in several languages. Journalists who were reporting about the shooting were able to receive information on Twitter very quickly.

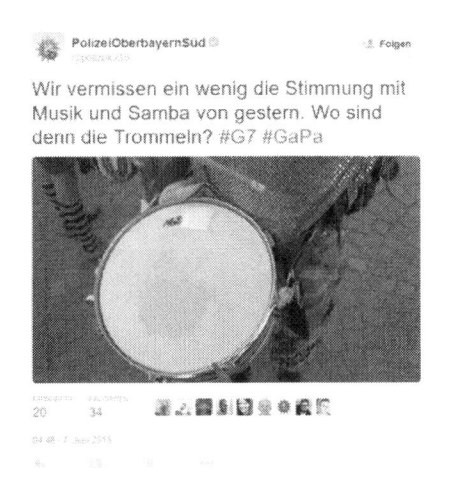

Figure 02-14 Tweet by police department "Oberbayern-Süd"

An additional downside: everyone can become a sender on Twitter – a circumstance that does not facilitate journalistic work. The senders can't be used as journalistic sources because they are often unknown, they may be biased or, at worst, they spread untruthful or "fake" news. After the crash of the Germanwings Airbus in the French Alps in March 2015, several fake news and fabricated lies appeared within only a few hours – alleged photos and videos of the crash and the inaccessible debris area (fig. 02-15).

Figure 02-15 Storyful's tweet

How can we verify Twitter messages? The colleagues at the Social Media Desk of ARD Aktuell in Hamburg (Tagesschau, Tagesthemen, Nachtmagazin, Tagesschau24, der Wochenspiegel as well as tagesschau.de are produced here) follow a strict roadmap when they are dealing with ambiguous sources. According to Michael Wegener, the head of the Social Media Desk, the procedure is similar to a circumstantial evidence lawsuit.

The newsroom starts with so-called "editorial verification". It follows the traditional 5 W's: what is the content of the Tweet? What can be seen on possible pictures or videos? Where and when was the Tweet created? In this case, the geotagging feature of Twitter and Facebook may help. If Tweets or Facebook posts, for example, show pictures from Syria, then there are often comparable pictures of these locations. ARD Aktuell consults these to verify whether the location is really the one that is supposed to be pictured. In addition, a Tweet is usually followed by another Tweet: do other sources twitter the same piece of information? Do similar images originate from different accounts? Or is there only a single Tweet, a single image that is shared frequently?

Furthermore, the source needs to be verified: is the source known because of a personal connection or because the Twitter account had been verified with the blue badge (The verification is a rather intransparent process during which Twitter asks selected users to proof that they are who they say they are)? Had someone already collaborated with the source? How credible is the source? Does it have many or only a few followers? What do others say about this source?

Next, the newsroom directly contacts the sender: on the one hand they may directly ask questions concerning the verification, but they may also ask for the permission to publish an image or a video. If they don't have the permission, the legal institution of "real time reporting" still allows the publication. In summary: if information is relevant and does not work without the Tweet, the Tweet may be shown.

Another important step is the verification with the support of experts – for the colleagues at ARD Aktuell those may be ARD correspondents in studios at home and abroad, scientists as well as official sources such as police, fire brigade etc. These sources are well informed about a certain topic or a location and may help to decide whether and image is "real" and information is correct. Are the details, the date, the location, and the context correct?

Entire books were written about the verification of content in social media. Since this book deals with mobile journalism and the use of social media as "news agencies on location", the topic of verification is not going to be discussed in more detail. Please make sure that you don't become a transporter of false information while being on location. Twitter, Facebook and others may give reason to investigate in more detail on location. But it happens very rarely that they can be used as direct quotes in a report.

The most important steps of verification

1. Verifying content with the support of the 5 W's, GeoTags or comparison with other sources
2. Verifying sources
3. Contacting sender
4. Contacting experts

Additional resources

Books

Stefan Primbs, Social Media für Journalisten: Redaktionell arbeiten mit Facebook, Twitter & Co. (Wiesbaden: Springer VS, 1st edition 2015)

Links

Sean Aday, Henry Farrell, Marc Lynch, John Sides, John Kelly and Ethan Zuckerman, Blogs and Bullet. New Media in Contentious Politics.http://www.usip.org/sites/default/files/pw65.pdf

John F. Nebel, Twittern zur Aufstandsbekämpfung.http://www.metronaut.de/2015/03/twittern-zur-aufstandsbekaempfung

Craig Silverman, Verification Handbook. An Ultimate Guideline On Digital Age Sourcing For Emergency Coverage."http://verificationhandbook.com/downloads/verification.handbook.pdf

3 What's in a reporter's bag? "Mobile Journalism" equipment

Summary

The right phone, the right accessories: tripods, add-on lenses, microphones, external batteries, lighting etc. How your smartphone turns into a (budget-friendly) OB-van

The key point in mobile journalism is the selection of the right equipment. It defines the "mobile journalist": He or she produces journalism with a "device that is in everybody's pocket" – instead of a professional mic, camera or the four-star laptop. The smartphone is not only a symbol for the change that journalists are experiencing, it also stands for the change happening in journalism as a whole. News content is increasingly produced and also consumed on a smartphone. It's impossible to automatically meet the usage habits of mobile news publications by simply turning to mobile production, too. Yet you may learn about the expectations and requirements of mobile usage here and there. You may get even closer if you produce with the device that the audience has already been using for consumption. An example: shooting vertical videos is still beyond the reach of professional camera teams. But the smartphone journalist is able to choose the phone as well as the camera position for every single shot.

Hardly anything is developing faster than the smartphone market – and the market for its accessories. Four or five years ago it was almost impossible to imagine that news reports would be produced with a smartphone. Seven or eight years ago phones would not have withstood the requirements of high-quality audio recordings. In this respect the following paragraphs do not qualify as absolute pieces of wisdom. They are mere tips for the journalist who wants to purchase a smartphone as well as accessories. As work methods differ from one journalist to another, so does the equipment. While one person prefers a particular phone, the other one swears by a specific microphone or light attachment.

"Less is more" – an opinion shared by many #mojos. What would be the benefits of "mobile journalism" if a reporter still showed up on a set with multiple bags, boxes and other stuff? "Mobile reporting" is inherently related to simplification. Mojos are able to act fast, be flexible and mobile – sometimes as a "one-man-show" or "one-woman-show". It's important to keep this in mind when you want to buy equipment. An external microphone, a lightweight tripod and light attachments are useful, for sure. Yet it's also reasonable to give smartphone journalism in its purest form a try and to explore how to achieve good results without any accessories. Because this is the opportunity of "mobile journalism": a small device that can be found in almost any bag records sound, takes photos, shoots videos, edits and, in the end, also even transfers the material. And any of us can suddenly be part of a developing "breaking news" story.

3.1 Networks and Connections

Using your smartphone as a reporting device means you will be using a lot of data. Sending an edited two minute piece could result in 1 GB or more. When you also upload material to Twitter, Facebook and do some livestreaming, you could be using up to 2 or 3 GB a day. The mobile plans that mobile journalists choose for their phone is important: if you plan to focus on producing and uploading videos with your smartphone, you need to pay attention to the amount of data that is included in your plan. It might be necessary to switch to a different plan to avoid a sudden reduction of the transfer rate or an exorbitant price increase in a "breaking news" situation. When you are abroad, local SIM cards can be useful, allowing you to use a mobile hotspot (see 3.9.). Also, some colleagues experience that they can use a 4G network when buying a local SIM whereas they only get to use 3G while roaming with their home SIM card.

Another possibility is the use of multinational SIM cards that provide network access in several countries, such as SIM cards by Truephone or Skyroam. Access to many Wi-Fi networks is offered, for example, by the fee-based iPass-network: during a crisis or an emergency mobile networks might be overloaded or even temporarily unavailable. In this case iPass offers fast and reliable access to many Wi-Fi networks worldwide, such as at airports or in hotels. Apart from that Google announced in 2015 that they would launch SIM cards that can be used across borders.

Data traffic via satellite might also be a solution: small satellite terminals such as the Cobham Explorer 510 or the Hughes 9202 enable connectivity anywhere as they don't depend on Wi-Fi or mobile networks. Yet data rates are often low, and the costs are high. The delay between sender and receiver may often be more than four seconds which makes live conversations difficult, especially in radio broadcasting. In addition, the respective hardware is quite costly: small senders and receivers may cost € 2,000, maybe more.

3.2 Too many choices – which phone should you buy?

How you are using your #mojo-phone determines the key purchasing criteria: a high-quality camera is important for successful photo and video recordings. In addition, the phone should have enough storage that can be upgraded with memory cards since video and voice recordings take up a lot of storage space. Battery power is also important; the best choice is an exchangeable battery (which is hard to find nowadays) so that the phone does not suddenly run out of power in a "breaking news" situation. The display should also deliver acceptable results in difficult light situations. On top of that it is helpful if external sources are easily available for use so that you can add music or eyewitness videos, for example, to your reports. The phone also needs to be sturdy enough to keep up with the everyday life of journalists.

Android or iPhone? This fundamental question divides mobile journalists evenly. One group swears by Apple smartphones and iOs – with clear advantages: for a single phone that is available worldwide it is possible to design apps that are almost tailor-made. And since mobile journalism, in particular video production, depends on maxing out the possibilities of a phone, it was the iPhone that had a clear advantage. Many apps that are essential for mobile journalism today were released for the iPhone first. Only then were they developed for other devices. Several apps are still only available for iPhones, while developers successfully transferred other apps to the Android world. Why? Because the Android market offers a big economic advantage to the developers: significantly more people worldwide use Android phones than iPhones. Earning a lot of money with an app that costs almost nothing is more likely to happen on the market for Androids than on the iPhone market.

The iPhone stands for reliable apps and high-quality hardware: the iPhone 5 series already offers an 8-megapixel-camera (MP), iPhone 6S and 6S Plus as well as the new iPhone 7 offer as much as 12 MP. In addition, the rear cameras of the iPhones 6 S and 7 can shoot videos in 4K; the iPhones 6 and 5S in "Full HD" (with a resolution of 1920 x 1080). It is also possible to record slow motion videos ("slo-mos") in "Full HD" with up to 120 images per second with the iPhones 6S and 7 – with amazing results. Starting with the iPhone 6 the front cameras offer 5 MP and "small HD" (1280 x 720). The iPhone 7 is equipped with "full HD" which is important if you plan to do live broadcasting by yourself.

Considering the strong position of the iPhone for photo and video it comes as a surprise that up until now all iPhones only record with a frame rate of 30 or 60 fps (frames per second) while the European TV standard PAL delivers 25 fps. If videos are not recorded with 25 (or 50) fps and with the camera apps that we are going to recommend in chapter 5, they will become jittery when they are converted to TV usage. (There are some people, however, who wonder whether 25 fps is still going to be important for much longer since the internet standard is 30 fps. Maybe even Apple counts on the irritating PAL television to disappear soon).

The dual lenses of the iPhone 7 are especially interesting: for the first time an iPhone offers the wide-angle lens as well as a 2x magnifying telephoto lens that allows you to take impressive photos with considerably more depth of field and more sharpness. Yet Apple's decision to drop the headphone port causes problems: accessories, such as microphones, can only be used with the help of an adapter that splits the iOs-Lightning connector into audio and Lightning.

An alternative to the iPhone is the iPod Touch 6G: it is less expensive than the smartphone but equipped with similar camera characteristics (full HD for the rear camera, "small HD" for the front camera). Apple's music/video player also offers up to 128 GB storage. As such it can be a valuable #mojo-tool if it's connected to the internet with a mobile hotspot (by using a Wi-Fi-router or the smartphone, see chapter 3.9.).

Requirement	iOs	Android
high-quality photo camera	up to 12 MP with a pixel size of 1.22 μ	up to 12 MP with a pixel size of 1.4 μ (Galaxy S7) or 23 MP (Sony Xperia Z5)
high-quality video camera	4K with 30 / 60 fps	4K with various frame rates
sufficient storage space	a maximum of 256 GB, no memory cards	various sizes, SD-memory cards used frequently
sufficient battery power	approx. 1,960 mAh	3,000 mAh and more
high-quality display	Full HD	4K
usage of external media	limited, in some cases complicated	yes
sturdy	yes	yes

Figure 03-01 Android vs. iPhone An overview of important features

Android phones are often much cheaper than iPhones. This is why the iPhone doesn't play a significant role in India, many Asian countries or Africa. In these areas mobile journalists rely on Android phones, which are often the so-called "China phones" produced by Oppo, Elephone or THL whose specifications may strongly deviate from bigger Android brands. The consequence: the larger number of different Android models makes it difficult to develop reliable apps that work on all phones. An example: some apps use the phone's camera control down to complicated hardware specifications. Mobile reporters may get frustrated because certain functions don't work on specific phones or only work with limitations.

The Android phone does not exist. The market is extremely fragmented, especially when considering manufacturers that are not part of the few big players such as Samsung, Sony, Motorola (with the Moto series), LG as well as Google's model phones in the Nexus series (which are produced by different manufacturers with strict hardware requirements). There are several interesting exotic phones for mobile journalists out there, such as the LG V10 and V20 (and the recently announced successor LG V30) that allow video recordings with manual camera control. Older models such as the Samsung Galaxy K Zoom, the S4 Zoom or the Asus ZenFone 2 Zoom offer optical zoom – which are considered to be real outsiders. If you compare their specifications with the most recent smartphones, these phones lack too many important features; a purchase would not be justified.

The decision for an Android phone is more complicated: if you go for the "bigger brands", you won't have any major problems when using video apps such as FilmicPro (see chapter 5). The website "DxO Mark", for example, provides an overview of smartphones and their camera quality, while also testing the image quality of DSLR and other cameras in detail. If you want to save money and purchase a powerful, but cheap phone from Chinese or Indian manufacturers, you should make sure that the phone is equipped with a good camera and sufficient battery power.

Windows phones are the third option: the Lumia series lives a marginal existence with low market penetration which has the following consequences: as of today, a live streaming app that would be worth mentioning is not available. The same applies to many other programmes, in particular for "digital storytelling" and multimedia applications. From a #mojo-perspective it's extremely disappointing that Windows does not put more effort into the Lumia series since the phones offer a high-quality camera with advanced possibilities for manual control. In contrast to Apple, Windows allows, for example, the pre-setting of the frame rate to 25 fps. It also offers numerous image formats and resolution options.

Further options are tablets and action cameras such as the GoPro as well as combinations of DSLR camera and smartphone. Tablets are easier to handle when it comes to editing, but they are not very handy for shooting. With the Padcaster (see 3.4) special #mojo accessories are available for the iPad. An action camera can also be a useful supplement. The live streaming app Periscope, for example, allows broadcastings with a GoPro that is connected to the smartphone. If you appreciate DSLR videography, you will love to experiment with transferring filmed sequences to the phone that allows you to edit and then upload the finished films. With "Osmo" the drone manufacturer DJI launched a camera that shoots in 4K and directly shows the stream on the smartphone display. The DJI Osmo is also equipped with a handle that stabilises the camera on three axes – it is both a camera and a Gimbal (see 3.5.).

3.3 External Microphones

If you want to buy only a single piece of attachment for mobile journalism, we would recommend an external microphone. The audio quality of built-in microphones for background sounds ("atmos") is usually sufficient: if you record street noise, crafts or the buzz at a conference with the smartphone microphone, you will only achieve acceptable results that can be used for broadcasting. It is the wind, though, that causes the biggest problems for the internal mic. The solution is a "wind cover" that can be slipped over both the mic and the smartphone (at the top or bottom, on the right side – whereever the activated microphone is built-in). Wind covers designed for bigger mics might fit – but there are also "windshields" available that are tailored to smartphones, such as Gutmann (approx. € 30) or Cubemic (approx. € 20) windshields or the wind blocker (approx. € 4). The iPhone's mic for video though is right by the lens so a windshield would cover the lens which is, let's say, impractical.

Built-in microphones often struggle with capturing interview sound: if a protagonist is not interviewed in perfect surroundings with a built-in mic, i.e. without any background noise or echo, the results will be disappointing. The interview passages will overlap with background sounds and the sound tracks will hardly be usable for radio broadcasting. The overall impression of a video film will also be influenced by poor audio quality. "It's not what you say, but how you say it" – this is not only a simple saying. This is where external microphones can actually help.

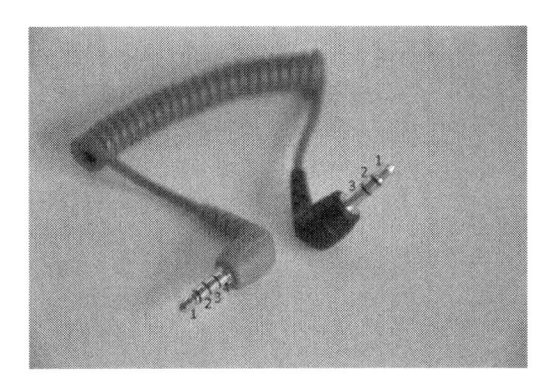

Figure 03-02 The right plug: the grey "TRRS" jack on the left works with a smartphone. An adapter cable like this could be an alternative.

Let's focus on a technical detail first: if you want to use your camcorder's audio equipment, for example, you might face unexpected problems: iPhone, Android and Lumia have a 3.5mm jack input that looks like the "normal" jack input of the camcorder. If you connect a microphone, you will have to keep this in mind: in contrast to the camcorder, the smartphone input is divided into four "rings" (fig. 03-02) (on the left in grey), while the "normal" plug only has three "rings" (on the right in black). The plug with four rings is known as the "TRRS plug". Mics should have a TRRS plug so that they work with the smartphone. If they "only" have a TRS plug with three rings or not even a 3.5mm jack input, you will need an adapter in order to use the mic. Please note: this adapter needs to have a TRRS output. Many external microphones that you can choose from today (certainly) have a TRRS plug.

TRRS has an advantage: one and the same connection can be used to get sound into as well as out of the smartphone. This makes it possible to listen to the sound during the recording (as long as this feature is supported by the app that is used). The simplest solution is an adapter cable – a so-called Y-cable that splits the TRRS plug with four rings into two 3.5mm connectors for mic and headset. These adapters are usually called "combo" audio adapter / plugs and are often available as a part of "gaming" headsets.

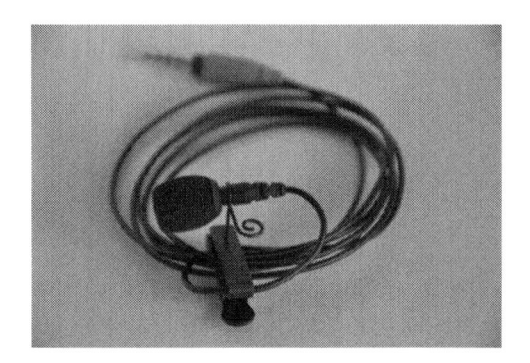

Figure 03-03 The Røde Smartlav microphone: wearable mic with TRRS plug.

The type of microphone that we use most frequently is a lavalier microphone. While the smartphone captures the background noise with the built-in microphones if needed, it is the lavalier microphone that improves the actual sound quality of the interview. A lavalier microphone is attached to the clothing, approx. 20cm away from the mouth. Since it is positioned very close to the body, it can capture lower frequencies. The direction is important: the small mic should be directed towards the mouth. Smaller changes may be audible since lavalier microphones are sensitive: if clothing is moving, they will record the rustling fabric. When you attach the mic, you need to be very accurate. The "Røde Smartlav+" (fig. 03-03) is a reliable smartphone lavalier microphone and costs about € 60. Since the mic cable is too short to capture high quality sound as well as a good image at the same time, you might need to use a TRRS extension (approx. € 5). The German manufacturer Sennheiser developed a series of higher quality lavalier microphones for iPhones: The "ClipMic Digital" and the "MKE2 Digital" convert digital sound for the iPhone with the help of a small adapter device developed for Sennheiser by the iPhone sound expert Apogee. These microphones are more expensive but improve the sound quality a lot. The Asian manufacturer BOYA offers lavalier microphones for the smartphone with an acceptable quality, but at a lower price range (starting at € 20). And please be aware: when you use a lavalier microphone, you will be able to capture good quality audio from the person wearing the microphone, but not from your own questions.

Conventional microphones may be used with an adapter, too: if you own VJ equipment or have access to your client or employer's technical devices, you can connect existing microphones to the smartphone. The company IKMultimedia developed several mics and accessories for audio recordings with a smartphone. The iRig PRE (less than € 40) is very handy. It is a small adapter that connects to the smartphone with a TRRS plug (fig. 03-04).

The iRig PRE also connects to iPhones. The iRig PRO, which costs twice as much, only connects to iOs phones by using Apple's Lightning connection. The sound quality is slightly better because the sound is converted into a digital format for the iPhone. Older iPhone models have a free headphone jack which is only a small advantage. The iRig comes with a small headphone output that allows you to listen to sound during the recording – if the respective app supports this feature. Microphones can be connected to the iRig with the conventional XLR plug. The iRig has a 9V monobloc battery that provides condenser microphones with the required phantom power. It also works without phantom power. A small side-knob adjusts the volume and helps to elevate low sound sources. IKMultimedia also offer the iRig PRO DUO for connecting more than one microphone to the smartphone.

Relatively new to the smartphone audio market is Rode. This Australian manufacturer offers an adapter just for iPhones: the iXLR is a relatively simple adapter that gets its power from the iPhone (or iPad) when plugged into the lightning port. Connect an XLR microphone on the other side and you are good to go. You can plug in headphones but be aware that you will only hear the 'raw' audio from the microphone. You don't get the audio as the software you are using records it.

For a lot of MoJo practitioners wireless audio is the holy grail since it would make our life a lot easier. There are two microphones worth mentioning here: First of all the Samson Go Mic Mobile. It consists of a handheld or lavalier microphone and a receiver that connects to your phone through lightning (iOS), USB-B or C (Android, WindowsPhone) or 3.5 mm (all systems). You can connect two wireless microphones to the receiver. These audio sources can be connected as a mixed track or you can set it up to have one source on the left and one on the right. This gives you the opportunity to split the audio into two separate audio tracks in editing.

Another wireless solution worth mentioning is the MikMe. It is an external recorder that connects to your iPhone through Bluetooth. It records the sound on the MikMe itself but automatically syncs to your phone when using the MikMe app. The biggest problem with the microphone is that it is rather big and feels a bit awkward to hold. On the plus side is that the audio quality is excellent.

Figure 03-04 The iRig PRE connects conventional microphones to the smartphone with a XLR cable.

Directional (or shotgun) microphones are helpful. They capture interview sound bites if it's impossible to use a clip-on mic: for a street poll, for example, you won't use complex wiring for every single person. In addition, a clip-on mic with a cable might be in the way if a reporter wants to capture lively and situative sound bites during which a protagonist is active, such as the automotive manufacturer who runs back and forth between the equipment. Apart from that a directional microphone may help to capture the "right" atmospheric sound. An example from a training for journalists in Myanmar: my awesome colleague Phyo Wailin filmed a short clip about a man who opened and sold fresh coconuts at a roadside stand close to the Shwedagon Pagode in the capital Yangon (compare with fig. 01-05). The traffic was loud. With his smartphone Phyo couldn't capture much more than the noise of passing cars. With a directional mic, however, he would have been able to capture the movement of the knife. In addition to connecting a directional mic with the iRig (see above) the "Røde Videomic" is another good option (approx. € 60) (fig. 03-05), with a windscreen and mount are included.

Figure 03-05 The Røde Videomic windscreen and mount.

There are several other options: Tascam offers a good stereo microphone with its iM2 that fits into the iPhone's Lightning adapter. Alternatives for good sound are good-quality USB-mics. The BBC reporter Nick Garnett, for examples, relies on the Samson Meteor which he connects to his iPhone using the camera adapter. Android phones need to support the so-called "OTG-host" mode (many new phones fulfil this requirement) so that mics can be plugged into the mini USB port. The respective app needs to support the USB mic, too. One of the many available options is the "Røde NTB-USB". Good results can also be achieved with the "iRig-Multimedia Mic HD-A". Florian Reichart, who collects many technical details for mobile journalists on his blog "smartfilming.blog", recommends the "t.bone MB 88U Dual" by Thomann for only € 39.

Earlier last year another wireless mic for the iPhone was released: the Sennheiser Memory Mic is in a sense a remote recording device for your audio. But if you use the app that comes with the microphone and use that to shoot video it automatically syncs the sound with the video. The distance between the device and the phone is not an issue. After starting the recording you can move as far away as you want. Just remember to bring the microphone back in range after you are done shooting. It then needs to connect to the internal WiFi from the Memory Mic to send the sound to the phone and sync. The biggest downside of the Memory Mic is how it looks. It is either a white or a black box that will always be very visible in your shot. Sennheiser is working on a new version that will allow you to connect a lavalier microphone.

Bluetooth microphones are another option, though I'm taking a rather critical standpoint: on the one hand the sound quality of simple phone headsets is often not good enough for journalistic purposes. At best the microphone produces recordings that sound like better phone conversations, without any bass, without any spectrum of frequencies that should normally be as broad as possible. In my opinion the Bluetooth pairing between headset/mic and phone is also still prone to errors, in particular if apps for sound and video recordings are used (as it is usually the case in "mobile journalism"). On the other hand, many apps (such as Easy-VoiceRecorder, see chapter 4.2, or Filmic Pro, see chapter 5.3.) support Bluetooth microphones.

If you are live streaming, it is important to control the audio quality (see chapter 7). Yet apps such as Facebook Live or Periscope don't support audio return channels that could be monitored. Thus, it might be risky to use external pre-amplifiers such as the iRig PRE since the sound might either be too low or too loud (aka distorted) when send to the phone during the live stream. For such usage IKMultimedia developed the "IKlip A/V", a smartphone mount with XLR connection for microphones. It is disappointing, though, that it is still not possible to control the broadcasting sound with this device. Apart from that the mount –

partly made of plastic – does not come with a hot shoe that would allow the attachment of light or other accessories.

A solution for audio monitoring during live streams is provided by small audio mixers that were developed for sound recording with DSLR cameras. They also provide the option to use and balance several sound sources, e.g. a lavalier microphone for the "host" and a directional microphone for interviews.

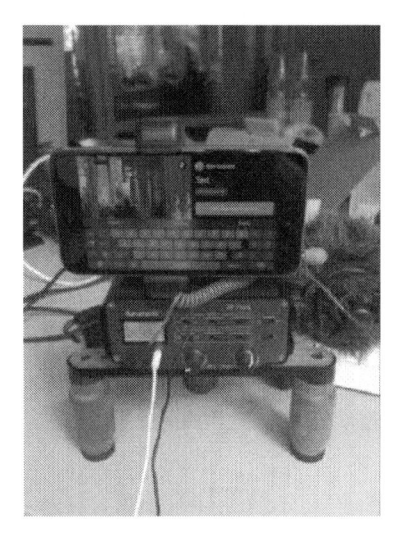

Figure 03-06 Audio control with the Saramonic audio mixer SRPAX-2.

There are several options available on the market, such as the Saramonic SRPAX-2 (fig. 03-06) that offers two XLR and two jack connectors as well as phantom power for mics. The device also comes with a threaded socket for a ¼-inch tripod screw on its base as well as its own tripod screw that allows the attachment of a smartphone mount (see chapter 3.4.). There is also a slide for hot shoe adapters at the side. The smaller Saramonic "Smartmixer" even has a built-in smartphone mount but it does not allow to balance several microphones. There is only one control knob for all channels. Further options are, for example, the Tascam DR60D MKII or the Fostex AR 101. The suggested audio mixers can also be useful for video recordings with more complex sound – such as recordings with two conversational partners or sound from a public sound system. But please always remember #mojo's premises: the simpler, the better. You should only purchase these devices if you've already reached your limits more than once when using external mics.

Recording 360 video is relatively easy now, as there are lots of consumer product on the market that give you the abillity to capture some great looking video and stills (see chapter 9). Capturing some 360 audio to go with it is not that simple. Microphones on the market that will get you sound coming in from all angles are really expensive. The cheapest high end solution is the Sennheiser Ambeo Smart Headset (ca. 250 €). The name sugests it is a headset, and it is -but it is a lot more than that. It has a microphone on the outside of both earpieces that record the sound the way you hear it. So anything happening to your left, comes from the left. Anything happening in the front, comes from the front. And so on. It can even record a sound moving around you and reproduce that exact same movement in your video. So far it only has an iOS version, but Sennheiser is apparently working on an Android version too. The version for iOS is plugged into the lightning connector and works with all available filming apps, including FilmicPro. And the video you record with it does not have to be 360. You can get that nice suround sound feel that the ambeo headset records into a normal video as well.

3.4 Tripods

"Use what nature offers you" – a rule of thumb mentioned frequently in trainings for video journalists and equally applicable to smartphones. You can place your smartphone on stones or lean it against a glass (or attach it with a hair tie and you have an impromptu tripod!). Put the phone on its display and you get a snapshot of the clouds. Stick it inside a glass while the glass it being filled with coffee beans for a "special effect shot" (see chapter 5.3.). Too many accessories and too much technology can be limiting – its small size makes new filming situations and perspectives possible, especially when you compare it to large TV cameras. "Less is more" – please keep this in mind, especially when it comes to heavy tripods. A reporter whose focus is on audio recordings won't need a tripod for his smartphone. And even a video reporter could do without a tripod if he had to. In chapter 5.2 I'm going to introduce a "hand-held tripod", i.e. I'm going to explain how you can shoot relatively steady images with the smartphone but without any accessories.

If you want to buy only one tripod, I would recommend a small and flexible mini tripod. It complements nature perfectly – in an interview situation the small tripod can be placed on a stack of books or the top of a car so that the smartphone is already on eye-level with the interview partner. Many #mojos rely on the Manfrotto table tripod "Pixi" (starting at approx. € 25) which provides stable and safe support. Until recently Manfrotto also offered a collapsible "pocket tripod" that can still be purchased second-hand. There are several more photo tripods that offer sufficient support. I love the "Gorillapod magnetic" (approx. €25): a tripod with flexible legs that can easily be wrapped around objects so that you can bring the smartphone in unexpected positions for an interesting perspective. With its magnetic legs you can safely attach the Gorillapod to street signs or on car tops. Critics may say that the tripod is unstable because of the flexibility of its legs, but that is simply a matter of taste. During the May 1st protests in Hamburg I produced many pieces to camera with the Gorillapod (fig. 03-07). This made several colleagues and people walking by laugh (mainly in a positive way), but still: I was not only flexible, but was able to produce camera pieces for the colleagues of NDR.de as a one-man-show and from anywhere. I didn't have to set-up and dismount a big tripod, not to mention having to carry it with me all over the place.

Figure 03-07 The Joby Gorillapod with magnetic feet, used during protest reporting

Bigger tripods may help, too – in particular during interviews in standing position which frequently happen in daily media life. Glen Mulcahy, an innovator at the Irish public station RTÉ and one of #Mojo's pioneers, recommends the "Manfrotto 560B" monopod (approx. €130) on his blog "TVVJ". It has three retractable feet and can stand on its own. In addition, he recommends the "Hähnel C5" tripod that has an integrated monopod. It is very small when folded, but only reaches a maximal workable height of 1.45m. This seems to be a little bit low– for an interview of a protagonist in standing position the tripod should be at least 1.75 m and up to 1.80 m so that the smartphone films on eye-level and the eye-line is correct (see chapter 5.2.). I've had positive experiences with the "Rollei C5i" tripod (fig. 03-08) that reaches a workable level of just below 1.80 m. Its ball head (fig. 03-09) allows quick corrections of the image frame (in contrast to a 3-way pan head that allows for more precise settings but takes up more time). The additional horizontal rotation (1) with the ball head makes pan shots still possible. It is possible to align the tripod stage horizontally and vertically with a spirit level (1) beforehand. The C5i also has a centre pillar that is adjustable in height. You can use it to adjust the workable height quickly without having to extend or retract three legs and align the camera with the built-in spirit level. Apart from that the C5i tripod can be turned into a monopod. If you are using a monopod, please pay attention to the horizon: standing on only one leg means that you can stop being level

Figure 03-08 The Rollei Fotopro C5i.

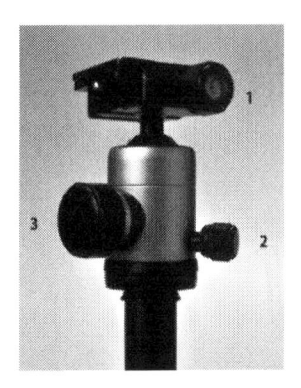

Figure 03-09 The ball head of the C5i.

3.5 Smartphone Rigs

Unlike cameras smartphones don't come with a threaded socket for tripod screws. That's why the connection between a tripod and a smartphone needs a "helper": a smartphone mount, a so-called "rig" or "grip". The market is already flooded with these attachments. Many wobbly selfie sticks are equipped with equally wobbly mounts. But there are a few products that are very practical for mobile journalism. Mounts for professional purposes should come with a thread that holds ¼-inch photo screws. The mounts mentioned below fulfill this condition.

Figure 03-10 Joby Griptight.

Figure 03-11 Shoulderpod S1.

From my perspective the cheapest and yet still useful model is the smartphone mount "Griptight" (approx. € 12) that the Gorillapod manufacturer (see above) Joby introduced to the market (fig. 03-10). The company recently launched an XL-version for bigger smartphones that exceed 5 inches. A clip that can be opened easily holds the smartphone in place. I've heard that the "Griptight" is likely to break after the third use, but I've been using my mount for years. If you combine the mount with the flexible Gorillapod, the result might indeed be a little wobbly.

A much nicer and more reliable option is the Shoulderpod S1 (fig. 03-11), not only because of its history: two amazing Catalan designers from Barcelona, Enrique Frisancho and Ana Maria Vicens, founded a design office in 2008, right before the beginning of the economic crisis. As customers failed to appear they turned their private passion for smartphone photography into a product. They realized that their smartphone took great pictures but was difficult to hold and could not be attached to a tripod. They came up with the Shoulderpod 1 that can be precisely adjusted to the respective size of the smartphone with a screw and which holds the smartphone tightly. It can also be used as a table stand for a smartphone and be combined with any common tripod. The #Mojo crowd loves the S1, especially because it was designed with care and an eye for details. Meanwhile the Shoulderpod family has grown: now there is a wooden handle as well as a wooden plate (R1 Pro) that allows the attachment of the S1 as well as light and sound accessories. The result is a "smartphone" rig for more complex usages. The Shoulderpod-series is very versatile – figure 03-05 shows an example of the R1 Pro which can be used in combination with an audio mixer.

Figure 03-12 Beastgrip Pro.

Rigs offer support for more accessories – but they also take a step backwards, away from the smartphone as a compact all-rounder to more complex accessories. In my opinion the "Beastgrip Pro" which was the result of a popular kickstarter campaign (fig. 03-12) is a good rig. It. In the photo the rig is combined with an add-on lens (see 3.6.) and the Røde Videomic with a windscreen. A big advantage: you can now hold the three devices in one hand. Holding a rig is much easier than holding a smartphone with your bare hand. You can also attach the Beastgrip to a tripod. More smartphone rig are the popular Padcaster that was developed specifically for the iPad, but can be combined with other devices such as a GoPro. Then there is the iOgrapher for iOs phones as well as several "cases" that were developed for the use of add-on lenses (see 3.6.). Fairly new on the market is the smartphone rig produced by Meike, a manufacturer from Hong Kong that allows you to attach additional lenses as well as a ring light.

3.6 Gimbals

"Gimbals" are always optional, never mandatory. They stabilize a camera during a shoot. With small motors and electronic they compensate any hand movements with a three-axis construction (left/right, top/down, sideways). They always keep the horizon straight and they pick up hand movements at the handle with smooth and steady pan shots. Gimbals are standard equipment on most camera drones. They compensate not only flight movements and any balancing efforts during strong wind situations, but also permanent vibrations. Without a gimbal, drone recordings could only be used after extensive editing and image stabilization which in turn have a negative influence on the resolution. Gimbals have also been introduced to sports videography with action cameras (GoPro etc.), providing steady images even when the movements are abrupt.

In mobile journalism gimbals can help to provide calmness and stability, especially when a camera is moving. A report that follows a protagonist, such as during a walk along a poster wall or the visit of an exhibition, or the piece to camera while the reporter is experiencing something at the same time – in these situations a gimbal may offer enormous benefits and produce images that are similar to those of a steadycam. "Steadycams" are part of professional TV equipment: expensive, heavy and complicated to use. In contrast to that gimbals are small and light – they stabilize much less weight since it is the smartphone that is the camera – but they also have a stunning effect on the filmed image.

The downside: Gimbals aren't a "small piece of equipment". They need to be handled carefully and are often stored in a separate bag or a small case that adds to your personal equipment making it bulkier. Cables that are plugged in, as for example for external microphones, often interfere with the functions of the gimbal. I usually decide on a case-to-case basis whether to bring my gimbal. When I know that I will have time for "special effect shots" (see chapter 5.3.), I'll bring my gimbal case. If you partner up for a shoot with a colleague or have your car parked nearby, you should also consider bringing it. But if you follow a demonstration and have to be mobile and ready to work at all times, you should leave the gimbal at home. The gimbal needs power, too – another battery that needs to be charged – and which could be flat just when you need it.

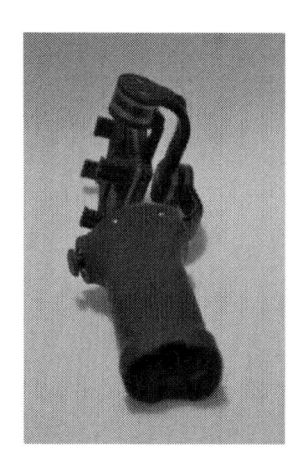

Figure 03-13 The CamOne Gravity Sports 3D.

When you buy a gimbal, take the size of your smartphone into consideration. The CamOne Gravity Sports 3D at a price of approx. € 220 (fig. 03-13) is a solid and sturdy gimbal that holds any phones up to the size of an iPhone 6S+. A Nexus 5 would be too big. A smaller version holds GoPros and similar action cams. Cam One developed their first gimbals for aerial drones and used this knowledge to develop a reliable model for mobile usage. The #Mojo community also loves the Lanparte HHG01 which is more expensive (approx. € 300) but doesn't offer any significant advantages. As of now the market is exploding – manufacturers that offer products at an equal price point are iKan (Fly X3 Plus), Feiyu (G4 Plus) or Husky (HY3M) which specialize in bigger smartphones. Crowd funding platforms such as Kickstarter or Indiegogo also feature promising gimbal products. The most recent one was the Proview S3 for just € 130.

A company in Munich developed a combination of a gimbal and a steadycam: the Luuv stabilizer is aimed at sports and action filmmakers. The selling point: the basic version "solid LUUV" (approx. € 200) doesn't require batteries thanks to the cardan suspension (it is heavier than a gimbal because of the balancing weights). The "ultra LUUV" (starting at € 480) combines cardan motion compensation with an additional electronic gimbal. The result? A more stable image than provided by a "simple" gimbal because steps and movements can be better compensated.

The drone manufacturer DJI launched a 4K camera, the DJI Osmo, that is directly connected to the gimbal. They use the X3 camera that is also installed in the DJI drones – this is the reason why DJI sells the Osmo handle separately (without camera). Additionally, DJI offers the gimbal without camera, but with smartphone mount – the "DJI Osmo

Mobile". An advantage: the handle control of the DJI Osmo Mobile is compatible with video camera apps such as "Filmic Pro" (see chapter 5.4.) which allows a smooth start and finish of a shoot without having to touch the display. Cameras and gimbals of other drones can be used in hand-held mode, such as Yuneec's Q500. GoPro launched a similar product with the Karma drone.

3.7 Add-On Lenses

Add-on lenses are available for almost any smartphone model at various price points. I have to admit though that I don't use them very often. I lose valuable time when I need to attach and remove lenses; the advantage that the smartphone offers would be almost gone. And I'm usually the one who moves around on set so I don't need a lens to bridge distances. On top of that almost all smartphones shoot with a wide angle so that wide-angle lenses are more or less dispensable. Personally, I don't use extremely wide angles very often in journalistic settings. The same applies to fish eye lenses that are not only very popular but are also part of almost any lens set. I can think of only a few topics to which they'd add another layer of content: the literal keyhole perspective occurs hardly ever in journalistic video reports. Telephoto lenses consume a lot of light, produce blurry, unsatisfying images or even dark corners (if the models are not compatible with smartphones).

My favorite lens is a macro lens because it allows me to get very close to the object and to capture structures, surfaces or drawings. This can be relevant on the level of content. Lenses that deform anamorphically could also be interesting. They capture an image that is wider than the standard wide-angle image by compressing it. Certain camera apps such as FilmicPro (see chapter 5.4.) support the use of these videos. The movie "Tangerine", for example, tells the story of homosexuals in Las Vegas and was filmed with Filmic Pro with the anamorphic lens by Moodoglabss.

A lens needs to be mounted to the smartphone camera. There are several available options. Manufacturers of smartphone rigs already have pre-installed threads for add-on lenses in their mounts. The Beastgrip Pro, for example, compatible with Android, Windows and iOs phones, offers a 37mm threaded mount and sells several lenses in a bundle (see fig. 03-14). Other case-/rig or lens manufacturers focus on the iPhone, such as Mcam (and its ALM lens series), ExoLens, Yopo, Ztylus, Manfrotto Klyp, Optrix PhotoProX, Moment Mobile Photography Lenses and the high-quality iPro iPhone lenses by Schneider Optics. All of them offer a rig/case with thread mount and lens combination.

Figure 03-14 The Beastgrip add-on lenses (fisheye, extreme wide-angle & macro)

Other lenses work without a rig: the Olloclip products for iOs phones are very popular (approx. € 80). They directly attach to the iPhone with a clip. This is useful, yet it also means that the distance of the lens from the iPhone is fixed and is not compatible with other phones. Apart from that clip-on lenses are wobblier than lenses screwed to a case or rig – an error source if the lens shifts during a demanding shoot. The anamorphic adapter made by Moondoglabs (see above) can also be put on the iPhone, but is incompatible with other phones. There is a large selection of other manufacturers of clip-on lenses such as Makayama, Mobi-Lens, Lensbaby, Phocus Accent or XCSource. In addition, there are systems that attach the lenses magnetically to the phone such as Photojojo, VicTsing or Wonbsdom.

System cameras take it one step further. They use the smartphone as both a display and the camera control: Sony pioneered with its QX-series (fig. 03-15). The lenses can be attached to various smartphones (including Android phones!) or they can be used separately. The QX-lenses connect to the smartphone via Wi-Fi; the display now works as the viewfinder. The "add-on camera" offers a couple of advantages (optical zoom, better lens performance) but lacks in other areas (additional battery, slow Wi-Fi-connection with a delay between lens and smartphone of up to several seconds). Other lenses can be attached to the QX-1 (approx. € 270) with Sony-E-Mount. Kodak launched similar products with its SL10 and SL25.

Figure 03-15 The Sony QX-series (photo © Sony Corporation),

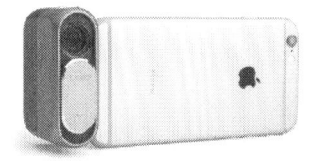

Figure 03-16 DXO One (photo © DXO), right

The DXO one (fig. 03-16) only works with the iPhone. It uses the Lightning adapter to connect to the phone and doesn't have to deal with long delays caused by the wireless image transfer. The 1-inch-sensor takes excellent images, but the camera only shoots video with a rate of 30 images per second – a disappointing fact since the European TV standard PAL is 25 images per second. The DXO one costs about € 500. And as mentioned before: for mobile journalism these additional modules are only optional and never mandatory. I still follow the rule "less is more" – it fosters curiosity and is simply more practical.

3.8 Light

"Natural light is your friend": at a shoot I always try to work without any artificial light as long as possible. First it is never easy to position light correctly. Then I'm often too lazy to carry additional lamps. And finally it usually happens that the batteries of the particular lamp that I would need in a given situation are flat. During the day an outside shoot is never going to fail because of insufficient light. It rather fails because of too much light or because of a wrong filming direction in relation to the light. The rule of thumb: stand with your back turned to the light (see chapter 5.3.). Inside a building it is easy to create good lighting for an interview situation with interior light and a standard lamp. But sometimes the available light is not sufficient. Examples: filming members of the audience at a club concert or interviewing them after the concert. In such a case small lights are useful that can be attached to rigs or cases (see chapter 3.4.). In a situation with good lighting an additional light may even add an interesting sparkle to the eyes of the interviewee.

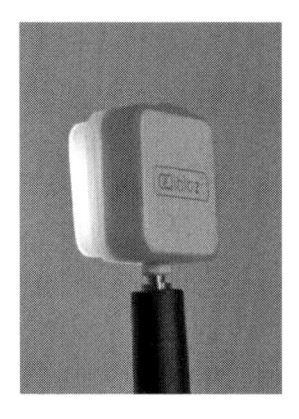

Figure 03-17 The iblazr.

The iblazr product line is an example for a custom-tailored smartphone use (fig. 03-17). The iblazr-light is smaller than a matchbox and the 4 LEDs produce a reasonable light at an adequate distance. Since smartphones mostly shoot with a wide angle, the distance to the protagonist during an interview is usually not very big. In addition, the battery lasts for many days of filming. The light can be charged with USB within 20 minutes. A small 3.5mm jack input connects the iblazr not only with the charging cable but also with the adapter that allows the attachment of the light to the hot shoe of the smartphone mount (case/rig). The first iblazr generation is no longer available. The iblazr2 is a little bit bigger and more sophisticated. The set that includes a charging cord and several color filters costs about € 100 in the online shop of the manufacturer concepter.com.

There are many copycats with similar products on the market. Starting at € 4 so-called "selfie" lights are available online that can be attached to the 3.5mm jack plug of the smartphone. But please keep in mind: this is the input port for external microphones (at least with Android phones). If you want to buy a light with a jack plug, you need to think about its attachment (With plastic glue I DIYed a mount that I can screw into the ¼ inch thread of the Beastgrip. It is made of a ¼ inch threaded bold of a tripod and a headphone adapter plug.). The Rock smartphone lamps are also interesting. Irrespective of the model they can be attached to the phone with a clip and they produce a lot of light with a circle made up of 10 LEDs.

Typical video and photo lamps that are attached to the hot shoe of the mount may also be used. In mobile journalism colleagues had positive experiences with the Metz Mecalight LED 160 (approx. € 20), the Manfrotto Lumimuse series (3 LEDs starting at € 40, 8 LEDs starting at € 80) or the iKan iLed 120 (€ 150). Many manufacturers such as Neewer or no-name companies offer practical and cheap alternatives online. Please make sure that the lamps come with their own batteries and don't rely on any additional power sources (batteries). The lights should also be continuously dimmable. It's another plus if you can also change the color temperature so that the lights can adapt to the natural light situation inside and outside and the recordings are true to color (and don't have a blue or red undertone).

Color temperature in Kelvin (approx.)	
1600 K	candle flame
2600 K	light bulb (40 W)
2800 K	light bulb (100 W)
4000 K	fluorescent light (neutral white)
4120 K	moon light
5000 K	early morning / evening sun
5500 K	mid morning / afternoon sun
5500-5600 K	electronic flash
5500-5800 K	midday sun – cloudy
6500-7500 K	cloudy sky
7500-8500 K	fog, dense mist
9000-12.000 K	blue sky, shortly after dawn / shortly before dusk, "blue hour"

Figure 03-18 Different colour temperatures

3.9 Batteries and Charging

A smartphone journalist needs fully charged batteries – pun intended. This also applies to the phone itself. Though the news may be relevant, and the story may be told in an intriguing way – without a charged smartphone "mobile reporting" is impossible. And it is this "mobile reporting" that consumes battery power above average. If you shoot and edit videos, upload data and stream, you do not only reach the performance limit of your phone but you also strain the battery. On top of that you'll need accessories that consume a lot of energy – external light, mobile hotspots, gimbal etc.

Most phones lack power: iPhones don't provide much more than 2000 milliampere hours (mAh); certain Android phones run up to 6000 mAh. Nevertheless, in a "breaking news" situation each of these devices will reach its limits and die within a matter of hours. If you are on the road, Powerbanks can help – mobile charging devices that need to be charged beforehand. If you are streaming during a "breaking news" situation, you will have to plug them in quickly. There's a myriad of models – the smallest ones don't even provide a full phone charge, but are light and can be a big help if the final minutes of a shoot are in danger. Bigger battery blocks provide more than 20,000 mAh hours, but are heavier. You should try to find your favorite type: if you charge on a regular basis and don't stream very often, smaller Powerbanks might be the best fit for you. Unfortunately, I often forget to charge my devices. That's why I use the Anker PowerCore with 20100 mAh that can charge an iPhone about six times. It has two outputs so that I can charge two devices simultaneously. The weight of the Powerbank is about 350g – a heavy lump in my equipment which has already saved my stories more than once.

Figure 03-19 Charging station with five USB ports.

"Always charge all your devices" – that should be the norm. This means: once the shoot is wrapped up, you need to charge all your devices at night in your hotel so that they reach full capacity again overnight. This includes the Powerbank. If you drag along a charging device for every single device, you will become desperate quickly while looking for sockets in the hotel room. A good replacement for many different charging devices is a charging station (fig. 03-18) that can charge three to ten devices at the same time. "Anker" among others launched reliable products: the Anker PowerPort with 5 USB ports (40 Watt) at approx. € 20 is both small enough for #mojo equipment and powerful enough for #mojo purposes. There are many other models on the market – before you make a buying decision, make sure to check the specifications in Watt (W) and Ampere (A). All ports should provide at least 2A each when they run simultaneously. If they don't, charging a device might take forever or fail altogether. Car chargers that can be plugged into the cigarette lighter and provide the final charge on the way to the shoot also should provide at least 2A. High-quality chargers adjust the power to the device that needs to be charged.

Too many cords: if you work with Android (or Windows smartphones) and iPhone at the same time, you will need different charging cables. And if you want to charge all devices simultaneously, you will need several cords. Cords that combine both must-have connections (Lightning as well as Mini-USB) into one make for less clutter in your bag (fig. 03-19). Cord winders are also available – you will never have to fight with tangled cords again.

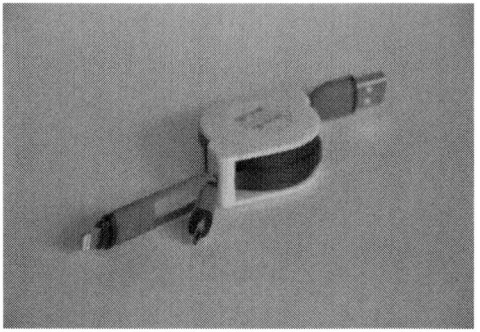

Figure 03-20 Charging cord for Android/Windows and iPhone.

3.10 Drones

Drones have become more and more interesting and usable for journalists. In this context drones refer to quadcopters (aerial vehicles with four rotors) and multicopters (aerial vehicles with more than four rotors) whose lift is relatively stable because of the multitude of their motors. They are big enough to carry small cameras and they are equipped with stabilizing programs and small gimbals (see chapter 3.5.) so that they produce relatively stable images. Some drones have cameras and wireless connections that allow the pilot on the ground to monitor the content and quality of the image from his smartphone. Other drones have mounts for action cameras, as for example cameras of the GoPro-series. These drones also allow limited image transfer to the control unit on the ground.

Figure 03-21 DJI Phantom 3. Photo: obs/DJI

This area has evolved at a fast pace in recent years. Until only recently drones were expensive, difficult to handle and could often only be operated with an official permission if their weight exceeded 5kg. Meanwhile semi-professional aerial vehicles are easier to operate, provide amazing image material and are also affordable. The market leader is the manufacturer DJI whose drones of the Phantom series (fig. 03-18) make it easy for the pilot to capture great images. They range between € 800 and € 1500 and are equipped with a "home" function if they get too far away from the pilot or if the battery is running low. Good soft- and hardware solutions provide for a steady flight even during a moderate breeze. DJI just introduced its most recent drone: the "DJI Mavic" is foldable and can be transported in the photo bag. It is flexible, light and shoots stable videos in 4K. The action camera manufacturer GoPro launched a competing product, the "Karma" drone but it can't keep up with the DJI Mavic. Other makers are Yuneec, Walkera, WLtoys. As far as I know they are yet to launch a comparable all-around package.

Does it pay off to purchase a drone? Aerial images can be a marvelous addition to a report: they can provide an overview to the audience or make distances, buildings or surroundings more visible. A general rule of thumb: don't incorporate an aerial image just because it's an aerial image – though this might sometimes be very appealing. Then let beauty beat content. Since drones are flooding the market right now, the effect is likely to wear off in the near future. If you enjoy technology, you can create a USP for yourself with a comparably low investment by using a drone in journalistic settings. Everyone can fly a modern drone. More experienced pilots often recommend to start practicing with a cheap quadcopter to get a feeling for the flight quality of a drone and to switch to an expensive model with a camera only once you've mastered the skills.

Please note the following rules and regulations: every pilot should check his liability insurance, no matter if the drone is his hobby or part of his profession. The majority of conventional insurances do not cover damages caused by drones. An additional insurance is required – since 2005 insurance is compulsory for unmanned flying objects.

A special license is required for drones that weigh more than 5kg or are used for commercial purposes. It is the latter aspect that usually applies to film shootings with a journalistic purpose. It is the regional aviation authorities that are responsible. In Hamburg this is the Office of the Interior. In Germany the rules differ from federal state to federal state with Hamburg being one of the strictest. The Office of the Interior mostly grants fee-based permissions on a case-to-case basis and requires a demonstration in which the pilot has to prove that he knows how to fly a drone. As of late a multi-permission with strict regulations is available. A list of regional aviation authorities is available at the Federal Aviation Office (Luftfahrtbundesamt) (see "Additional Links").

There are even more regulations to be observed: in Germany unmanned flying objects have to stay in the pilot's visual range. The use of binoculars is not allowed. This means that the range of the drone is limited to a radius of 200-300 m from the pilot. You also need a permission to start and land drones on third party land. Property and personality rights have to be observed during a flyover. As a general rule a drone mission is only allowed in the so-called "uncontrolled airspace". This excludes prohibited areas, such as the 1,5 km zone around international German airports. According to a summary of Stiftung Warentest it is not allowed to fly drones over "the government district, nuclear power plants, gatherings, residential areas, industrial facilities, scenes of an accident, disaster zones or military facilities" (see "Additional Links"). Larger no-fly zones have been established in cities such as Hanover, Frankfurt, Leipzig, Dresden, Dusseldorf or Dortmund.

The German Federal Ministry of Transport plans to limit civilian drone use even further since there were several incidences close to bigger airports in which drones were involved. Rules and regulations in Europe and other foreign countries differ from those in Germany. A pilot should always check the legal situation before he starts planning a mission.

3.11 Miscellaneous

No limits to accessories – my rule of thumb: I only buy those accessories that fit into my #mojo reporter bag. My bag has started to bulge here and there and in weak moments I'm asking myself whether I need a slightly bigger bag. But I always discipline myself since for me "mobile reporting" goes in hand with easiness and mobility – a formula that is in opposition to the imminent back pain that a video journalist or the camera person experiences when they have to carry tripod, heavy camera and light at the same time. So it's really up to you to decide which accessories you frequently use and need. Journalists who write longer stories, such as for online media, but leave the laptop at home, might appreciate a small Bluetooth keyboard that facilitates text input. The market offers several foldable models that are easy to transport in the accessory bag. There are a few more smart ideas and solutions that I'm going to describe below.

Figure 03-22 My favorite accessories: The DIY egg timer camera pan motor, the OTG stick and the iXpand.

Storage space is always limited: small sticks can help in this emergency situation (fig. 03-19). Sandisk launched the first solution for the iPhone. The iXpand flash drive connects with the Lightning adapter. They don't increase storage space, but they allow you to move files to the storage stick with an app to free up space on the phone. Material on the iXpand can be edited on the computer via the USB plug. The 16GB model costs more than € 40, the 128 GB model more than € 110. Similar products are available by iDisk, iDrive or Phonestar. There are cheaper options for Android phones: if they support the OTG service as most more recent smartphone models do, you can insert a small USB stick that increases storage space. You can then move around files with the file manager of the smartphone. Most sticks have both a mini USB port as well as a USB connection for the computer.

The second big problem is network coverage. It fluctuates a lot, especially in rural areas and during situations of heavy use. In addition, access abroad is often expensive (roaming fees). With most phones the SIM card defines the provider (if the phone doesn't have two SIM card slots). And if you switch the SIM card, people won't be able to reach you under your usual number. If you have the flexibility to use a different network than is defined by your SIM card, you have a solution to this problem. Mobile hotspots (Mifi) build a 3G or 4G/LTE connection with a mobile phone card that can now be used via a WLAN connection. Reliable devices made by Netgear or TP-Link can be purchased for about € 100. The costs for an additional mobile data plan or a data SIM need to be added to your list of expenses. If you use a MiFi-hotspot in addition to the smartphone, you can use two channels at the same time with apps such as Speedify (the 4G connection of the phone and the mobile phone connection of the MiFi-hotspot via WLAN). Professional live streaming apps made by LiveU or Dejero (see chapter 7.11) also use this "bundling", i.e. a bundle of mobile phone and WLAN connections that can be used simultaneously.

And now there are no more limits to creativity. Smartphones are light and as daily objects they turn into useful accessories. I created, for example, a device that turns very slowly and makes good, moving time-lapse recordings. With a high-strength glue I attached a ¼ inch screw to a cheap egg timer. Now I'm able to attach a smartphone with every smartphone mount. Within 60 minutes the egg timer moves 360 degrees. And then there are apps such as Hyperlapse (iOs, Android) that make really fun recordings. #Mojo goes in hand with the love to experiment. Have fun!

Additional Resources
Links

DxO Mark Mobile: The Reference for Image Quality". Accessed March 12, 2016.http://www.dxomark.com/Mobiles

Florian Reichart, Blog "Smartfilming.com",http://www.smartfilming.com.

Glen B. Mulcahy, Blog "TVVJ",http://tvvj.wordpress.com

Nick Garnett, Bloghttp://nickgarnett.co.uk.

Luftfahrtbundesamt. "Anschriften der Landesluftfahrtbehörden". Accessed June 24, 2016.http://www.lba.de/DE/Presse/Landesluftfahrtbehoerden/Landesluftfahrtbehoerden_Uebersicht.html?nn=701672

Stiftung Warentest. "Das müssen Hobby-Piloten wissen." Accessed June 24, 2016.https://www.test.de/Drohnen-Das-muessen-Hobbypiloten-wissen-4727469-0/

Interview with Marc Blank-Settle: "May I use your WiFi, please?"

> Marc Blank-Settle worked for the BBC for many years before he started to train journalists. Today he is a trainer at the BBC "College of Journalism". He is one of the pioneers in the field of "mobile journalism" training. Over the years he has taught thousands of colleagues how to produce quality content for radio and TV with the iPhone.
>
> Twitter:@MarcSettle

As a smartphone journalist who is out and about you are relying on three things: storage capacity, power and best possible connectivity. What do you do if there is no connectivity?

The three pillars of "mobile journalism" are storage capacity, power and connectivity. This is not influenced by the apps that you are using or the story you want to tell. Connectivity might be of particular importance, especially if you want to upload large video files. If you were to upload even only one minute of video content – we can disregard the app or the resolution here – you will have a problem if your connection is slow. Which means: yes, a "mobile journalist" always needs to make an effort to find acceptable network coverage. There are a few tricks: go into airplane mode as soon as possible and then re-activate network connections. This trick has helped me several times. I simply replaced the

2G or 3G network that I previously had by connecting to an 4G network. In other words: simply cut all connections first and then reconnect in a second step.

Is this a simple "trial and error" method or can you explain why it works and if you can really count on it?

I wish I could say that this method is scientifically proven. Unfortunately, it is not. I've not only done it many times but also recommended it to other people. It works more often than it fails. I would always give it a try. It only takes 5 seconds: turn on the airplane mode and turn it off right away. That's it. There are other apps that inform you about the quality of your connection or the locations of the nearest radio tower and Wi-Fi-networks. A really good iOs app is "Open Signal. Since there are many radio towers in the city, it might be enough to just interrupt the connection, walk a couple of feet and then reconnect. In rural areas you might have to walk much further. Some apps don't work with bad UMTS connections. In such a case the app can also help you find the needed network.

I've been working as a journalist for 20 years. When I started I knocked at other people's doors and asked: "May I use your phone to call my editor, please?" Back then there were no mobile phones. Nowadays it might still be worth knocking at doors. My question today is different: "May I use your WiFi, please?" This might be very helpful if you can't even find an UMTS network in rural areas. The Wi-Fi network of the nearest farm can help. Maybe you pay them a couple of Euros to be able to send your material on the way. As I mentioned before: it is the quality of the connection that is essential for a #Mojo to be successful in his job.

Does the BBC really encourage you to knock at someone's door? Have you only had positive experiences so far?

Yes, for the most part. As the BBC we are well known throughout the country. And people are mostly happy to help us. The transmission rate of a private wifi network at someone´s home can be bad, too, especially in rural areas. But that's just bad luck. Some people allow you to use their network for free, others ask: "Hey, and what are you going to pay me?" I don't pay for this out of my own pocket. It's simply a way of having as many options as possible and to have a back-up idea in emergency situations. This is much better than this: if there's no network, I have to stop working.

Does it make sense to use a different mobile hotspot than the one used by the smartphone?

This is very wise. And also: a smartphone without a SIM lock that can be used with any network provider can be useful, too. If the phone only works with one SIM card, problems might come up if your own network is blocked. Many journalists have two phones with different providers so that they have connection with at least one phone or that they can compare which phone offers better connectivity. I once trained journalists in Wales. There are quite a few hills, mountains, valleys – and network coverage differs considerably. Here journalists generally use smartphones that work with more than one provider so that they have several SIM cards available and can try various networks. In contrast to smartphones mobile hotspots normally don't have a "SIM lock" – they can be used with different networks. Some colleagues disagree because they don't want to carry along another device that needs batteries. But a mobile hotspot should be so small that it doesn't interfere with the job too much.

Are there other accessories that might help?

My recommendation: an external storage stick which is available for any phone model. If connectivity is really bad, the reporter can always copy his material to the stick and send it to the newsroom with a messenger or taxi.

There are apps that try to use both a mobile phone and a Wi-Fi connection at the same time. Speedify is one of them. What has been your experience so far? Does it work?

I signed up for Speedify and gave the service a try. Initially, I wasn't impressed with its performance. But they´ve got a lot better by now. There are other services such as Dejero or LiveU (see chapter 7.12.) that bundle more than one channel of transfer. This seems to work much better, but only with a receiving server at the other end. Speedify tries to do the same without that second server.

If connectivity were really bad – what else would you recommend? Should I hold the phone high up in the air?

This depends on the content you want to send. Social networks can deal with low bandwidth. There are services that turn a text message into a Tweet, for example. If all else fails, this could be an option to still report about an incident. A similar service is available for Facebook. So instead of sending simple text messages to single persons, you can send them to a service that converts them into postings on Twitter or Facebook, if the data network is bad or doesn't work. In fact the biggest problem is big amounts of data, especially video content.

Will 5G change anything – the mobile standard beyond LTE that shall be introduced in 2020?

Supposedly 5G is going to change everything. It's the next "big thing". We wont' know if this is really going to be the case until the end of the decade. An important question is whether the promised download rate – such as a movie within seconds – will be matched with comparable upload rates. This would be essential for mobile journalism. A further question refers to the location of 5G: can we only use it in bigger cities? When is it going to be rolled out in rural areas? We already experience today that even UMTS is not available everywhere.

What's your opinion – is "mobile journalism" still useful if one of its main pillars – connectivity – is missing, as for example in rural areas?

You have to ask yourself which resources you have at hand. If you have a high-quality camera, a team and an OB van, you will achieve better results than using a smartphone with bad connectivity. Most people though don't have an OB van parked in their lot. And for them a smartphone can turn into a pocket news headquarters, even without good network coverage: because smartphones can record in radio or TV quality, edit and send – maybe after returning to the office. The smartphone enables the journalist to always be a journalist. If something happens and the camera crew happens to be in the same place by coincidence – great. But how likely is this scenario? This is what I want journalists to understand: with the smartphone they can always report when something is happening.

Is "mobile journalism" easier to implement and distribute if there is a lack of resources (e.g. camera crew, editing studios)?

We usually have a camera team available when something happens. But there aren't as many teams as there are stories that we want to tell. In this aspect the smartphone offers a big opportunity to us at the BBC. An opportunity to tell stories that are different and new. If you have a small budget, as a blogger for example, you can't afford a crew. Smartphone journalism might be your only chance to produce audio or video content. And you can directly share your content on social media – what a great opportunity!

As a Mojo-aficionado, do you wish that all camera crews would stay in the office for one week and that only smartphones would be allowed?

At first sight this seems like a wonderful idea. I'm not convinced though that we would be able to offer reports to our audience that meet their expectations with regard to image and audio quality. Because smartphones have their limits – difficult light situations, for example. You can use external lights, but in the end we all need to identify the limits of the smartphone and know how to deal with them. Yet a smartphone can be useful to shoot the reverse shot in an interview situation, for example, as a second camera so to say.

What are your Mojo must-haves?

I think that a handful of devices that fit in a small bag are more than enough: additional storage, a small microphone, and a small tripod. A light can be useful, but it is not always necessary. An external battery is a must, maybe a mobile hotspot, too. You can spend a lot of money on additional lenses, such as the Sony lenses mentioned in chapter 3.7. But all of these items add extra weight to your equipment, making it heavy and expensive. I now know: a few accessories for little money already improve your footage considerably.

Marc Blank-Settle's equipment (2016): clip-on microphone, light, tripod, storage extension for iPhone, smartphone grip, clip-on lens and external battery.

4 Radio broadcasting on the move

Summary

Which apps are helpful when you are doing interviews and recording background atmosphere with a smartphone? How can we produce fully edited pieces to camera and complete packages from audio clips? Which apps support live reporting with a smartphone? How can we publish radio reports?

"Mobile journalism" has already become a daily routine for many radio journalists, even more so than for their TV colleagues: the era of tape recordings is long gone. Flash recorders and other storage media have been introduced. Smartphones are storage media, too, with the advantage of a built-in broadcasting feature. More and more stations redesign their workflows in such a way that they can broadcast live feeds provided by their reporters via phones (and please keep in mind: the feed doesn't have phone quality, but meets broadcasting standards). The difficulties that video journalists deal with – poor image quality (often due to bad mobile phone connection), high storage needs and battery usage – are put into perspective with regard to audio productions that use less storage and battery power. Today most mobile phones can easily manage various audio codecs that are important in radio production.

The change in radio broadcasting is well underway: many stations now dispatch OB vans only to cover major events by several reporters working for several programs. A single reporter would now only rarely appear with complete equipment at a press conference or a book presentation – mainly because his mobile phone offers him similar options as the OB van did 10 years ago. "Mobile reporting" in radio broadcasting is not only cheaper than traditional production since expensive technology and additional people can stay at home. "Mobile reporting" offers other advantages, too: a reporter with a smartphone is more mobile than an OB van, as, for example, during a protest march or at an event that takes place in a larger area. As a mobile journalist you can easily decide to switch locations or even hop onto a boat or bus, when the story needs you to. My advice: decide on team constellations on a case-by-case basis. Even if a smartphone is the cheaper means of production, it might be worthwhile to have a second team member – a technician or a reporter – on location as a support. Sharing tasks is helpful to be on air not only faster but also with better quality. With a smartphone radio broadcasting is possible for everyone. If a personal DAB or UKW transmitter is not available, the finished audio reports can be published online. There are several well-suited platforms that are offering such a service.

The built-in smartphone mic is a good choice for many recordings: this mostly applies to iOS-phones and better Android-/ Windows models. Smartphone microphones capture background noises ("atmo") in usable quality. As described in chapter 3.1 it is possible to slip a conventional wind cover of a ball-shaped microphone on the phone to avoid wind noise during external recordings. There are also resourceful providers that create wind covers specifically for smartphones.

If the built-in microphone does not provide the desired quality, an external microphone might solve the problem (see chapter 3.2.). In interview settings I would recommend lavalier (or "clip-on") microphones or handheld, often directional microphones. With the help of a tripod a directional mic may be placed closely to the interview partner, such as on a table. Handling noise can be avoided as well. Cords should always be positioned "with space". If they are positioned too tightly, movements might lead to clicking or other noise.

4.1 A little bit of theoretical background: audio formats

To make sure that important recordings are successful, basic knowledge of audio and file formats might be helpful. If you plan to save recordings, you need both a format and a container – a process that is very similar to preserving fruit: fresh fruit may be cut into pieces, soft-boiled or cooked into jam. Then the result is filled into a jar, a tin or another container. A good overview of the most important formats and containers is provided on the blog "e-teaching.org" (see Additional Resources below) that I used as a resource for the summary below.

Containers for audio formats are marked by file extensions, e.g. ".mp3", ".wav", ".m4a", ".ogg" or ".wma". While the label on the jar of jam provides information about the expiration date, the cook or ingredients, audio containers might be labelled, too – with "meta data" such as the name of the author, song title or date of recording.

The most important audio containers

WAVE: files with a ".wav" extension usually store uncompressed digital data that is available in PCM-format (see below). ".wav" files are often the best choice and are recommended if recordings are processed later on, such as during editing.

AIFF/CAF: These containers developed by Apple may store various formats; most often uncompressed audio files which is adequate for mobile journalism. The CAF-container stores considerably more meta data than AIFF and is not limited in volume.

MP3: The popular "mp3"-container generally includes compressed recordings in MPEG-1 Audio Layer 3 or MPEG-2 Audio Layer 3. An ".mp3"-file is considerably smaller than a ".wav"-file but with an identical audio length. It is better suited for data transfer if phone connectivity is bad. On the other hand data is lost during the storage process.

MP4/M4A: The MP4-container originates from Apple's QuickTime file format. MP4-containers may store video and audio in addition to images, graphic elements or text. The file extension ".m4a" is more precise for containers with audio data compressed in the AAC coding process.

WMA: Microsoft competes with the "ASF" container format that is labelled with the extension ".wma" if it stores coded audio content.

OGG/OGA: In contrast to MP3 and MP4 the OGG-container is a free container that is not limited by software patents and can be used for various media content. For audios the audio codec "Vorbis" and the file extension ".oga" are generally used.

The container includes information about the sound: the spoken word, music or atmospheric sounds need to be "translated" into a digital format to be stored. Eventually frequencies often translate into "0" and "1". This conversion into "on" and "off" is made possible by different codecs – tiny programs that do not only convert sound into digital information but that also produce real sounds from digital information. There are various codecs that each "understand" specific formats, comparable to an English-German dictionary that only helps to translate from English to German (and vice versa).

The most important audio formats

PCM (pulse-code modulation) converts sounds into digital information without any major losses. This is perfect for further processing during editing if, for example, low-pitched sounds need to be raised or bird sounds intensified. As a consequence PCM files are much larger than compressed audio files.

Flac (Free Lossless Audio Codec) compresses without any losses and is not linked to any expensive software licences.

MP3 (MPEG-1 Audio Layer 3 and MPEG-2 Audio Layer 3) is one of the first compressed codecs and was developed by the Fraunhofer Institut. MP3, in particular, is very popular. It codes sounds but it uses compression: certain information is omitted – which is hardly audible – to minimize recordings. LAME is an open codec, similar to MP3.

AAC (Advanced Audio Coding) also codes with losses and minimizes music on CD, for example, to a sixteenth part of its original size. The process succeeds MP3 and is the preferred choice for some users since it offers a stronger compression at a better sound quality.

WMA (Windows Media Audio) is a lossy coding process developed by Microsoft. WMA is widely used because it supports the music industry's DRM (Digital Rights Management) among other things.

Vorbis is an open source code that compresses with losses, but is not patented and can be used without any licence fees.

4.2 Android: Recording and Editing

There is a large selection of apps that allow you to record with your Android smartphone. In my opinion the following criteria are important: the app should support the most important audio codecs, in particular enabling lossless uncompressed recordings (PCM/FLAC as .wav- or .aiff/caf). Usage needs to be simple and straightforward. A visible audio meter should help during the recording, for example in regulating an external microphone. It would be ideal if the sound could already be monitored during the recording (by using an iRig Pre, for example, see chapter 3.3.)

A program that fulfils all of these prerequisites is "Easy Voice Recorder Pro". The pro version has a couple of important add-ons, such as stereo recordings and offers the possibility to adjust the input volume (gain). When you open the program, you could start recording right away (fig. 04-01), though I recommend the following preliminary steps: with the magic wand (1) you open a drop-down menu (fig. 04-02) in which you can adjust the input level of the microphone, for example (1). You can configure the app so that it skips silent parts (2) – a rather problematic step for journalistic recordings since silence transports information, too. You can see all the presets in the overview (3). Back in the main menu (fig. 04-01) the three menu items direct you to the most important basic settings (fig. 04-03).

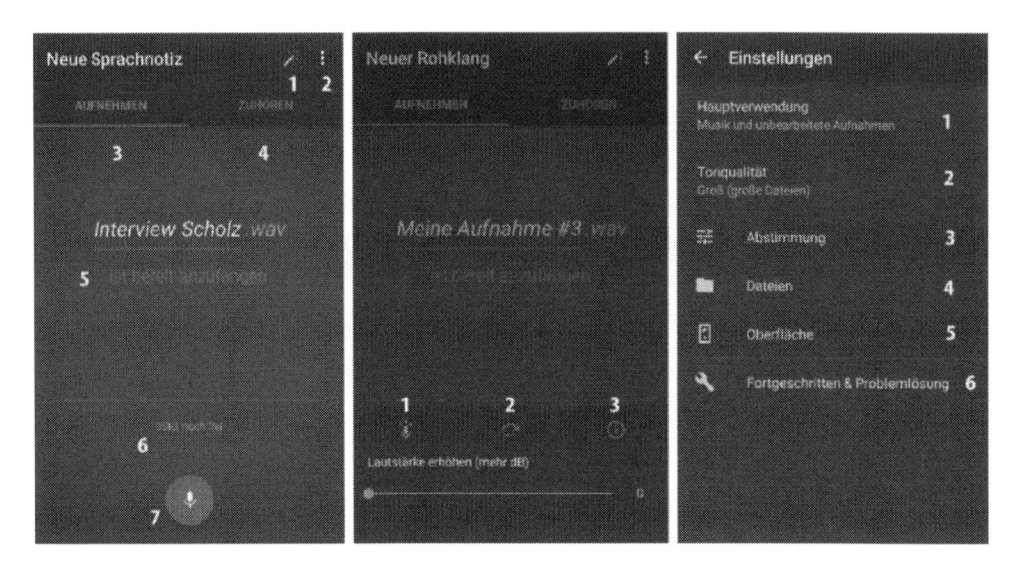

Figure 04-01, 02, 03

I would recommend making recordings that are as lossless as possible, without any compression or pre-set filters (an exception: if storage is limited and you need smaller files). As the main purpose (1) select "music and unedited recordings". Then select "large" in the sound quality setting (2) (which leads to bigger files). You can determine the format in the "Settings" (3) menu (fig. 04-04). Select the "main line" as the microphone as it records raw material – unless you are using a Bluetooth microphone (see chapter 3.2.). It also gives you the option to activate stereo recording. It is important to determine both the recording container as well as the format – which is ".wav (PCM)". Please keep in mind that these recordings take up about 5.5 megabyte (MB) of storage per minute while all other formats produce smaller files due to compression (at 48 kHz m4a, mp4 and aac need approx. 0.9 MB per minute, 3gp between 36 and 92 kilobyte per minute which is not good enough for professional recordings). The sample rate should be as high as possible with a normal rate of 48 kilohertz (kHz) which in turn produces the largest possible files: a .wav file at 48 kHz takes up 5 MB, at 8 kHz only 0.9 MB. The bit rate only needs to be defined for the AAC format.

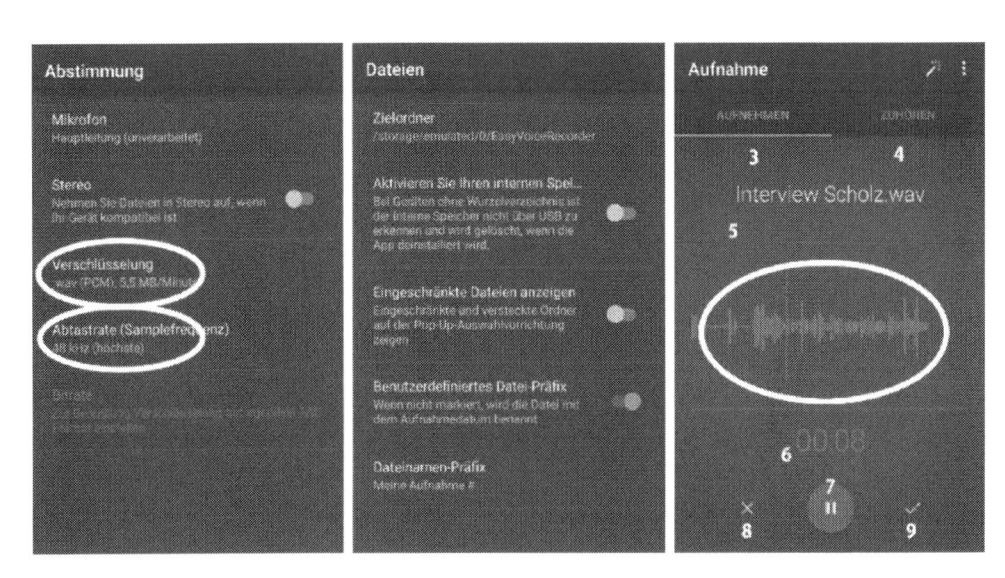

Figure 04-04, 05, 06

Configure the storage location in the "Files" menu (fig. 04-03, (4)). Here you can define the target folder (fig. 04-05) which is helpful if you want to save sound bites of a particular project in a specific folder. If you put some time into organizing your material early in the recording phase, you will save a lot of time during editing. Some devices require an activation of the internal storage so that recordings can be copied to the computer and are not deleted if the app is deleted. Easy Voice Recorder saves recordings by default by adding the date of recording to the file name. You can change this by saving a "custom file prefix". This would allow you to easily identify all files of a single project.

After these basic settings you can start recording. In the main menu (fig. 04-06) you can now name the file (5). This name appears in the title of the recording, following the date or the user prefix. The recording starts and pauses when you tap the recording button (7). The audio meter (circled) starts to move from left to right indicating whether the recording is correctly balanced: the blue bars should get bigger and smaller; red bars indicate overmodulation. The time code (6) reflects the current length of recording. After the recording this needs to be either checked (8) or discarded (9). In the "Listen" menu (4) the finished recordings can be continued, listened to, renamed, discarded or transferred to other apps (Cloudspeicher, for example) or to editing.

A further recording app for Android that I can recommend is RecForge Pro. It is less clearly organized and shows weaknesses in the translation quality of the menu items. RecForge Pro supports listening in during the recording. The titanium recorder allows the most important basic settings and supports uncompressed WAV-recordings as well as microphone amplification. There are several more recording apps for Android.

There are also several programs available for editing. The free Lexis Audio Editor (also available as a paid app for Windows phones, see chapter 4.4.), for example, only offers a single track. Blends and mixed tracks, such as atmo and sound bite or sound bite and music, can only be realized with limitations and involve several steps. On the other hand Lexis offers a large selection of tools that allow you to easily accomplish a few short editing steps.

http://www.lexisaudioeditor.com/

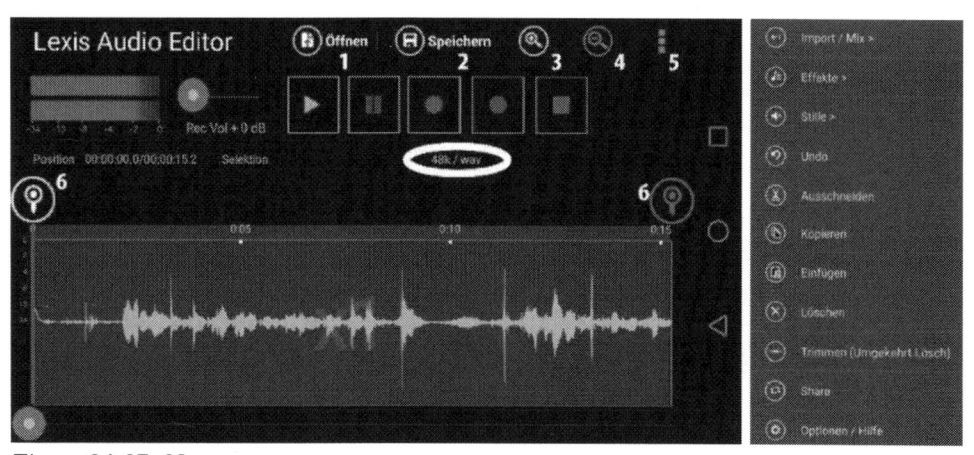

Figure 04-07, 08

Lexis starts with the editor window (fig. 04-07). It is important to configure the basic settings first by selecting the respective menu items (5). The menu (fig. 04-08) also includes many important functions for editing. In the "Options" menu (at the bottom) select editing with the highest bitrate (320 kilobytes per second) and in a lossless, not compressed .wav-format. In the Editor menu Lexis displays the selected format option (circled).

Next you can open the first audio track (1). With the two selectors (6) on the right and left you can mark the range that will be copied, cut or edited. In the menu (5) you can

4 Radio broadcasting on the move

import further tracks that will be added to the end of the file. You can mix tracks (e.g. atmo with piece to camera) – but you only have an "all-or-nothing"-option – it is not possible, for example, to exclude individual parts of the track. Here Lexis reaches its limits. The timeline can be enlarged (3) or minimised (4). After you are finished editing, you can save the track (2).

Editing is much more convenient with a multi-track audio editor. Audio Evolution Mobile Pro was developed for the music business and offers a wide range of functions (the free version should only be used to test the program). Journalists won't need all the options offered by the program. They make its usage rather confusing, even complicated. The big advantages of Audio Evolution Mobile Pro are the availability of multiple tracks and the supported audio formats. The app also supports MIDI-devices so the start screen is unnecessary for #Mojo purposes: confirming the MIDI-device (none) with OK brings you to the timeline (fig. 04-09).

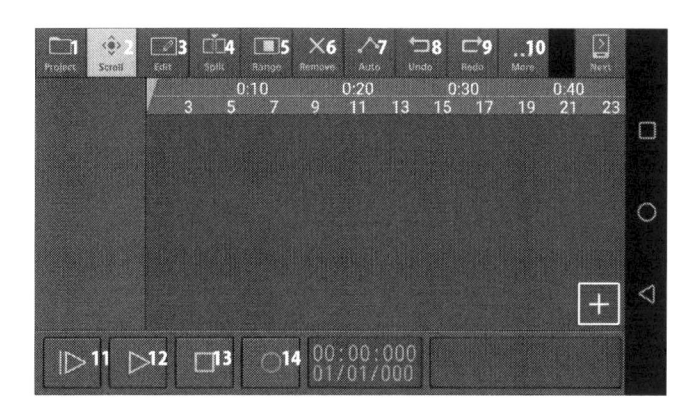

Figure 04-09

The timeline offers different editing options. You cannot only start a new project with (1), but you can also import clips and export finished clips. "Scroll" (2) means that you can move the timeline to the right and left with a simple touch. "Edit" (3) moves single clips that have been marked; "Split" (4) divides clips. With "Range" (5) you can label, move or copy clips. (6) deletes single clips. Audio Evolution Mobile also offers the possibility to adjust the volume within a clip (7). In addition, it also features the important undo- (8) and redo-(9) function so that there aren't any irreversible steps. While "More" (10) offers further options, (11) plays the present timeline, and (12) starts at the playhead. (13) stops the playback and (14) lets you add your own recordings within the app (e.g. your off comments).

Before you start recording, you should configure the basis settings. In the "Project" menu (1) you can define the sample rate in the "Options" menu. Select radio broadcasting quality and standard, i.e. 48.000 hertz. Then you can start and name a new project in the same menu (4) or open an existing one (5) (fig. 04-10). The first menu item allows you to import an "audio / MIDI file" (1) or a "song from the music database" (2) (the app accesses the music files that are stored on the phone). After you've added several clips, they appear with visible audio meters in different colours in the timeline (fig. 04-11). In the right bottom corner (circled) there's an overview of the parts of the timeline that are currently displayed in the editing window. You can enlarge or minimise the scale of the clips that are displayed by zooming in or out of the timeline with two fingers. The green playhead button (1) indicates where the playback was stopped. The plus symbol (2) allows you to add more tracks.

Figure 04-10

4 Radio broadcasting on the move

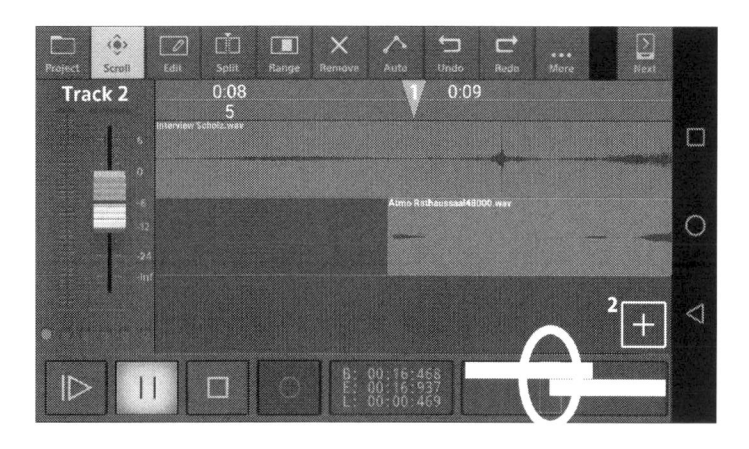

Figure 04-11

This app needs getting used to: first select the type of editing in the tool bar; only then select the clips that you want to edit. In comparison with many other apps this is the reverse order. Other apps let you mark the clip first and then you can select the tool to edit this sample. If clips have been moved to the right position, you select the menu item "Auto" for a crossfade first and label the positions within the clip that need fading (fig. 04-12). The tool bar on the top changes with the selection of the "auto" menu: two new options appear that allow you to select new positions (1) or move existing ones (2).

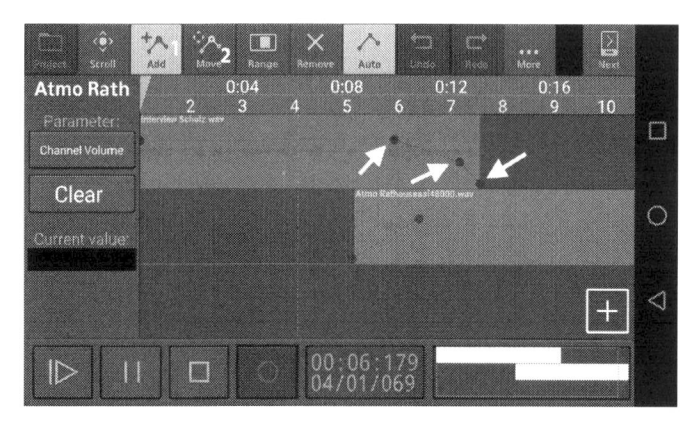

Figure 04-12

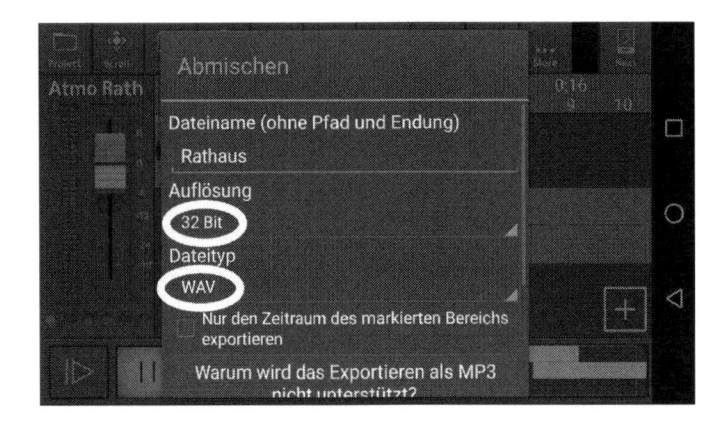

Figure 04-13

You need practice to get used to working with Audio Evolution Mobile Pro. Once you've mastered it, the program is a wonderful tool: you can record, create and mix audio clips consisting of sound bites, atmo and text by a speaker since single clips can be accurately moved and edited. Once a clip is finished, it is exported via the "Project" menu ("mix / dub project"). In the menu (fig. 04-13) you now need to define the "resolution" (32 bit) as well as the file format once again: the lossless but storage intensive ".wav"-format would be my recommendation. The file is saved to the project or music directory and can now be published or forwarded.

http://www.extreamsd.com/index.php/products/audio-evolution-mobile-for-android

After the most recent update the "N Track" app is a good alternative, too: its free version already offers four audio tracks and allows you to mix finished clips. With the subscription (approx. € 2 per month) you can export uncompressed audio files in .wav format with 32 or 64 bit. "N Track" as well as "Audio Evolution" are both more than an audio mixer: the small recording studio supports MIDI tracks as well as other functions that are not necessary for mobile journalism and that might make the app quite confusing.

4 Radio broadcasting on the move

4.3 iOs: Recording and Editing

There is a large selection of recorders in Apple's app store. Many are unsuitable, some are ok, only a few are excellent. And you know by now that these programs should record with good audio quality. In addition, they should offer the selection of different format and container settings and allow to listen to the sound during the recording. Usable recorders are, for example, the "AVR" app as well as the "Recorder" app" or "Recorder+" (be careful – there are many apps with similar names).

A free and simple option that fulfils all major functions is "Voice Recorder", often used by journalists – Voice Recorder almost has the status of a legend. But its best recording quality (PCM in -.wav container, 353 kilobits per second) is only at 22.050 hertz while the generally required standard in audio broadcasting is at 48.000 hertz. Yet the recordings are still very good.

Voice Recorder starts with the file menu (fig. 04-14): storage is empty when you start the app for the first time. You need to define important parameters before you start recording. These can be accessed via the wheel icon in the top left corner (1). In the settings menu (fig. 04-15) you can then define the format – VoiceRecorder offers .wav files as well as AAC, MP4, CAF and AIFF. Back in the file menu you can start a new project file (2) or you can search for files (3). You can access recorded audio clips from your desktop computer or tablet via Wi-Fi (4) – a very useful option. When you touch the microphone button (6), Voice Recorder switches to the recording window and starts recording right away.

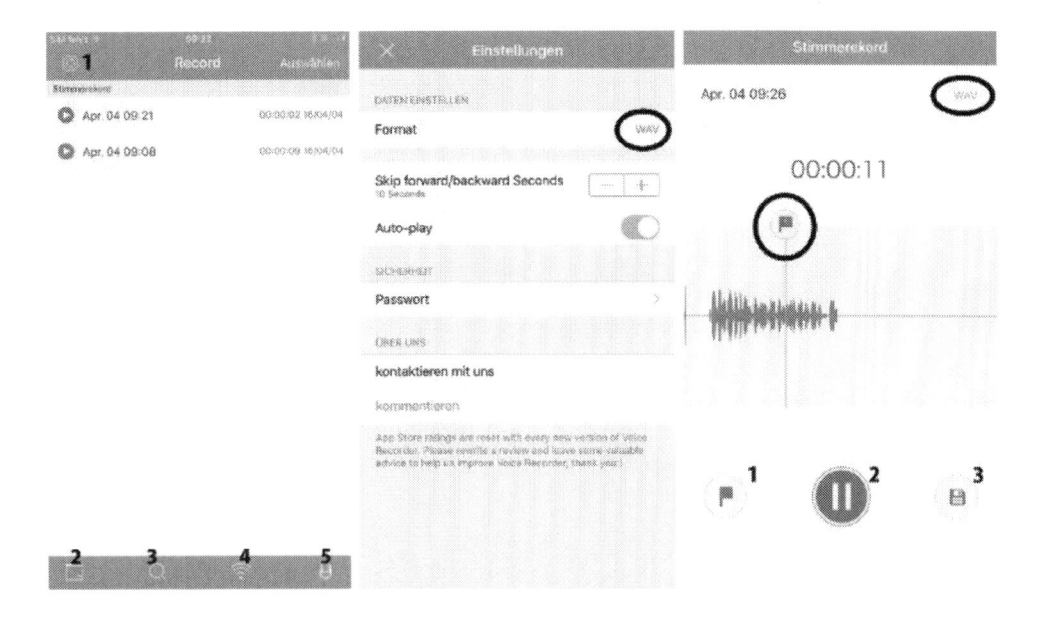

Figure 04-14, 15, 16

An audio meter appears during the recording (fig. 04-16) that allows you to monitor the level of recording. You can set markers with the flag symbol (1 and circled) that make it easier to edit the material at a later step (please keep in mind that these markers are not transferred to other programs). The recording format is displayed in the top right corner (circled). The recording can be stopped (2) and saved when completed (3). The recording appears in the file menu where it can be listened to or transferred to other apps for further editing.

https://itunes.apple.com/us/app/voice-recorder-free/id685310398?mt=8

Another good app for recording and editing is the "Hindenburg Field Recorder". Named after the airship that crashed in 1937. From the app developer's perspective this was the first big moment of live broadcasting on the radio. In addition to the iOs-app there are several desktop programs made by Hindenburg that process content. Unfortunately, the app is quite costly – yet it offers a large range of functions. It relies on the .wav format which is good for #mojo-purposes. But there aren't any other options. This might be problematic if a report can't be transmitted as a .wav-file due to bad connectivity. In such as case a second program would be necessary that compresses the .wav-file and converts it to another format.

4 Radio broadcasting on the move

The Hindenburg Field Recorder starts with the recording screen (fig. 04-17). The wheel icon (8) lets you configure the most important settings. Select the reporter view in the settings menu (fig. 04-18) because it provides a better overview during recordings. Put the sample rate to 48 kHz. You can listen in to recordings and adjust the input volume (gain). The pro-version supports 24-bit files (can be selected), but it normally works with 16-bit recordings. At the bottom of the settings menu you can delete all projects at once – a convenient feature during spring-cleaning season.

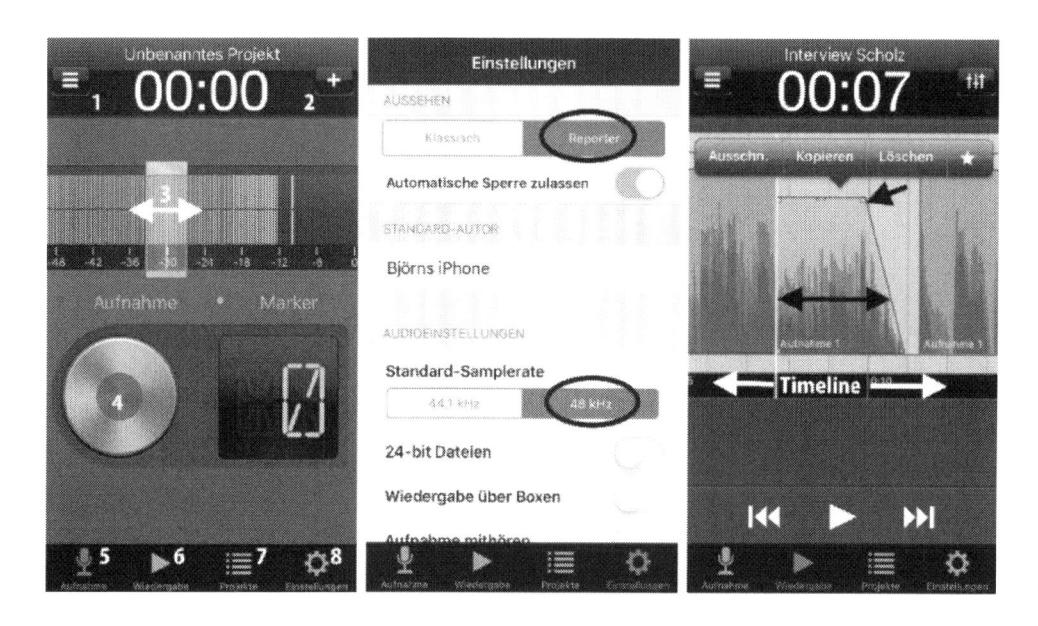

Figure 04-17, 18, 19

Start a new project with the plus symbol (2) in the recording menu (fig. 04-17). The input volume can be adjusted with the slider (3): a recording should display a blue amplitude, with a maximum of yellow heads. If the amplitude turns red, the recording is over-modulated. The recording starts with a touch of the recording button (4). While it's running, you can set markers with the recording button – which is now yellow – that are displayed in the menu on the top right (1). This makes editing at a later step much easier. The recording stops when you move the pause icon in the slider to the right.

Now the recording is available on the "Play" screen (fig. 04-19). It appears as an audio meter and can now be edited. Using the tools isn't easy, especially not when you use the app for the first time: many functions are hidden behind a double tap. An example: with a double tap on the timeline two markers appear that allow you to mark a segment. With another double tap an editing menu appears that allows you to cut, edit or delete the segment. The volume of a marked segment (displayed in orange-brown) can be adjusted by moving the corners (black arrows). A clip may get a lower overall volume or fade at the beginning or end.

In the project menu the blue clip can now be shared – as a project or for editing with another Hindenburg program on the computer or as a .wav-file. Here Hindenburg offers useful options such as "send via email", a direct FTP-upload or an upload to Soundcloud.

https://hindenburg.com/products/hindenburg-field-recorder

Further apps for recording and editing are, for example, the TwistedWaveRecorder and -Editor, the recording and edit app Hokusai or "voddio" – technically a video editing program that also edits multiple audio tracks. A problem, however, is that the voddio app hasn't been improved and the most recent update was not very solid. The BBC reporter Nick Garnett (see interview below) relied on audio editing with the multi-track editor voddio for many years, but now favours a new app that meets (almost) all needs a radio/audio reporter might need: Ferrite.

The paid app "Ferrite" combines the best features of many programs: it is a good recording tool with a multi-track editor. Because of this the app is highly recommended by most professional mobile journalists. Even the free version is good enough to produce shorter audio pieces. But lossless audio (ALAC-container/CAF-format) can only be produced with the premium version. If you are using the free version, you only get lossy m4a-audio container in AAC-format. Up to three audio tracks are free while the paid version offers up to 32 tracks.

4 Radio broadcasting on the move

Figure 04-20, 21, 22

The library is the starting point of the Ferrite app (fig. 04-20). As with the other apps mentioned above you should configure the basic settings first by tapping the wrench icon in the top right corner (1): the context menu (fig. 04-21) lets you import audio or open the user guide. The second menu item leads to the settings menu (fig. 04-22). Ferrite distinguishes between the recording format and the output format. If you want to produce lossless content continuously, you need to select "lossless (ALAC/.CAF)" as both the recording and the output format. The latter option is only available to users of the paid app.

Simple clips can be recorded in the library – with a tap on the microphone, labelled with an arrow (fig. 04-20). The small wheel lets you adjust the input volume (2) while using an external microphone. Below the recording screen Ferrite displays recordings that are available and that can now be edited (3). A tap on the info icon (4) shows the most important file parameters – here you can modify the file name, for example. The file can be saved to the phone or transferred with a tap on the "sharing" icon (5). (6) deletes files (please note: clips are unrecoverable after deletion).

105

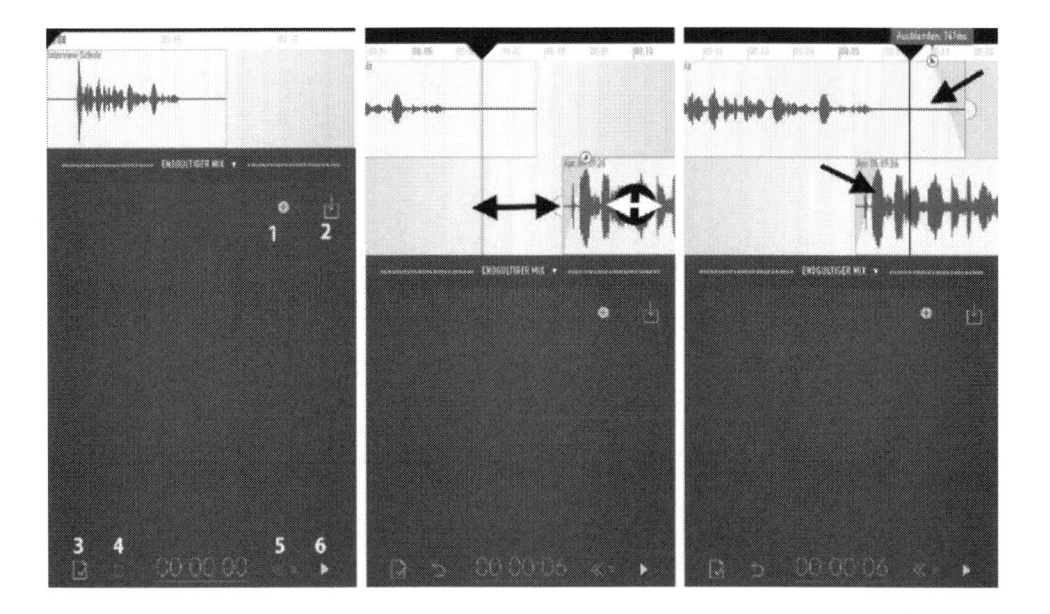

Figure 04-23, 24, 25

Ferrite turns into a multi-track editor when you open the editing screen (fig. 04-23): the selected clip will be opened on the first track. More tracks can be added with the plus icon (1). With (2) you can add another clip to the new track in the timeline. When you are finished editing, you need to click the checkmark (3). You always have the option to undo the last editing step (4). You can navigate the timeline with (5) and play the content of the timeline with (6).

Editing clips is easy: trim the content at the beginning and end of a clip with the handle (fig. 04-24). A tap on the clip opens a context menu that allows you to copy, cut, delete or move the clip to the play head position. You can also grab the clip and move it within the timeline. The audio volume can be adjusted by clicking the small arrows at the corners of the clip (fig. 04-25). If you move them to the middle of the clip, the beginning or end of the audio will fade. In addition, Ferrite offers "Auto Ducking": music is set to automatically "duck under" another track if a piece of a segment is layered with a sound bite. The professional version of Ferrite offers more filters and effects that are explained in the comprehensive app manual. After you are finished editing, you can save or share the clip as described above.

https://www.wooji-juice.com/products/ferrite/

4.4 Windows: Recording and Editing

For Windows phones there are hardly any useful recorders that allow the adjustment of the recording quality. The "VoiceRecorderPro 8.1", for example, codes sound in the lossless ACC-format with only 98 kilobits per second at 44100 hertz. Other apps are "Audio Recorder", "Free Recorder" and "Voice Recorder Pro +" – all of them don't record in satisfactory quality. The Lexis Audio Editor is also available for Windows phones but you can only edit a single track. I can recommend the "Recording Studio" app. It is free but needs practice.

An app that has everything is offered by Microsoft for a little money: with "Wave Master" you can define the quality of the recording while you also have a comprehensive audio editor at hand that is similar to Windows Movie Maker (see chapter 6.4.). The program starts with the project manager. With the plus icon you can start and name a new project. In the next step Wave Master automatically displays the editing window (fig. 04-26). Now you should configure the basic settings (4): a menu appears that directs you to the most important "Options" via "Settings" (fig. 04-27). Recording quality should be "high" and Wave Master should export a .wav audio format to avoid any losses caused by compression. Wave Master exports PCM at 48.000 hertz, but only about 1500 kilobit per second.

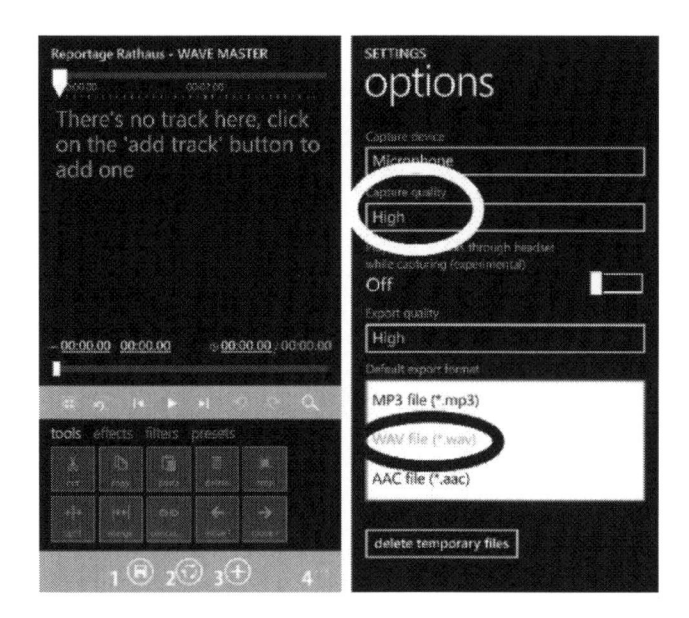

Figure 04-26, 27

You can add your first clips with the plus icon: a white submenu appears and allows you to add an empty track, to record (circled) or import a track (fig. 04-28). The recording mode opens another window (fig. 04-29) in which you can record an interview or "ambient sound", i.e. background noise, with either the built-in or an external microphone. The recording button (1) starts and pauses the recording, the "Stop" button stops it (2), "cancel" cancels (and discards) the recording (3).

4 Radio broadcasting on the move

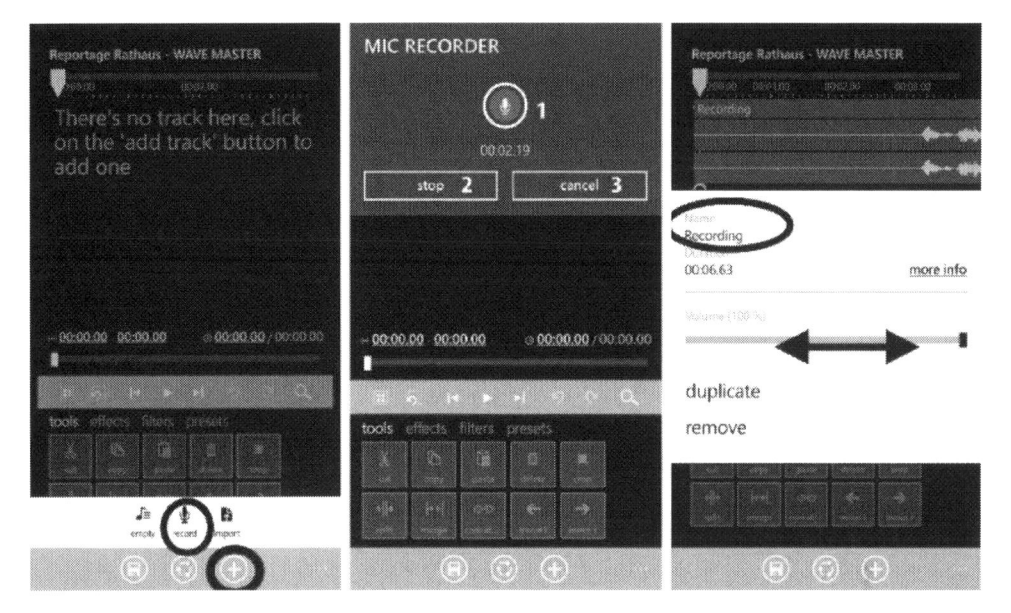

Figure 04-28, 29, 30

The recorded or imported clip appears in the timeline (fig. 04-30). By touching the clip for several seconds an additional window opens in which you can name (circled) and place markings to the clip. This makes editing easier. In addition, a clip can be copied, and the volume of each clip can be adjusted in relation to other recordings (arrow).

109

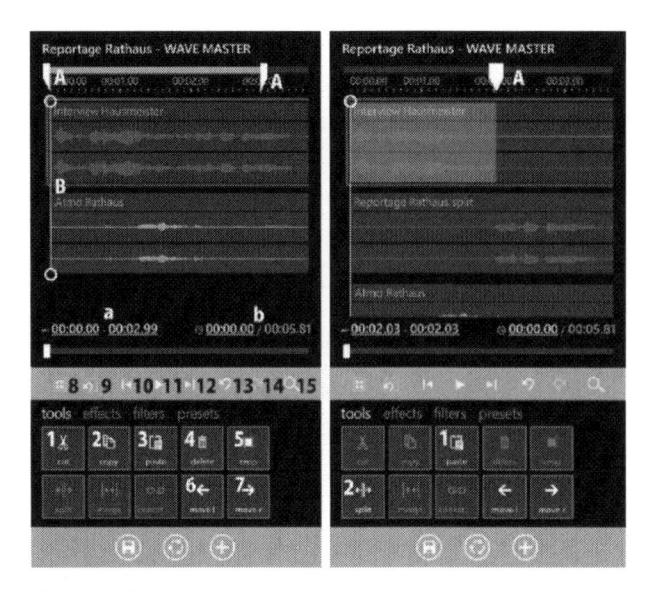

Figure 04-31, 32

The timeline features two different tools (fig. 04-31): the play head (B) and two markers (A) that select a segment for editing. The time codes (a) indicate the start and end of the segment to be edited (between the markers A), the time codes (b) indicate the position of the play head as well as the overall length. "Edit" refers to the selected clips (colour coded) in the respective segment – in the given example only to track 1 ("Interview janitor in red"). The marked segment can now be cut (1), copied (2) or deleted (4). In addition, a clip can be inserted to the marked segment from the clipboard (3). "Crop" cuts everything that is outside of the marked segment. You might have to get used to the fact that you can't move any clips with a simple touch: Wave Master doesn't accept any "empty" regions. This means that each clip is as long as the longest clip. What is important, though, is the position at which the actual content can be heard (the rest is filled with silence). With "Move" (6 and 7) you can move the audible clip content within a track. This is quite complicated so the "undo" and "redo" (13 and 14) function might come in handy. The blue bar facilitates the definition of the working segment: all clips can be selected (8) or all labels removed (9). (10) jumps to the beginning of the clip, (12) to the end, (12) plays the clip. With (15) you can adjust the scale of the timeline.

The editing marks (A) can be moved onto each other to mark a specific point on the timeline instead of a region (fig. 04-32). Now new tools become available: the clip can be subdivided at the respective position (a new track is created that contains the content of the marked clip). In addition, you can insert audio content to this exact position which then overwrites the clip content. The disc icon makes the finished piece available. It can be saved to the phone (a file menu opens), the cloud or can be directly published on Soundcloud.

4.5 Publication

Many journalists publish their content on their employers' channels: a radio station, a website etc. All they have to do is make sure that their audio tracks get to their client. With regard to audio files this is no rocket science since the files are significantly smaller than videos. A .wav file is so small that it can be sent via email. It can easily be sent via FTP transfer (e.g. iTransfer Pro for iPhone or FiIezilla for Android phones) or via platforms such as "We Transfer" (iOs- and Android app). If you want to publish audio on your personal platform, you need to plan your social media strategy carefully so that an actual audience will discover your clips (more information on this topic is provided by Stephan Primbs in "Social Media für Journalisten"). If you do so, there is a good chance that you reach an audience with your audio tracks.

Podcasts are becoming more and more popular. You can publish a podcast on your personal blog; Wordpress and others offer specific plugins. There are numerous – some of them free – platforms that let you share audio, such as Podbean or iTunes: in order to strengthen their own product, Apple bought and closed the independent podcasting platform Swell in 2014.

Figure 04-33

Soundcloud is still very popular for audio content (fig. 04-33). Its big advantage: Soundcloud links cannot only be shared on Twitter, for example, but they can also be listened to. The Soundcloud app lets you not only consume audio, but you can also upload your own tracks. Soundcloud is commonly used and I think that it is a good platform to publish "raw" audio tracks as an addition to a personal blog. There are a few more good options that link audio with photos or other visual media. We are going to present some of these ideas in chapter 8 ("Digital Storytelling"). In addition, there are several apps that link and send short audio clips to Twitter, such as Chirbit. The new app "Anchor" (iOs and Android) is also popular. It is a social network that hosts two-minute podcasts and shares them with other social networks. Unfortunately, it is not possible to upload pre-produced tracks with the Anchor smartphone app. This is only possible on demand with a desktop tool (as of August 2016) – bummer!

4.6 Live streaming and apps with an input server

Radio is a live medium, too: many stations appreciate that they can quickly have a connection to the correspondent who is on location. The simplest option (which is almost too simple to be mentioned here) is a simple phone call – because in the end a smartphone is nothing more than a good old mobile phone. There were times stations wanted journalists to use a phone for a live talk to establish an ISDN connection and to get a much better quality, even when a "music taxi" – an ISDN codec for transmiting audio – was available. So when an event unfolds before your own eyes, it might be worthwhile to call your station's editor-in-chief to discuss whether a live report on the phone could be the right choice for now.

With the data connection of the smartphone it is now possible to establish high-quality audio connections with minimal delay: the station needs to be equipped with an input server that can read the sender's codec and converts back to audio signals. This complex (and expensive) technology enables live connection with minimal delay between sender and recipient. If latency is too high, a conversation between the studio and the reporter on location is impossible because too much time passes between question and answer. In Europe the "Luci-Live" app has many customers. One of them is the ARD: their "MUPRO" app based on Luci-Live makes live talks with audio return flow as well as the transfer of finished radio reports possible. In the Netherlands the app is used by several public

4 Radio broadcasting on the move

broadcasting companies to report from all over the world. The paid app only works with an input server and as such it's not a good option for #Mojo individuals. In the USA Comrex developed a similar system. Both companies want to add video live streaming to their portfolio to meet the growing demands of multimedia journalists. A third alternative is an app called Report-It. Just like Luci-Live it needs a login name and password that you can only get when your company has a license.

Live streaming is also possible for journalists that don't work for a station. The "Mixlr" app works for audio as do Periscope or Facebook Live for video: after installation the user can go live and send a stream to his Mixlr page (fig. 04-34). The user can alert potential listeners to the live report on Twitter or Facebook by turning on the Facebook/Twitter icon. Before the start he can choose a category for the live stream so that it is easier to find on the Mixlr homepage. During the broadcast it is possible to send further Tweets or messages or to use the chat function of the Mixlr platform. The delay between sender and recipient is about 10 seconds – still acceptable for live comments during a football match. A delay of 10 seconds would certainly be too long for an interview with the studio (a second phone would be needed as a return line with the questions of the host).

Figure 04-34

113

Additional Resources

Books

Stefan Primbs, Social Media für Journalisten: Redaktionell arbeiten mit Facebook, Twitter & Co. (Wiesbaden: Springer VS, 1. ed. 2015)

Links

"Audioformate und -Codecs im Überblick". Blog e-teaching.org. Accessed March 30, 2016. https://www.e-teaching.org/technik/aufbereitung/audio/audiocodecs

"Ferrite Recording Studio User Guide V 1.2". Accessed April 3, 2016. http://service.wooji-juice.com/ferrite/user-guide/ferrite-user-guide-1.2.pdf

Wytse Vellinga. "Mobile Storytelling" Blog. Accessed April 3, 2016. http://mobile-storytelling.com/

Interview with Nicholas Garnett: "A reporter needs to be on the road."

Nicholas Garnett is the North of England reporter for BBC Radio 5 Live. Previously he reported for other local BBC and commercial stations in Great Britain. Nick considers himself a "crash test dummy" for radio broadcasting technology: there's hardly any technology out there that he hasn't tested yet. Since 2009 Nick has relied on his iPhone to record and edit interviews and to send the final reports to the station. Nowadays he records eight out of ten live talks with his smartphone. Nick reports for the BBC from all over the world. His station sent him to Paris after the attacks on the satirical magazine Charlie Hebdo, in 2015 he arrived in Nepal shortly after the earthquake and was also sent to Tunisia after the terror attacks in the same year.

Twitter:@NickGarnettBBC

Since when have you been working as a reporter with your smartphone?

It started at the turn of the millennium. Until then radio reporters were driving around with big OB vans, with huge UKW-transmission towers on the top. Then we switched to satellite transmission all of a sudden: I got a mobile, portable satellite and was now able to send from anywhere. Since then the equipment has become smaller and smaller. When the iPhone 3G and 3Gs were launched in 2009, the first developers started to write programs that allowed us to record and edit audio. At that moment I got rid of my digital Nagra recorder. I stared using a beta version of the app "Luci Live" in November 2010 and was now able to report with my smartphone in broadcasting quality. That was the breakthrough moment. Although Skype was already available, Luci Live was the first software that we could really trust. Since then I've only been reporting with my iPhone, about 80 per cent of my live reports.

Would you refer to your early work as "mobile journalism" as we know it today? Or had you been doing this type of work for a long time already before the actual expression was introduced?

I think that the expression "mobile journalism" wasn't used until 2014. To tell you the truth: I hate this term and it's going to disappear sooner or later. Once we've trained enough journalists, this way of working is going to be the standard. I can't wait for the day when I'm not an "outsider" anymore, but the "mainstream". I really wish that every journalist learned this technique. It's not the tools, but your attitude towards journalism that matters.

I truly believe that news is not made in the newsroom but "on the road". If you are a reporter and you sit in the newsroom, you are in the wrong place. Sometimes I even say that I haven't set foot in a newsroom in more than 5 years. Though that's not really the truth. Once in a while I need to go to the station to pick up a couple of batteries and pens. But I don't really like going there – it's a waste of time. A reporter needs to be on the road.

I'm always out and about and I listen to what people are saying. I see for myself how they change their behaviour. This is what makes a reporter's life worth living. And when you are finally reporting, you don't sound like an idiot. Because you now know how people think about a topic. The same holds true for more important topics: sometimes reporters suddenly appear out of nowhere and don't know what they are talking about. I'm always outside, with the people whom I report about – and this is made possible by the new technology.

Do you remember the first report that you produced with your iPhone only?

That was in Scarborough, a coastal town in the North-East of England. People wanted to spread the sand from the beach on icy roads. I left my computer at home and only had my phone with me. I had already played with the multi-track editor "Voddio", but never dared to actually produce content with it. And there I was: after a 2.5 hour-long drive I arrived in Scarborough, without a computer. So I went to a coffee shop with a Wi-Fi network, sat down, had a cup of coffee, and started to produce my report with the smartphone. I had never produced anything in my life that involved so little effort.

This moment changed my life: I never ever have to carry along my heavy equipment. And I can drink coffee while I'm working. My first live broadcasting was the election of Ed Miliband as the former leader of the Labour party. At that time I was on the road in his constituency. It was raining cats and dogs and there was a heavy storm that blew my satellite dish off the car. My only chance to make a live broadcasting was Luci Live. Once again I had already played around with the app for a couple of weeks, but never dared to use it. So I didn't tell them! I just connected to the studio and they didn't know how I was coming up on air. Thank goodness I didn't 'fall off air

What are the disadvantages of "Mojo"?

Everything in life is a compromise and you have to improvise on a regular basis. I spent a lot of time trying to make sure the quality is good enough to broadcast. In the past the audio / sound engineer arrived with the OB van, put on the kettle, had a couple of biscuits and then he even held my microphone: I didn't have to do a single thing. Now I have to do – and take care of – everything, the content as well as the quality of coverage, for example. And when you are finally done with all the technical preparations, you suddenly ask yourself: what am I going to say during the broadcast? This is a major concession, a big disadvantage. I can deal with it because I'm an experienced journalist. But it can become a problem for journalists who are just starting their career.

Do you have less time for a story?

There's never enough time.

So with regard to content "Mojo" also comes with disadvantages. Can you think of any content-related advantages with this form of production?

Yes, of course. Here's an example: on Sunday I'm driving to Walsall to talk to several nurses about their opinion on the National Health Service in the middle of England. I'm only going to pack my phone, my headphones and a wind cover that I'm going to slip on the microphone of the iPhone. That's less intimidating and my interview partners are getting less nervous and talk to me more openly. People are less afraid of a phone because it only looks like a small phone. I don't have to place a big box under anyone's' nose, with a gigantic, frightening microphone. I often interview people that have been in less favourable situations. It's easier for them to trust me because there's no distance between us – a distance caused by an unknown and strange object that is the microphone.

Do people sometimes forget that you are doing an interview with them?

Yes, they are more relaxed. They answer more openly and honestly than they would when talking to a TV camera or a bulky radio microphone.

Are there any people that show a negative reaction because they expected more people to take care of them during their 15 minutes of fame?

Yes, that happens. Sometimes I need to show them my professional software so that they don't think that I'm still a student in training. But if you succeed in establishing eye contact with your interview partner, having a real conversation with only your phone between you / yourselves – then your interview partner won't be concerned anymore. If you arrived with a big team, he or she would never forget that the interview was recorded.

You are a radio reporter with a smartphone – is it an advantage that you could also report for TV if it was suddenly necessary?

In the summer of 2015 my newsroom/office sent me to Calais to report about the refugee situation. They closed the Channel Tunnel that day because refugees repeatedly tried to get inside. That caused major congestions so that the TV broadcast van never made it to Calais. The Morning Show called me and asked if I could help them out with a live interview on the phone. I told them that I could do even more. That was at 7.24 in the morning. At 7.36 am I had mounted my phone to a tripod and was prepared for a live broadcast. And it worked even though there was only an UMTS-connection, not even LTE. When I was asked to report after the earthquake in Nepal, I was able to use a mobile phone network that was surprisingly stable. So I could offer several live streams from the area of the earthquake on Periscope.

Can you think of any stories that you would rather report with conventional equipment instead of the phone?

For TV reports I would sometimes love to use a camera or a DSLR camera, especially when it comes to fast-moving objects or people. For radio reports I would prefer conventional technology if connectivity were an issue. An example: if I were reporting from a packed football stadium in which many people were using their mobile phones. My connection to the station could be repeatedly lost. This happens to some colleagues frequently because they try something that they shouldn't: at bigger sport or news events I would still set up a satellite dish if there were enough time. Nowadays they are so small that you can easily take them along.

What do your colleagues think of you and your reporting style?

The smarter ones see it as an opportunity to get on air and also work like that. For them it's an additional tool in their toolbox. And then there are always people who think that the quality is not good enough or that the delay is too big. They complain about digital artefacts on the station, audible dropouts. But these colleagues are not the ones who are spending their time on the road looking for good stories that sometimes lead you to the faraway corners of the world. If it works, it's always a miracle – which I'm very thankful for in my role as a reporter. If I had to report live for 40 minutes via a satellite connection that costs $ 5 per minute, it would cost a whole lot of money. Doing the same via a mobile network would be less costly. I'm not a 20-year old reporter anymore. I simply tried to keep up with the development. It's my aim, too, to be as useful as possible for my employer.

You are a journalist. Yet as journalists we are using the exact same technology that everybody else could use – with the same result. Won't we be digging our own professional graves?

I agree, but only to a certain extent. Because it's impossible to tell someone who is standing right next to the collapsing World Trade Centre: You are not allowed to report. You are not a journalist. Everyone can capture images, videos, and news. But what we do with the material afterwards is going to remain in the hands of journalists. Even more so because this is where we make our money. There is so much material out there, on YouTube for example. But people still turn to TV or radio to find out what has really happened when there is a major event. This is not going to change. But yes: everyone can gather newsworthy material. I really appreciate that. During the Ebola crisis in Africa the BBC struggled to report on location – it was too dangerous for the reporters' health. We equipped the doctors at the Ebola centres with iPhones. I filmed a short video and explained how they can shoot a good video. The results were brilliant!

What would be the consequence? You wouldn't be on the road anymore where the story unfolds, but inside, in an office curating the material?

This may happen.

Are you looking forward to this?

No, not at all.

What are your equipment must-haves that you would never forget?

I would never ever leave my phone at home, and neither the extra battery. I often pack a big rechargeable battery that charges my phone 15 or 20 times. The battery really is the weak spot of mobile journalism. On the other hand: usually I'm on location for four or five days. In the past I had to use a connection for power supply at some point. Today I can work with my phone for such as long period of time. New technology doesn't only replace old technology. It has a lasting effect on the way we work.

Nick Garnett's equipment: iPad mount, selfie stick, two Sennheiser headphones, a Sony headphone, Anker USB charging station, iPhone 6+, iPhone 6S, iPad Pro 9.7 inch, 2 x mobile Hotspots, 2x dust proof iPhone case, iRig microphone, iRig pro-adapter, old Nokia phone, Shoulderpod S1 and R1-Pro, LED light, Fuji pocket camera, Blackmagic HDMI recorder, XLR-microphone, two sets of ear buds (for the reporter and the guest), headphone-/microphone splitter, Anker Powerbank, wind cover, Comrex radio device, Shure adapter, tripod, additional / replacement microphone, cords for light and charging, shower cap to protect phone against the rain. Not pictured: MacBook Pro and a big bag with cords.

5 TV on the go: Filming

Summary

What are the rules for shooting moving pictures with a smartphone? Which rules can be transferred from VJ or conventional shootings with a camera crew? Which apps are useful when you are filming with a smartphone?

More ease, a faster way to respond and the potential for cost reduction – these are the reasons given by Laurent Keller, the Editor-in-chief of the Swiss regional station "Léman Bleu" in Geneva when he explains why his TV station completely switched to "mobile journalism" in news production (see chapter 1.1.). At "Léman Bleu" the days a team of three or four people appeared on location for a shoot, intimidating the protagonist who doesn't have any TV experience, belong to the past. "Mobile journalism" is neither complex nor conspicuous, even less so for news.. For an interview all you need is a phone, a tripod and a microphone. And since selfies have become standard practice people are now more used to smile or talk to a smartphone – in contrast to talking to the big cameras used in conventional television.

"Mobile journalism" significantly reduces time and effort, especially with regard to moving image production. The necessary equipment fits into a small bag, and the space needed (for people and technology) at the location of the shoot is extremely low. The results are absolutely good enough for TV. A smartphone camera delivers good quality images, partly even in 4K. A professional camera definitely delivers better quality – brilliant colours, better images in difficult light situations and more depth of field. However, for a news report you don't always need all of that. So "mobile journalism" in TV becomes a matter of consideration – which depends on the topic and the location (see the interview with Philipp Bromwell at the end of the chapter). The key feature is the professional use of the phone. If you know the right tricks, you mobile video will turn into something that can be broadcasted.

In comparison smartphones are rather cheap and can also be used as a "secondary camera" on location. For example for the long shot in an interview or the set-up shot ("B-roll") that introduces the interview guest with an off-text right before the sound bite. In addition, a shoot with two or three smartphones is going to be much cheaper than a multiple camera shoot with professional equipment.

5.1 Fundamentals

Always turn on airplane mode when you shoot or edit with your smartphone (fig. 05-01). Otherwise incoming phone calls might disrupt your work or even destroy your material. Even a text message or social media notification can cause serious issues. Once you send your footage to the newsroom, you temporarily need to turn off the airplane mode. A reporter who works with his smartphone on a regular basis may want to carry along a second phone for emails, phone calls and internet access.

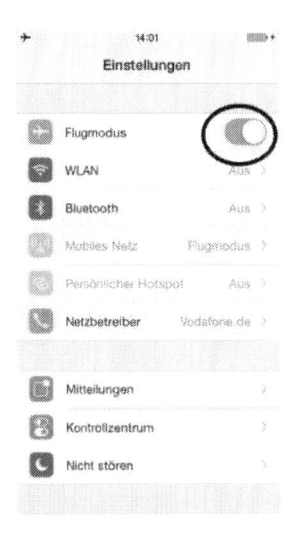

Figure 05-01 Turn on airplane mode!

It's also important that you have sufficient storage capacity on your phone. Both the filmed content as well as the apps take up a lot of storage space. Editing apps need even more memory space when you start a project. The need for storage is another argument for using a separate reporter phone, especially if a large amount of video content needs to be produced (see also: storage expansion in chapter 3.11.). There are several websites that can help you calculate the file size of different video formats. On the basis of the recommended TV quality video settings the following rule of thumb applies to the video app "Filmic Pro" introduced below: 1 second of video content corresponds to approximately 4 MB of storage space.

Storage needs of videos in broadcasting quality

Resolution: 1920 x 1080

Frame rate: 25 fps

Bitrate: 32 MbpS

Audio: 48 kHz

➡ 1 second corresponds to approx. 4 MB.

The most important basic rule is rather straightforward: Always clean your camera lens! Usually the lens gets pretty dirty because the phone is in your bag or in your pocket without any protection. If you clean it before each shoot (with a lens cloth, for example), your results will be visibly better. This is pretty obvious, but let's be honest: who does clean the lens of their smartphone on a regular basis?

5.2 Image composition, eye line and handheld tripod

If you want to shoot material for a broadcast with your smartphone, you need to follow certain principles. Many of these principles can be transferred from VJ-shoots or shoots with professional cameras to smartphone shoots. Yet others only apply to smartphones. Some rules even intensify: since storage space and battery run time are limited and a review of the material is not as easy, self-restraint will pay off because it restricts the flood of material. You need to compose you images before you actually start the recording. And make sure you have some idea of what kind of shots you need for your story. This will help you in keeping the number of shots low. This also applies to any other camera shoot, but the consequences of the rule violation will hurt more when you are filming with a smartphone. You also need to change the familiar and tested way of how you've been using your phone to some extent.

Image alignment is another aspect that needs attention if you produce moving images with your smartphone. Our eyes are arranged next to each other; human spatial perception is wider than it is tall. These given facts function as an orientation for television and most moving image services on the internet. Whether the horizontal image is going to establish itself online, hasn't been proven yet: normally many people use their smartphone vertically. This can be observed when looking at the majority of personal videos. When these videos are used for television, which might happen with videos by eye-witnesses of an accident, for example, ugly, static borders appear to the left and right of the narrow video. The live streaming app "Periscope" initially only allowed vertical live images. BILD, a German newspaper, picked up on this visual appearance and now produces a daily web video show in a vertical format. The BBC produces a number of vertical videos each day that you can find in their news app. These vertical videos are not shot in vertical format initially but are cropped versions of their regular video content. By doing so they hope to reach an audience that would otherwise not see their content. Other apps rely on square images, such as Instagram..

It's almost like a war zone between the users of different types of content – with an undetermined outcome. Most buyers of videos are still in need of horizontal material. Several apps that allow you to produce professional videos exclusively offer a horizontal setting. Exceptions are Filmic Pro for filming (see chapter 5.4.) and for editing on iOs LumaFusion (see chapter 6.2.) or the Android app PowerDirector (see chapter 6.3.) for editing that also produce moving images in a vertical format. In the following I'm going to explain how you can produce moving images in a horizontal format. Though this should not be an excuse to avoid finding your own answer to this important question: Are you already producing vertically or still horizontally?

If you film longer takes without a tripod, you should use a "hand-held tripod" for your phone. The right hand holds the smartphone in such a way that the thumb can operate the shutter release button (always on the right side!) and the hand doesn't get in the image. The left hand takes hold of the right wrist to stabilize the image. The so-called "spider-like grip" – the common way of holding a smartphone – is much more prone to shaking and blurry images (fig. 05-02, fig. 05-03).

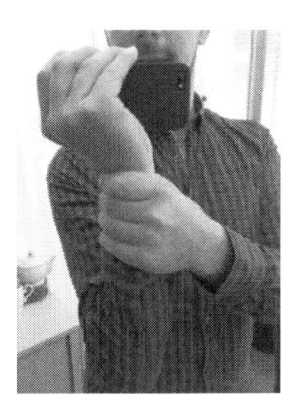

Figure 05-02 The handheld tripod.

Figure 05-03 The spider-like grip.

Zoom with your feet: In contrast to many professional TV and photo cameras most smartphones don't have an optical zoom (see chapter 3.2. for exceptions). This means that smartphones zoom in by enlarging the captured image – at the expense of image resolutions and image quality. If you film moving images with your smartphone that have broadcast quality, you will have to do without the zoom. You can enlarge an object or a protagonist by moving closer – "zoom with your feet".

"Natural light is your friend". A general rule: don't use the light and flash of your smartphone. They do not only produce harsh and selective light but also create hard shadows behind your conversational partners. Since "mobile journalists" usually don't tend to arrive with a professional lighting crew, they need to rely on natural light (sunlight, reflection) and available artificial light as the most important light sources. The rule of thumb: identify the light source that dominates the room and turn your back to it. Ideally you could use a second light source to glamourize the hair of your protagonist for example. There should also be a sparkle in the eyes of your protagonist. This avoids the "dead eye" syndrome. A small spot can help but it needs to throw the light on the protagonist from the side and not directly from the smartphone.

Figure 05-04 "Rule of Thirds": The golden grid makes protagonists look good. Screenshot taken from Benjamin Unger's report.

As in a VJ or team shoot the "Rule of Thirds" is of great help with regard to image composition: some camera apps are even able to lay a grid on top of your image. According to the rule an interviewee will not be positioned directly in the centre of the image but in such a way that his body axis is placed along the left or the right line of the grid. When he looks from the right to the left, his body axis would be placed on the right line – and vice versa. His eyes would be placed on the intersecting point of the right and the top lines (fig. 05-04). Interview partners should always look at the camera (fig. 05-05) and never away from it (fig. 05-06). In addition the camera needs to film on eye level to avoid any undesirable effects: a perspective from below (frog's perspective) may have an arrogant or superior effect on the viewer. If you film from above (birds-eye view), the protagonist often looks podgy, small, under pressure, pushed into a corner. But you can always use both perspectives purposely, of course.

Figure 05-05 The correct eye-line

Figure 05-06 The wrong eye-line

5.3 How to divide scenes: The Five Shot Rule

The "Five Shot Rule" helps you to select your shots: if you divide each sequence into the five shots described below, you will always have several options during editing to put your film together. When you are on location try to develop a feeling for the right number of shots. This also helps to keep the flood of material down and to use the limited storage space of the smartphone wisely. The actual order of the "5 shots" is flexible. During the shoot as well as during editing you will chose a different order for different sequences. It is the content and the story that are still key: there are journalists who in theory divide actions into sequences with different meaningful shots instead of dividing scenes into "shots". They don't want to risk shooting details that are insignificant for the storyline if they only think of positions. In my opinion the end result is often the same – given that journalists remember that all they want to do is to tell a story. Then these "5 shots" will always turn into meaningful sequences.

The Five Shot Rule

1. Who is doing something? Close-up of the protagonist

2. What is being done? Close-up of the activity

3. How does the protagonist act?

    (An over-the-shoulder shot connects actor and activity.)

4. Where does the activity happen? Room – medium or long shot

5. Unusual shot – exciting, imaginative (yet meaningful) perspective

Who is doing something? These shots get close to the protagonist and show his face in a close-up that captures his face and upper body at most, doing what he is supposed to be the doing in the scene (fig. 05-07). The examples are taken from a film that Benjamin Unger from the German broadcaster NDR made about a man who creates wooden sculptures with a power saw. Benjamin, who works at the NDR Regional Office for Mecklenburg-Vorpommerania and also participates in the "Next News Lab" in Hamburg on a regular basis, shot this film with his iPhone 6 only and strictly followed the Five Shot Rule.

Figure 05-07 Five Shot Rule: Who is doing something?

The following shot shows the activity – what is being done in the scene? Our protagonist works on the wood with his power saw. Straight forward! (fig. 05-08).

Figure 05-08 Five Shot Rule: What is being done?

A connection between the actor and the activity can usually be achieved with an "over-the-shoulder shot" of the protagonist. This shot (fig. 05-09) establishes a connection between our protagonist and his sculpture. We can see his work almost from his perspective. This is how close we get (this is also called a POV shot – "point of view", without the shoulder and a partial view of the head). A (less suitable) replacement for this shot could be a medium shot over the shoulder that connects actors with their actions.

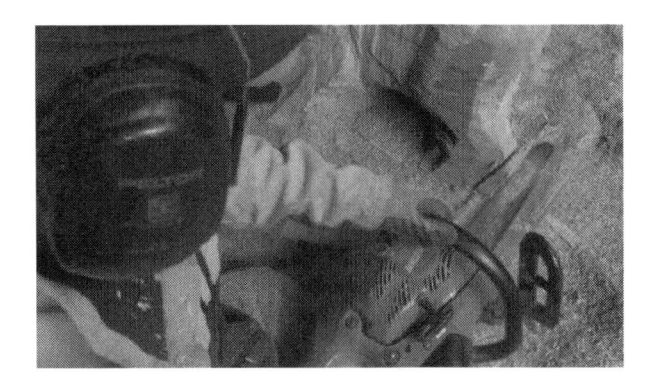

Figure 05-09 Five Shot Rule: How does the protagonist act? Over-the-shoulder shot

Where does the activity take place? A shot that is a little bit wider can help to locate actors and actions in a room (fig. 05-10). The recording in our example is not ideal; it's slightly indecisive and does not follow the rule of thirds perfectly. And a very attentive observer might wonder what's beneath the covers in the far right corner. But this is also a step in the overall learning process: not every shot can be perfect. A good story always outweighs little imperfections in image composition.

Figure 05-10 Five Shot Rule: Where does it happen?

The four shots described above are obligatory while the next one is optional: the Unusual – or "wow" - shot (fig. 05-11) shows the action from a surprising perspective. Benjamin chose the bird's eye perspective, which illustrates a big advantage of "mobile journalism":

130

to hold a smartphone above the head of a protagonist is easy. If a cameraperson had to haul up his professional TV camera to this height and film downwards, the team would have to bring along a lifting platform. On a more serious note: the smartphone is perfect for unusual shots because it is small. The possibilities are endless: have you ever filmed out of the sound hole of a guitar to portray a musician? Or from a glass while it's being filled with beans or chocolate? These are the real advantages of filming with a smartphone. Benjamin even shot a second unusual shot: close to the ground, with a wooden block in the front and the power saw in the background.

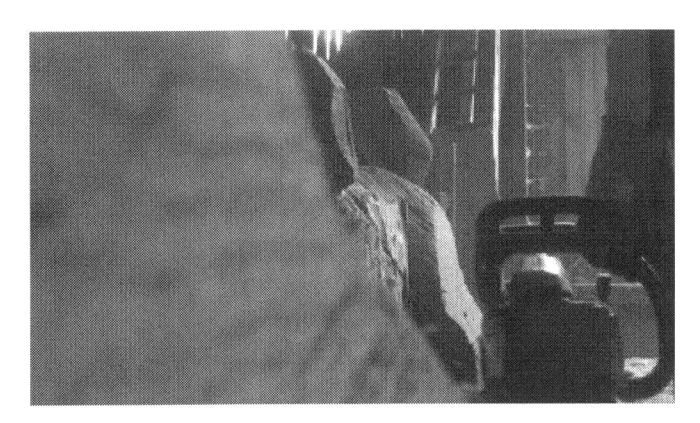

Figure 05-11 Five Shot Rule: The "Wow" shot

If you are a beginner, you should hold on to these fixed positions and avoid any pivoting of the phone (and never ever zoom in, see above). This makes it not only easier to concentrate on the five important shots, but also to edit the material instead of any half-heartedly shot movements filmed with a medium shot.

Another rule of thumb: if you are filming a fixed, static shot, you should count at least to 10. Otherwise you will risk that your shots are too short. In editing there might not be enough material between the blurriness caused by pressing record at the beginning and end.

10 tips for shooting with a smartphone

1. Put your phone in airplane mode

2. Clean the lens

3. Focus on a coherent image composition first, then start recording – save storage

4. Keep your phone steady – handheld tripod or tripod

5. Use natural light – turn your back to the dominant light source

6. Follow the Rule of Thirds

7. Remember the Five Shot Rule

8. Shoot "stills", avoid pans – count to 10

9. Zoom with your feet and never with the camera app (the resolution would suffer)

10. Stop the recording before you compose a new image – save storage space

5.4 Video Camera Apps: Filmic Pro

All smartphones have their own camera app that often works well with the built-in camera of the phone. At a first glance this app seems to be more than enough (see chapter 3.2.). But only a few of these "generic camera apps" allow the camera control that is needed for high-quality shootings: notable exceptions are Windows phones, which we will talk about later on in this chapter, and the Android phones LG V10, V20 and V30. Apart from these the majority of standard camera apps neither allow manual focus or exposure control in video mode nor the setting of recording parameters such as the frame rate. These are three tools that are extremely important for those people who want to film professional moving images.

Focus and exposure control separate the wheat from the chaff: amateur videos are often characterized by so-called "focus pulls", i.e. the image pulses at the edges because the camera automatically tries to adjust the focus of the image in regular intervals. The overall impression of the image is unsteady and unprofessional. In addition, exposure adjusts automatically – light values of the image change constantly. Both effects are a no go for professional moving image material. There are several apps that offer the required camera control, and I'm going to introduce the most important ones in the following chapter.

5 TV on the go: Filming

If you only want to purchase a single app for mobile journalism, and if you work with an iPhone or an Android phone, you should definitely consider "FilmicPro". The app developers (Cinegenix) have been improving this app for many years, at first for the iPhone and by always taking the user needs into account. Recently they also launched an Android version. However, the use of the app is still very much in development on this platform. The app doesn't work well on all types of Androids because of the different hardware. That's why you might experience some audio issues and dropped frames. But the team behind FilmicPro has been working hard to improve the Android experience.

FilmicPro offers full control of the smartphone camera, including manual focus, exposure, white balance and control of the audio input level. In mobile journalism it has been a rare occurrence so far that an app is available for more than one platform. FilmicPro is still one of the few notable exceptions that will soon be followed by other apps. Since the worldwide Android market is much bigger than the market for iPhones, it's also more profitable. The availability of FilmicPro on both platforms is a big advantage for us: using the app on either an Android or iPhone device is almost an identical process. That's why the following sections apply to both platforms.

FilmicPro offers a wide selection of basic settings that lets you adapt the app to different production settings. It might pay off to talk to the TV or internet provider that is going to buy your content, before you start producing a film. The following settings serve the use on the European TV market and can also be applied to online services.

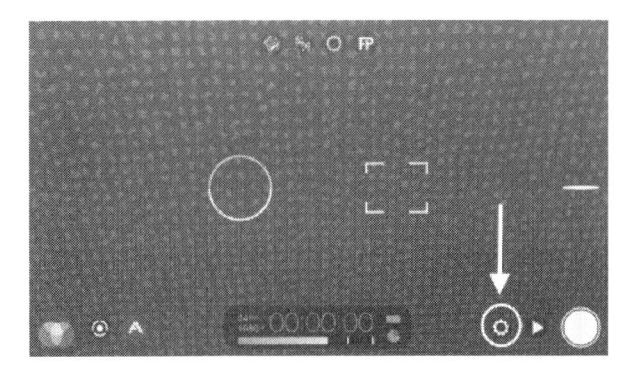

Figure 05-12

133

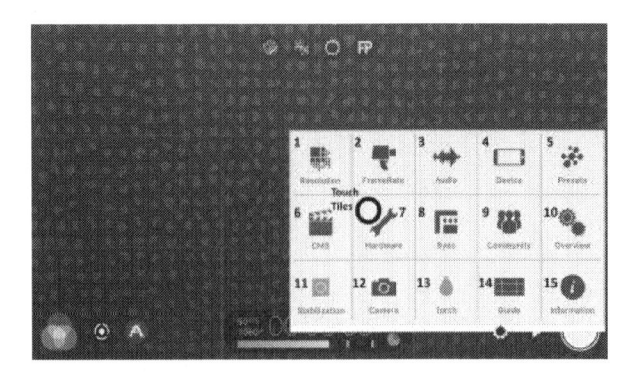

Figure 05-13

FilmicPro starts with the camera window (fig. 05-12). You need to adjust the basic settings before you start recording. Open the respective menu by tapping on the wheel icon (bottom right of the screen) and choose from two dozens options. With a click on the respective title you can browse the different categories (fig. 05-13): (1) adjusts the recorded resolution, (2) the framerate, (3) the audio codec FilmicPro is recording. (4) offers important options with regard to where the recorded material is stored, (5) defines personal presets. Filmic Pro offers its own system to manage recorded content (6, "CMS") and supports some hardware addition like gimbals or lenses (7). You can synch material with Flimic´s cloud (8), use the app´s own social network. (10) gives you an overview or the app ´s settings.

An important feature is the picture stabilizer (11): So far, Filmic relies on the iPhones stabilizer. While the stabilizer reduces image quality (visible especially in low light situations), you will not be able to produce professional footage without it when holding your phone by hand. Also, the stabilizer corrects movements you deliberately film, for example a smooth pan along a building: You will see that the movement gets irregular if the stabilizer is switched on. Therefore the advice is ambivalent: Never film without stabilizer while holding your phone in one or two hands – in this situation, avoid regular pans! If you really need to pan, put the phone on a tripod, switch of the stabilizer and do it – but don´t forget to switch the stabilizer back on.

The camera symbol (12) switches between front and back camera. Be careful: when switching back from front to back camera you have to make sure that all record settings are back in place. Sometimes Filmic might not switch the stabilizer back on or remain in lower recording resolutions if older iphone front cameras dont´s support full HD. The built-in phone light can be turned on and off (13), but it hardly ever contributes to the creation of a more professional image. For image composition (see above) you can trust the "Rule of Thirds" grid (14). A tap on the info icon (15) opens further information and app tutorials.

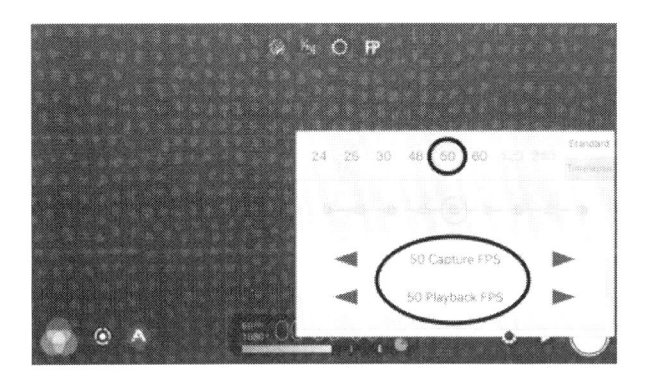

Figure 05-14

The setting of the frame rate is important (fig. 05-14). It defines the number of images that are filed per second. Many internet applications as well as the American TV standard NTSC work with a frame rate of 30 or 60 fps (frames per second). TV productions in Europe, however, require 25 fps or 50 fps (PAL), film productions 24 fps. If the recorded frame rate differs from the one needed for broadcasting, you need to convert the video first. This may result in minor image errors and will definitely change the overall quality for the worse. If you don't need to convert your material (or only in parts), you will also save a lot of time. Converting a film is time-consuming – this especially applies to smartphones. We recommend to film with 50 fps if you want to convert into European PAL standard as its codec (25i for "interlaced") shows 50 parts of a movement per second, squeezed into 25 frames (first the odd lines, then the even lines of each picture are shown by your TV set, adding up to 50 pictures).

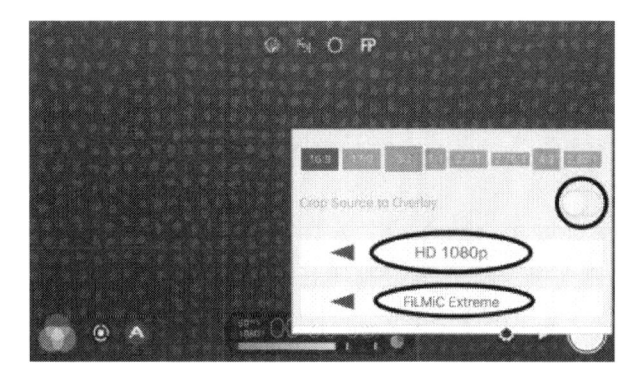

Figure 05-15

The quality of an image also depends on the image resolution (fig. 05-15) with which an app records – alongside the quality of the physical camera lens that also plays a role. The better the image quality, the higher the need for storage space, the bigger the video file and the longer it will take to upload a finished film. My recommendation: make sure to record in HD ("High Definition"). The two 16:9-formats are reasonable (1280 x 720, the so-called "small HD", or 1920 x 1080, which is "Full HD") (fig. 05-15). If your phone camera supports 4K and has enough storage space, it might be useful to choose this resolution: you can zoom in on the image without losing full HD resolution in the editing phase.

Filmic records in 16:9 format as default but can also record in 1:1 or 4:3 (amongst other formats). If you choose one of these formats at the top of the meno the app will show a white frame in the camera window. It indicates the chosen format, but FilmicPro will still record 16:9. This can be useful if you are producing for different distribution formats. An example: if the video material is posted on both Instagram and aired on conventional 16:9 television, you will have to record in 16:9, which is the bigger format. During the recording the 1:1 overlay indicates the recorded area while also marking the area that would be lost in the Instagram square. The author can already take this into consideration during the shoot. Only if you switch on the option "Crop Source To Overlay" will FilmicPro actually record in the chosen format.

In video encoding the bit rate should at least be set to "Filmic Quality" (32 Mbps – Megabit per second) or "Filmic Extreme" (50 Mbps). The bit rate determines (in broad terms) the amount of image information that is processed per second, i.e. the "depth" with which a spot in an image is described in the memory. The more bits per second, the better the image quality and the higher the storage need. The highest bit rate (50 Mbps) needs more storage, but especially in low light condition you will notice the difference even

5 TV on the go: Filming

compared to "Filmic Quality". FilmicPro also allows to record in "RAW" format to be used especially with professional post production after the shoot.

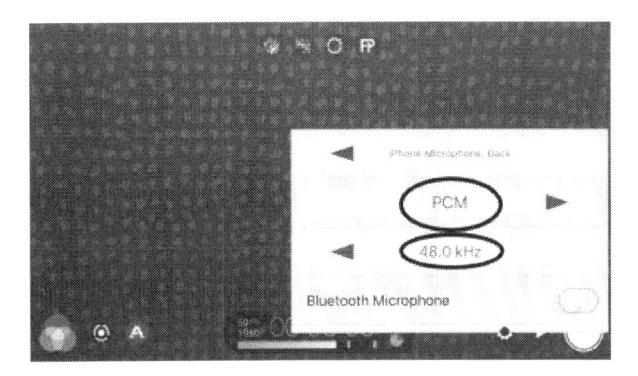

Figure 05-16

With regard to the audio format it might pay off to talk to the editors of the medium that is going the buy your material. The TV station of the ARD, for example, asks for uncompressed (PCM) audio at 48 kHz (Kilohertz). That might differ from one station to another. In addition, uncompressed recording also has the highest storage needs. On the other hand the options for audio compression (AIFF, AAC) are common formats that shouldn't cause any major quality losses. Selecting an audio format has only been possible in the iPhone version (fig. 05-16). The recently published Android app only allows the selection of the sample rate. Cinegenix promised to make these options available for Android in future updates.

FilmicPro also permits the use of external audio sources. These are usually automatically identified, but can also be purposely selected in the Android version. Apart from that the user of the Android app can decide whether the "audio meter" is displayed in the camera window: absolutely! This is one of the major advantages of FilmicPro in comparison to generic camera apps – you can control the sound of the recording and even listen in during the recording with "headphone monitoring", if you are using an iRigPre or iRigPro (see chapter 3.3.), for example.

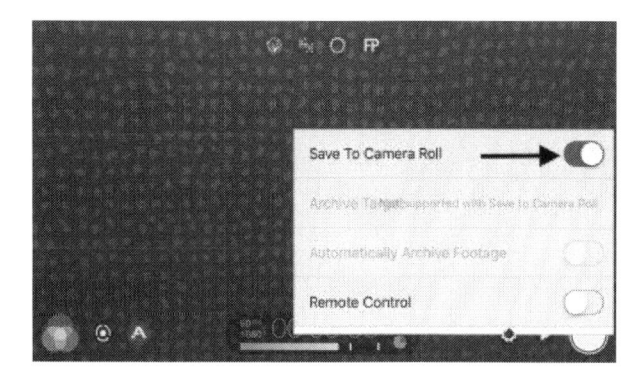

Figure 05-17

Another important question is the storage location of the recorded material. This makes editing easier because FilmicPro does not save the different clips in the camera roll of the iPhone, which can be directly accessed by the user. Initially the material is only visible in FilmicPro and needs to be exported in a time-consuming process. If you enable "Save to Camera Roll", all you material will be saved to the photo gallery of the iPhone by default. Videos can be quickly imported to other programs for further editing (fig. 05-17). Android phones don't have this problem: FilmicPro always saves content in the gallery of the phone. You can define the exact file path within the app so that you can save different projects in the corresponding folders. The result is a clear arrangement of files and folders.

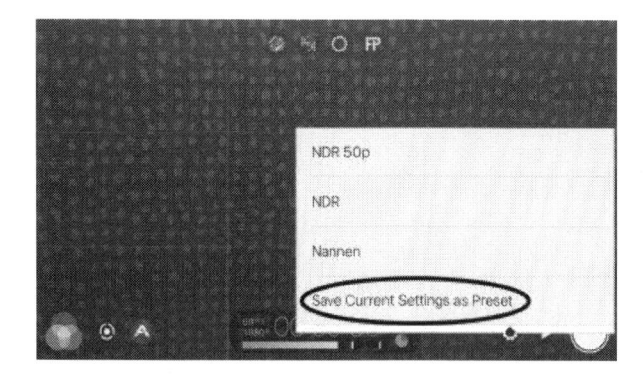

Figure 05-18

You can save your basic settings as "Presets". They don't get lost and can be updated with a simple click before each shoot (fig. 05-18). It is possible to define different pre-sets

138

5 TV on the go: Filming

for different scenarios – if you shoot for TV on a regular basis, but you also produce content with a lower resolution for internet streams from time to time, you can quickly switch back and forth between different pre-set alternatives.

FilmicPro also works with certain add-on lenses and other hardware, but I won't explain that in any more detail. One example: the Osmo Mobile can be paired with FilmicPro and you can start a recording by pressing the gimbal´s hardware button. More information is provided by the relevant menu options, the respective hardware manufacturers as well as on the FilmicPro website. Now that we have completed the adjustment of the most important settings, you can close the menu by touching the visible parts of the camera picture.

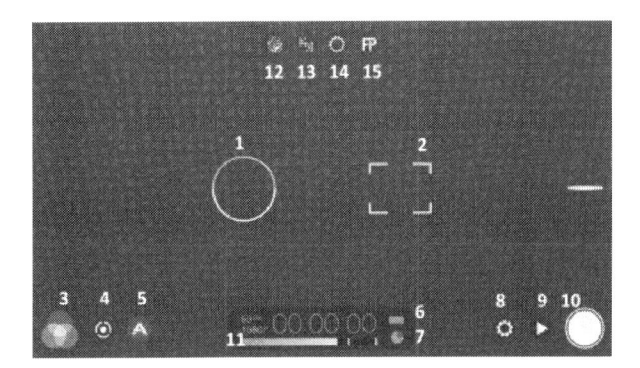

Figure 05-19

Starting point for recordings is the home screen – the camera window of FilmicPro (fig. 05-19). There are two important elements that immediately catch our eye: the "reticles". There is an exposure reticle (1) and a focus reticle (2). With your finger you can move both reticles to that particular image element that you want to be in the focus and that should work as a point of orientation for the exposure. With the reticles you can control the following: if you did an interview in front of a blue, sunny sky, the sky would be bright blue and the face in the front would be too dark. With the reticles you can correctly expose the face and even overexpose the background if needed. This doesn't cause any further problems as long as the meaningful image content has the correct exposure. The same applies to focus: the sharpness of an image needs to be with the acting protagonist and not with a bookshelf in the background. The app might sometimes need a couple of seconds to correctly adjust sharpness and brightness: after the right positioning you need to be patient and correct the image. Then, and only then, it's time for the next step.

Tap the reticles to lock focus or exposure. The symbols change to red and won't change again during recording. This has several advantages: the image is steadier, for example, because the phone camera does not attempt to automatically adjust the focus – a process that causes the edges of the image to shake. On the other hand as the author you need to know that – if worse comes to worse – your interview partner might become blurry if he moves away or towards the camera during the recording. That's the reporter's dilemma: a walk with the protagonist with a fixed focus asks for a constant distance between camera and object – which is almost impossible. An automatic focus might cause unaestethic shaky image edges ("focus pulls"). The further away an object from the camera, the larger the area of sharpness. This can be helpful. With FilmicPro you can also manually correct the focus, yet you need an advanced knowledge of the camera app.

When exposure is locked, the smartphone doesn't make any automatic exposure adjustments when the light situation changes. This is very useful because automatic corrections are often disruptive and leave an unprofessional impression. On the other hand a face might become too dark if the sun hides behind a cloud during an interview. These are the normal problems that every cameraman has to deal with, irrespective of the device being used. Yet it is important to know that only with the manual control of exposure and focus results can be achieved that meet professional standards.

To manually adjust focus and exposure you should press the reticles longer which will give you handles on both sides of the screen (fig. 05-20). You could also press the symbol (4) with the same effect. The handle on the left is for manually changing exposure; with the one on the right you can change focus. Both can be controlled by moving your finger over the handle. With the exposure handle you can also choose to lock either ISO or shutterspeed while manually changing exposure. The right handle for focus can also by used as a zoom handle by pressing "zoom". But we prefer not to use that as you loose image quality. When in manual mode, you can slide the focus bar from the right to the centre to reveal an extra handle. This controls the speed of an automated focus pull. To do this, tap the middle point of the right handle to set a focal point. Move the handle to the next focal point and tap the middle point of the handle again. Now you can start your recording and press one of the two focal points you selected and the app will smoothly move to the second focal point.

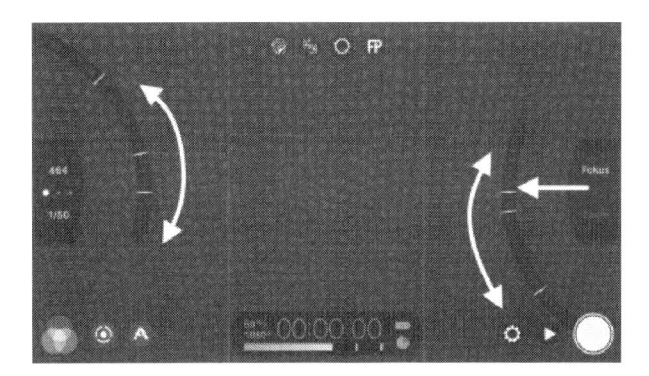

Figure 05-20

On the bottom left of the screen (fig. 05-19) you will find the white balance (3) which can also be locked(fig. 05-21). This is of particular importance if you are filming in rooms with mixed lights. In such a case the white balance would automatically attempt regulation when the camera moves from an area with natural light to an area with artificial light. Colours would change: a white wall, for example, might turn yellow or blue – an undesirable effect. In such a case choosing a "medium" value usually helps. Please don't change the value during the recording. There is a number of presets you can use on the bottom of the white balance menu. Next to these presets you can also take full manual control by changing the colour temperature and tint. This can be helpful if you use your iPhone as second camera as you can synchronize both Kelvin values. Make sure to fix the White Balance before shooting by pressing the "AWB" symbol which will change from blue to red. It is one downside of FilmicPro that you can´t see if the AWB is locked after you have left this particular menu.

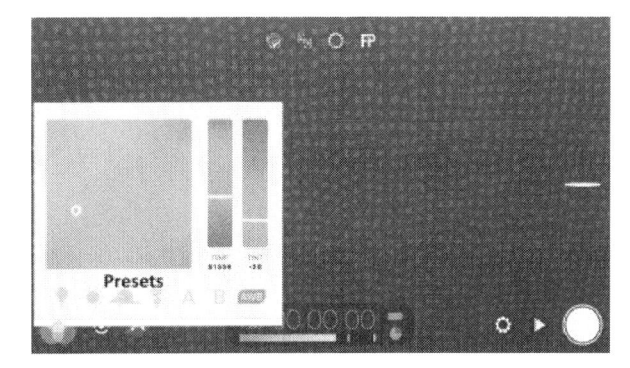

Figure 05-21

141

The camera window (fig. 05-19) displays more important functions: the battery capacity of the smartphone (6) and available storage space (7). One of FilmicPro's problems: if there is no more available storage, the phone will sometimes pretend to record more footage without saving any videos. You can control the above-mentioned settings with a tap on the wheel icon (8). With the filmstrip (9) you can look at the clips that have been recorded and start rough editing (only if you didn´t safe them to camera roll). You can start the recording by pressing the recording button on the bottom right (10): the timer in the middle starts displaying the length of recording. With another tap on the recording button you stop the recording. I would recommend recording several small clips, i.e. frequently press start and stop (an exception: if a scene unfolds in front of your eyes, never ever press stop!). In editing it's much easier to work with many small, short clips. The horizontal bar on the far right gives access to the digital zoom. We don't recommend to use this because the image quality will suffer.

With the audio meter (11) you can balance the volume. I've learned that FilmicPro is rather sensitive which means that you need to make sure that the amplitude is continuously in the green zone. As soon as the first yellow amplitudes appear, my sound was already overmodulated. Overmodulation means that the recording is, more or less, irreparable, i.e. useless. If the level can be defined manually (see for example the iRig Pre described in chapter 3.3.), I will generally start at zero, i.e. at the minimal level, to slowly get to an acceptable green medium value. Most of the time the default audio level is fine.

FilmicPro also offers monitoring functions that as far as we know no other smartphone app offers: When activating the "A" symbol (5), for more icons will show up in the top middle of the screen with function Video Journalists working with professional video cameras will regognize: FilmicPro offers a "Zebra" (12) indicating which areas of a picture are under- and overexposed as well as two more exposure functions (13, 14). Very helpful on a smartphone screen is "focus peaking" (15) which illuminates all lines that are in focus in green. By this you can make a more informed decision if you have adjusted the focus properly.

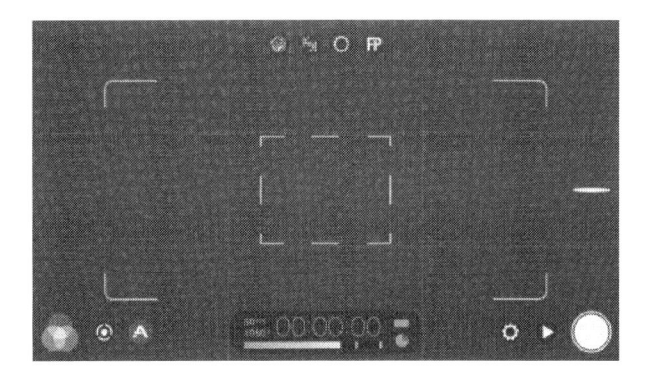

Figure 05-22

A new FilmicPro function is the automated full-screen focus and exposure (fig. 05-22) indicated by larger reticles. It can be activated and deactivated by double-tapping the reticles. In automatic mode FilmicPro offers some astonishly smooth focus pulls when objects are moving, much better than the iPhones own auto-focus. The same goes for the exposure function though by trial and error you will find situation in which the automated function works or doesn´t.

The finished recordings can also be edited in FilmicPro, at least to a certain extent (with an iPhone this is only possible if the recordings have been saved in FilmicPro itself and not in the gallery). FilmicPro allows simple trimmings that facilitate editing in another program. There is also some basic colour correction that might prove useful. You can find the clips by clicking on the "film" icon next to the settings wheel. If your iPhone saved the clips to the FilmicPro roll, you will have to select them in this menu and export them to the iPhone gallery. Now you can edit the material with external programs.

5.5 More Filming Apps

With its availability for Android and iPhone FilmicPro is one of the essential camera apps for mobile journalists. However, there are some alternatives that are often cheaper and provide a similar quality. These are of particular interest because FilmicPro has so far not been 100% reliable on Android phones.

Figure 05-23 Movie Pro

The range of functions of MoviePro (only for iPhones) (fig. 05-23) is similar to the one offered by FilmicPro. The app offers the required control of focus and exposure. It also supports external microphones, even Bluetooth microphones, and allows increasing or reducing the input level. Support and documentation, however, lack many important features. But MoviePro still offers a couple of advantages when compared to FilmicPro such as the presumably largest range of video formats for recording that is offered by an app: besides the most common resolutions there is a square format (1080 x 1080) that perfectly works for Instagram. The most recent versions of FilmicPro as well as Movie Pro both allow vertical recordings – this will be important if you plan to use your material in apps such as Snapchat. The pre-sets in MoviePro are easy to manage; changing from one preset to another is more straightforward than in FilmicPro.

But MoviePro is still not my app of choice: the description of the image recording quality is rather unusual. It's not measured in the commonly used Mbps (Megabit per Second) but in per cent. 400 % roughly correspond to 160 Mbps, 100 % to about 43 Mbps (which is good enough for journalistic projects).

5 TV on the go: Filming

Figure 05-24 Cinema FV5.

For Android phones Cinema FV5 had been the best app for producers of moving images for many years. But FilmicPro is now seen as a real alternative. Cinema FV5 (fig. 05-24) is still competitive: while FilmicPro has a good reputation and gained a lot of experience with iOs, Cinema FV5 has the advantage of many years of development on the Android platform. In contrast to FilmicPro this app is available and appropriate for a wide range of phones and it also runs smoothly. FilmicPro will expand the range of phones that it supports slowly and little by little.

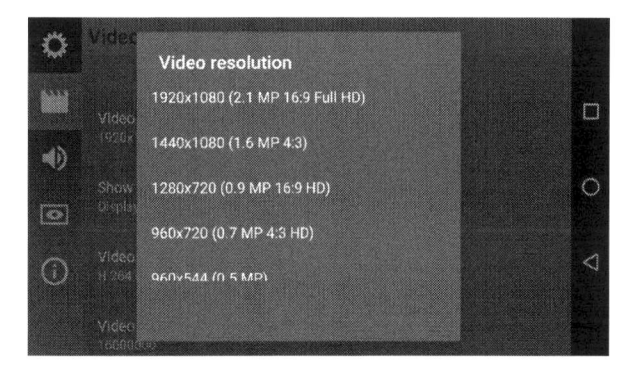

Figure 05-25

Cinema FV5 supports a large range of settings. Many different film formats can be selected (among them is a square format, not in Full HD 1080 x 1080, but only in 720 x 720, fig. 05-25). You can also adjust the frame rate (if supported by the operating system of the smartphone). Many other settings correspond to the settings offered by FilmicPro.

Figure 05-26

Cinema FV5 lets you correct exposure and focus manually. There are two reticles (fig. 05-26): with the green reticle (1) you can adjust the focus. It changes its positions when you briefly touch the screen. The white one (2) adjusts the exposure. It reacts when you touch the screen slightly longer. The main settings (3) can be accessed with a tap on the wheel icon. "Menu" (4) includes shortcuts to grids, (such as the "Rule of Thirds" grid), frames, histogram and stabilizer. The flash icon controls the smartphone lamps (which are often useless).

In my experience it can be problematic to listen to the audio recording (6). Cinema FV5 will only allow this if you have the necessary hardware (such as iRig Pre). In various workshops and when listening to my own recordings the recordings made by the phone were not authentically played back by the sound of the headphone. The sound was frequently slightly distorted. Additionally Cinema FV5 only displays the audio level once you tap on the headphone icon or only once you start the recording. This can be slightly annoying with regard to the required balancing process prior to the audio recording.

Figure 05-27 The generic camera surface of Lumia phones

Windows phones are always equipped with manual camera control – this is a big advantage of Lumia smartphones, at least of those phones with a good camera and a high performance. After you open the camera (fig. 05-27) you can switch from photo to film recording (fig. 05-28) with a tap on the video camera icon. When you move the camera icon to the left (direction of arrow) towards the centre of the viewfinder, three rings appear that let you manually control the camera: according to the basic setting all values are automatically regulated ("auto" icon in the circle). The outer ring allows you to manually adjust the white balance (1), but only based on very general symbols and not according to the Kelvin scale. The middle ring (2) regulates the focus while the inner ring adjusts (3) the exposure. You should always define these parameters first before you actually start recording. This will avoid any automatic adjustments during the actual recording (such as undesired "focus pulls").

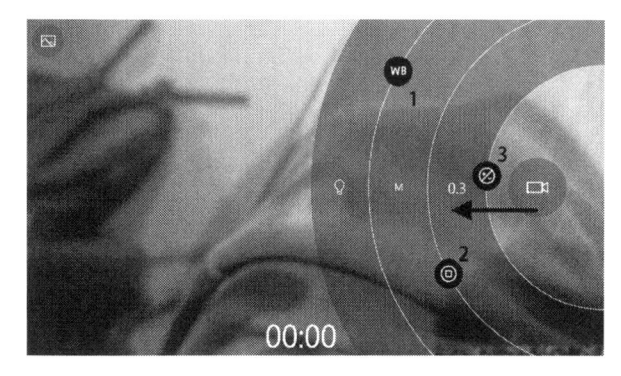

Figure 05-28 Windows Camera: Built-in manual camera control

The viewfinder offers many functions that were already introduced when we talked about different camera apps (fig. 05-29): a direct shortcut opens the gallery of the recorded videos (1). The app can also record images with the front camera (2) and can turn the smartphone light on and off (3). The Windows camera app comes with a slow-motion function (4) and displays the camera settings for white balance (5), focus (6) and exposure compensation (7). The three dots (8) direct you to the settings menu. The recording starts with a tap on the camera icon (9).

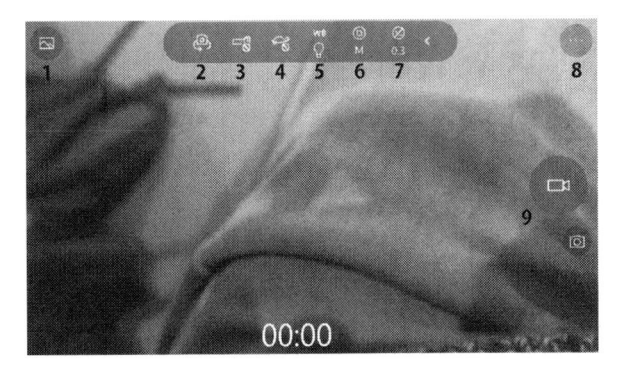

Figure 05-29

Before you start recording it is important – as always – that you adjust the basic settings. This can be done in the settings menu (8) of the viewfinder (top right) and with a left swipe to the "video" menu (fig. 05-30). Depending on the specifications provided by your client a frame rate of 25 images per second might be useful. The resolution should be set to at least "HD" (High Definition with 1920 x 1080 p). The Windows phone offers several recording formats, yet a square format is still missing.

5 TV on the go: Filming

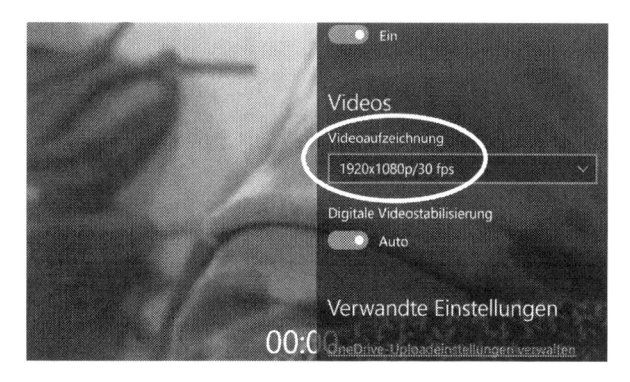

Figure 05-30

The Windows camera does not allow audio control, which can become a problem: there is neither a level nor a possibility for audio monitoring which makes it difficult to use. There are no real alternatives to the generic Windows camera app yet.

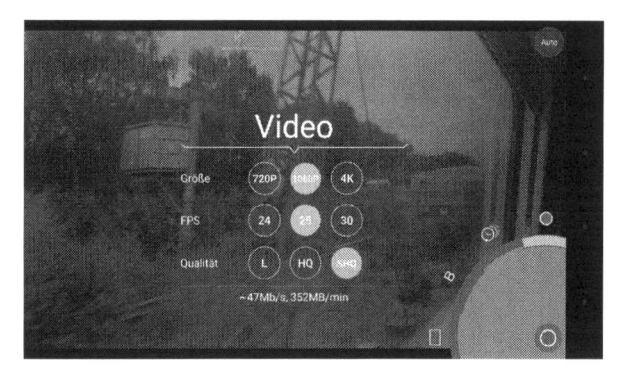

Figure 05-31 ProShot for Android and Windows phones.

A new star may be born with the introduction of the video app "ProShot" (fig. 05-31), available for Windows and Android phones. ProShot makes recordings with 25 images per second, with a frequency of 47 Mbit per second in 1080p (it even offers 4K if this is supported by the mobile phone). The Android version offers a larger range of functions and allows manual focus control as well as exposure control, at least to a certain extent: the exposure can be manually adjusted by choosing a certain image element, but it can't be locked. This means that the exposure would adjust to varying light situations – an effect that is usually not desired. I talked to the developers and they said that they were not able to change this as of now. They announced that they would also write a program for Windows phones with a corresponding range of functions. But not even the Windows version is very reliable yet.

A more recent and very promising Android app is "Cinema 4k": focus and exposure can be manually controlled (but reticles are missing). The app allows controlling the level of sharpness with a software zoom (the focus area can be enlarged and becomes more visible). It supports 25 images per second, grids (such as "Rule of Thirds") and, as far as I know, the app runs smoothly on many Android phones. Unfortunately, it doesn't yet offer the possibility to monitor the audio recording level.

Figure 05-32 A new star in the iOs universe: the camera app "Mavis"

A lot of potential has the iOs app "Mavis" which is fairly new on the market (fig. 05-32). The software was written by students of the University of Brighton. They initially focussed on programming a real time vector scope (displayed in the bottom left corner of the photo) and were successful. Since they learned a lot about programming the iOs camera during this process, they created a very persuasive app with extensive options for camera control. Mavis allows manual focus, white balance as well as manual exposure. It displays the audio level and allows to manually control the input level (gain). The app can also record in various formats, such as 25 images (fig. 05-33) per second in HD or 4K. It also offers "peaking", i.e. it highlights the part of your image that is in the focus a bright colour.

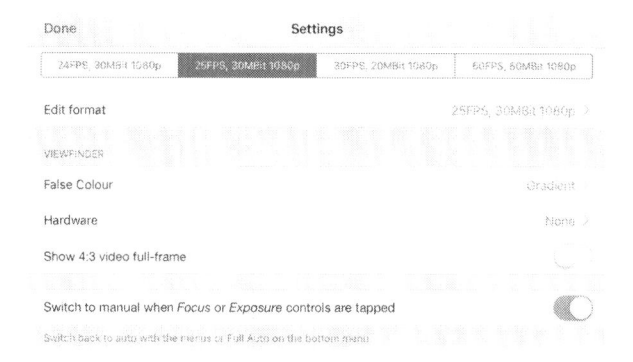

Figure 05-33

The viewfinder is much smaller than in any other app: Mavis uses a part of the screen for the buttons that allow the manual control (fig. 05-34). This has a couple of advantages: functions and settings options can be seen at a glance, though some users might describe Mavis as being cluttered. The first experiences made with Mavis have been really good. The app is stable, maybe even more stable than FilmicPro, and produces great results.

Figure 05-34

A further iOs alternative is the cheap app ProMovie Recorder developed by Liaoyuan Huo. It supports 4K recordings and offers full manual control (exposure, shutter, focus) in the most common formats (25 fps, 48 kHz audio). The surface is clearly arranged and easy to work with. You can test a free version of ProMovie Recorder that comes with a watermark. If you like the app, you can remove the watermark by investing about € 3.

In conclusion I would like to give a final recommendation: many colleagues use more than one app on their phone. Apps can crash (which usually happens without a good reason!). So you should always be familiar with an option B, the second app on your phone.

Interview with Richard Lackey: "Nothing I am doing is rocket science. It is the combination of it all and the process which is most difficult to learn."

Picture: Richard Lackey

Richard Lackey is a filmmaker, colorist (CSI), digital cinema technology and workflow specialist with an extensive knowledge and experience of digital motion-picture imaging and post production. US born, and UK bred, Richard has worked internationally since 2003, most notably Cape Town, South Africa, and Dubai, UAE. Richard started his career as a television editor, progressing from offline to online editing, and post supervision. Richard earned his first feature film credits as a post production coordinator and post producer before finally moving into a production role as a producer.

With a love for creating compelling imagery, and the technology that makes it possible, Richard has found a line between the technical and the creative, and is competent with both. Richard writes for a leading online technical portal cinema5d and is a full member of the Colorist Society International (CSI) and the Digital Cinema Society (DCS). Richard is currently working in business development and product management for UBMS, a leading cine, production and broadcast systems supplier for the Middle East and Africa in Dubai, UAE.

Twitter: @RickLackey

www.richardlackey.com

How did you get into filmmaking with your smartphone(s)?

This requires a bit of context, and it's more about why, than how. Professionally I am a digital cinema camera and post specialist. I've built up an extensive working knowledge of the technology and science behind digital motion picture imaging, especially color, and post workflow. It's my passion and the main driving force behind my career path to date.

However, I've grown frustrated and bored with a lot of the big camera tech. I believe it has really hit a plateau the past few years. It really doesn't matter what camera you pick up, from $1000 to $100,000 they are all capable of producing good enough images that what matters more than resolution, specs and formats, is the technical and creative skill and eye of the filmmaker.

Don't get me wrong, that's fantastic, it's finally about storytelling and not how expensive your camera is, but I'm a technologist as well as a creator, a balance of both. I'm interested in the future of digital imaging, in what's just over the horizon.

I believe the future of big cameras is small cameras, and a major shift from capturing images to capturing a lot of data about a scene, and reconstructing images computationally from that data with the help of very clever algorithms.

So, back to the question at hand. Finding myself bored and frustrated with the status quo of large sensor cinema camera tech, but as always, itching to shoot, I had just bought an iPhone SE. I was inspired to see what kind of video I could shoot with it.

I knew I wanted to shoot with post production in mind. For that I needed fully manual control over the camera, and the best bit-rate possible, so I downloaded the FiLMiC Pro camera app. What started as a throw-away experiment, became a massive turning point for me, and the start of a fascinating and rewarding journey.

This is how and why I got into smartphone filmmaking. Because it was, and is accessible to me, and to so many would-be filmmakers out there who may not even realise they already have a capable camera to start expressing themselves and their ideas.

What were the biggest problems you encountered on your first shoot?

To be honest I didn't really experience many problems because I knew how to avoid them in the first place. My technical background meant I knew what I wanted, and how to get it out of a limited device because I first understood how to get it from a unlimited device. I approached the iPhone with the same technical and photographic fundamentals I would approach shooting with a RED or an ARRI but acknowledging the limits of a tiny sensor.

Knowing, and understanding the science of the image pipeline and how to use the control that FiLMiC Pro gave me, allowed me to hit the sweet spot of the phone's sensor and processing. For instance, because I understood how temporal video compression works, I knew that I'd have far more useable detail encoded in the file, given a limited bit-rate, if I kept my shots quite still. Too much motion means significant changes in the image frame to frame, and that means losing quality. So, I kept my shots still.

Knowing I only had approximately 8-stops of dynamic range to play with, I purposely decided to avoid having the sun in the frame, so if I was shooting towards the setting sun, I framed the sun behind a building, or shot with the sun behind me. Being aware of the limitations, understanding the technology, and using the built in exposure tools an app like FiLMiC Pro gives you to know what your sensor is seeing, allows you to make informed, creative decisions that result in capturing the most useable image information possible for post production. The result is images people can't believe were shot with a phone.

How do you prepare for filming?

Usually I have some idea beforehand of the video I want to create and what the purpose of the video is. Most of the time I want to test something, a technique or more recently maybe an accessory like a lens, or exploring camera movement with a gimbal, or I am shooting something with a particular post production process in mind that I want to explore. I won't call them films, because they aren't really films yet.

My videos are usually shot in a particular location, a city, or part of a city that I might be travelling to for work, or on vacation. So I look on instagram for inspiration, I might spend some time on Google street view, looking at where I could go to get some interesting shots, often knowing I may have limited time. I use an app called TPE (The Photographer's Ephemeris) to check the path of the sun and what the light and shadows will be like at a particular time of day. If it's a work trip I might only have an afternoon or an evening free to shoot. A vacation is easier, I'll have more time, but at the same time I'm trying to be conscious of not making it into work, or becoming overly obsessed by shooting.

More recently I'm also trying to limit myself beforehand to some specific objectives that will build additional layers of knowledge and skill on top of what I've already learned. This might be spending time using a gimbal, or testing out a particular set of ND filters, or even planning an interesting night shoot that I know will give me video I can push further in post production to find improved noise reduction techniques. I try to focus on one or two things at a time so I can better keep track of the results.

Most of your work seems to require a lot of time after shooting. Can you explain what your workflow looks like?

Yes, I definitely shoot for post. Image capture and post production are inseparable. The shooting part is fast becoming the easiest part of what I'm trying to do, which wasn't necessarily the case when I started. Now I'm spending a lot of time in post. Right now I edit and color grade on desktop using DaVinci Resolve. Soon I hope to be able to edit on iPad with LumaFusion, and export an XML of the edit into DaVinci Resolve on desktop for the rest of my post work. I spend 90% of my time in image processing and color using Resolve.

My goal in post is to take what I've shot with the iPhone and create final images that look like scanned 35mm motion picture film that has gone through a professional DI (digital intermediate). This process is not just about throwing on a "film look" lut and calling it a day. This is a multi-operation process that is in constant flux, it's really a process of discovery and I enjoy it the most.

This is where pixels are being constantly destroyed and recreated, and where the power of sophisticated image processing algorithms (and soon more and more AI) is put to work to create images that end up containing far more perceived image depth, information and quality than was captured in the first place. A snapshot of my evolving post process right now includes a few distinct steps.

First I will analyse the source video for noise and artefacts. I may perform a rough pre-grade on a few shots before editing to see how they will respond. This will determine if a shot even has the potential to be polished to the level I am aiming for. If not, it gets thrown out immediately, and that feeds back to informing how I will shoot next time.

If the shot is dark and has some visible noise, then I start working on noise reduction. Noise reduction is a dark art, and it's very easy to make a shot look terrible, ruining all soul the scene may have had. I rarely need to reduce noise over an entire image, so often it is a localised process using various qualifiers and masks to isolate parts of the image. I'm using the Neat Video OFX plugin (https://www.neatvideo.com) in Resolve for noise reduction.

The second step is actual correction of exposure, color temperature, tint, levels, and color. This takes time and requires understanding how to read a waveform, RGB parade and vectorscope. This is also where entire sequences of shots are matched to a common and specific correct base point where white is white, black is black, exposure is correct across all shots, and everything lines up well for the next stages.

Third step may involve some localised adjustment of sharpening or sometimes even softening using masks, or a very clever OFX plugin I've been enjoying called detailr, made by Tom Huczek (www.timeinpixels.com). I use his false color plugin too, he's doing great work.

Fourth step is film emulation, this is a process of applying various modifications to the gamma and colors, and of course grain to emulate motion picture film.

FilmConvert (www.filmconvert.com) is a game changer when it comes to accurate film emulation, and I'm spending a lot of time with it now, exploring all of its parameters and adjustments. FilmConvert have developed a camera profile for FiLMiC Pro on iPhone, in normal, flat and log gamma flavors. FilmConvert actually changes my workflow substantially, as the initial primary color correction and shot matching is done within the plugin, rather than beforehand.

Finally I'll create a final creative "look" or stylised treatment of the colors, it just depends.

What are the biggest downsides of shooting with a phone?

Definitely the biggest downside is the limited dynamic range of a smartphone image sensor, which is just down to physics. The limitations of bit-rate and type of video compression that are imposed by the hardware and/or OS is another one. Lastly I would say the very deep depth of field, where everything is always in sharp focus. I don't really consider this a downside but some people definitely do.

What would be your main advice for someone who wants to start shooting videos like yours?

That's a tough one to answer because while nothing I am doing is rocket science, and every part of the process in shooting and post makes use of readily available tools, techniques and software, it is the combination of it all and the process which is most difficult to learn. I am learning and re-learning every time I try something new and fail.

I intend to share and teach as much of what I'm learning as I can, on my website www.richardlackey.com and in my videos on YouTube www.youtube.com/richardlackey so I guess my advice would be to catch the stuff I'm sharing and piggyback on work already done. I'm always trying to highlight other people who are also pushing in a similar direction.

What are you hoping for in the future technological development of the phone?

The future of digital imaging is computational. I think just a gradual progression towards virtualizing as much of the hardware as possible.

We're going to see phones with more cameras. We already have dual camera phones with a wide angle lens and a telephoto, although right now these are mostly being used as two individual cameras, with the exception of a computational digital zoom feature in some phones already, and some rudimentary depth processing for photo "portrait mode" effects.

Two cameras is not enough, we will see three, four, five and more. These cameras will have different purposes, some will be color, some monochrome, some high resolution, some lower resolution but more sensitive in low light. Maybe we will eventually see the maturity and adoption of true light field technology. All of these very different sources of image data will be combined into a single image, whether photo, or video entirely in software.

This will lead to the virtual sensor and virtual lens. We will be able to set up in software, perhaps in some future version of FiLMiC Pro, a virtual sensor of any size, a virtual lens of any type, focal length, and configure it with a virtual iris with as few or as many blades as we want, we will be able to select lens coatings from a drop down menu, or download complete lens profiles simulating a set of vintage Cooke primes, or a Helios with its swirly bokeh, or a Leica Noctilux and see all of the precise effects of those lenses in our images we'd expect from the real thing.

Other shooting parameters will become virtualized, such as video frame rate, ISO, and simulated shutter angle, even shutter type. The resulting motion blur will be simulated and all of these variables will be changeable in post after shooting.

It will be possible to generate stereoscopic images and video computationally from volumetric scene data, or simulate slight changes in the position of the virtual camera in six degrees of freedom in post production, or maybe rendered in real-time through a VR headset. We will have a choice whether we want to record only the resulting computed images, or the source data allowing full freedom to change anything in post.

That's where I see it going, and it's a done deal. It's only a matter of time.

Richard Lackey´s gear, left: Shooting in the desert of Al Qudra, Dubai with the iPhone XS Max, Polar Pro Iris ND Filters and Zhiyun Smooth 4 gimbal. Right: The Tarion Volador slider with iPhone 7 Plus in the Helium Core rig with Moondoglabs anamorphic lens and ND filters. Pictures: Richard Lackey

6 TV on the move: Editing

Summary

How can you edit your filmed material on the smartphone? Which apps are useful? How can you produce reports that meet the quality standards of TV or online platforms?

The smartphone is so much more than just a camera: it is a highly productive computer. "Mobile journalism" is so powerful because you can realise every single step that is required to complete a TV report or a clip for a website on a single device. The smartphone doesn't only offer many options for filming, but also has some very good programs for editing video. The easiest way to start your editing experience? Start with basic editing in a camera app: with FilmicPro or MoviePro you can trim your filmed material, i.e. you shorten a video at the beginning and end. This is how you easily condense your material before you import it to an editing programme. The advantage: the editing programs don't have to handle large amounts of data. They react faster and are more stable.

6.1 Fundamentals

It's the processing power of the phone that is of particular importance in video editing: only use the editing app and close all other applications to avoid crashing or the production of bad images.

If you followed the 5 Shot Rule during filming, you shouldn't have any problems in the editing process. Video editing is an art that many books have been written about. But with a few rules of thumbs in mind you will be able to tackle almost any problem. In the end it's always the story that counts: a single clip needs to convey meaning; a sequence consisting of several clips clarifies connections. This means that a single shot in a film should neither be too long nor too short, generally between 1 and 10 seconds (for one to three-minute reports about current events). Wide shots or documentary-like filmed actions often need more time. Close-ups, however, also work if they are shorter. The established rule of 3 seconds for an image now appears out-dated in a time of fast-paced commercials and internet clips. Changing settings and perspectives (camera locations) facilitates transitions while the exclusive use of similar shots leaves a "jumpy" impression and has an irritating effect. It is often difficult to insert content "into" pan shots or zooms: the majority of transitions only work from the beginning of a movement until it is completed. If there is movement in an image, the edits can be smoother because the eye of the observer is much more forgiving than in a still shot. Journalistic films are generally characterized by hard cuts; fades and other tricks are rare exceptions that may only be used for scene or time changes of the plot, if at all.

My experience is that editing the audio content is the biggest challenge in video editing: you should level and adjust the audio as early as possible in the recording process so that you don't need to spend a lot of time on it in the editing process. Unfortunately most editing programs don't always offer a visible audio layer for single clips. So authors can only rely on their ears. If you are monitoring audio with headphones, you will get a good hearing impression but it can still differ from the impression of the future listener. The listener will hear the sound coming from the speakers of the TV or smartphone. That's why you need to "pre-listen" to each clip without headphones. As an author you also need to make sure that you are working with a medium headphone volume: if the headphones are set to "full volume" after saving, the finished video might be set to a gain that is too low.

If you are editing the #Mojo-way, please keep this in mind:

1. Turn off any other apps
2. Pre-select your material, maybe even consider pre-edits (trimming)
3. Use your headphones at medium volume
4. Make sure to monitor the audio track on your smartphone speaker, too
5. Use common sense, especially with regard to audio track configuration
6. Include meaningful clips and cut non-meaningful sequences
7. Movements facilitate editing
8. Avoid fades and tricks

6.2 Editing with an iPhone

Fig. 06-01 A finished LumaFusion project with several video tracks

LumaFusion is the best editing app for the iPhone – there's no doubt about it (fig. 06-01). It was developed by LumaTouch, the company that already launched its predecessor "Pinnacle Studio Mobile Pro", a powerful editing program. Originally Pinnacle was developed for Corel as the "smaller brother" of the desktop version of the same name. And even though Pinnacle was relatively powerful, it was still very limited for pro video editing. But it had some features that made it the go to app on iOS for broadcast journalists. It offered, for example, a workflow with 25 and 50 images per second; many smartphone editing programs (such as iMovie) automatically work with (just under) 30 fps. If material had been filmed with 25 fps because it was intended for PAL television, editing with one of these programs would render it useless. First the images would be converted to 30 fps for editing. Then they would be reconverted before the actual broadcasting. The result: a visible quality loss. Pinnacle, however, was not only able to process material with 25/50 fps, but could also playout material with the same image rate. But Pinnacle only offered a single video track – in contrast to Kinemaster for Android, for example. It successor, LumaFusion (released in January 2017), takes video editing on iOS devices one step further by offering some amazing features: three video and audio tracks, an adjustable image rate and various functions ranging from professional editing of key frames up to a wide range of effects for image correction.

LumaFusion starts with the project view (fig. 06-02). In the middle you can see preview strips of projects that you have already edited. On a side note: during editing LumaFusion automatically saves intermediate steps so that nothing gets lost even if the app crashes. The camera (1) takes a screenshot of the project that is currently selected in the preview window at the top. (2) saves the project. The question mark (3) links to the online help centre. In the information menu (5) you can later view detailed information about your clips (image rate, format). Here you can also edit the clip titles to organize a project. The list icon (6) turns the project view on (blue background) and off (white background). An existing project can be edited as a whole with a single touch, e.g. you can delete it with a tap on the recycle bin (9) or duplicate it for further editing (8). You can search in the project view (10) and change the sorting sequence according to various features. The plus icon starts a new project, which can then be named in the new window. As mentioned repeatedly it is always important to look at the settings of the app before you start recording. In LumaFusion a tap on the wheel icon (4) opens the settings menu.

LumaFusion offers the option to define important basic settings for all projects. In the settings window (fig. 06-03) you can define the image format ("resolution") as well as the image rate ("frame rate"), either for the current project or as a default setting. If you are working for a TV station, you generally need to select the 16:9 format with 50 images per second (circled). LumaFusion also offers the option to edit videos in a vertical (9:16) or a square format (1:1, for Instagram for example) as well as several other formats. The audio quality for the PAL standard is 48 kHz (in accordance with the basic settings of FilmicPro). You can also define the file format. On top of that, it is possible to adjust the format of photos and videos that differ from the format of the project. You can also define the standard length of transitions, titles or photos that are created in the timeline.

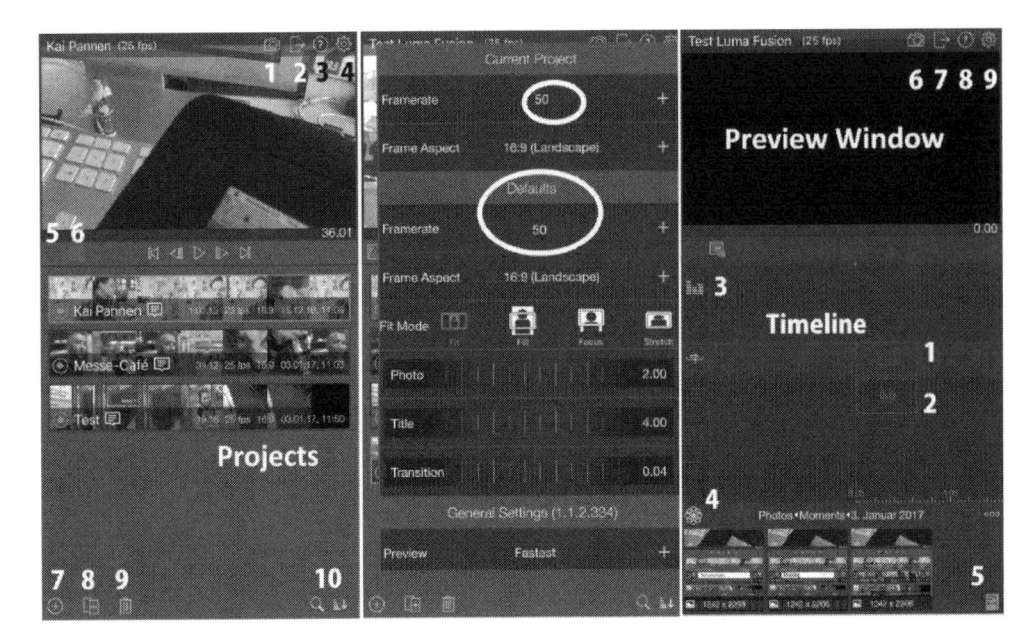

Fig. 06-02 to-04

The actual video editing takes place in the editing window (fig. 06-04). While Pinnacle Studio was mainly designed for vertical use, LumaFusion offers a wide range of vertical and horizontal layouts. You can switch between layouts with a tap on the icon at the bottom right (5). To make things easier we're going to focus on the vertical format, which is also the standard view. In our opinion it's more clearly laid out than the other formats, but of course that's a matter of taste. The editing window includes important menu items that we already know from the project view: the screenshot camera (6), the option to share projects (7), the help menu (8) and the settings (9). Below the menu you can find the preview window that is dominated by the timeline. The blue timeline offers up to three combined video-audio clips (1) which is a surprising feature when compared with conventional editing programs for computer desktops: here video tracks are simple image tracks without audio. Later on we are going to explain how you can work with only video and separated audio tracks in LumaFusion. Below the blue video-audio track you always find up to three audio tracks that are marked green (2).

The icon at the bottom left is important: the standard icon is the flower (4). Here you can select photos and videos from the phone gallery. With a tap on the flower icon a window opens that includes many brilliant functions of LumaFusion (fig. 06-05): in a broader sense it combines all sources that can be edited in the timeline: such as iTunes music (Please pay

6 TV on the move: Editing

attention to copyright laws when you use music in videos that you publish) or other sources, files that can be imported from cloud storage ("Imported") as well as titles and transitions ("Transitions", i.e. fades). If you touch the writing next to the flower icon – it describes the file path – you can directly navigate within the gallery.

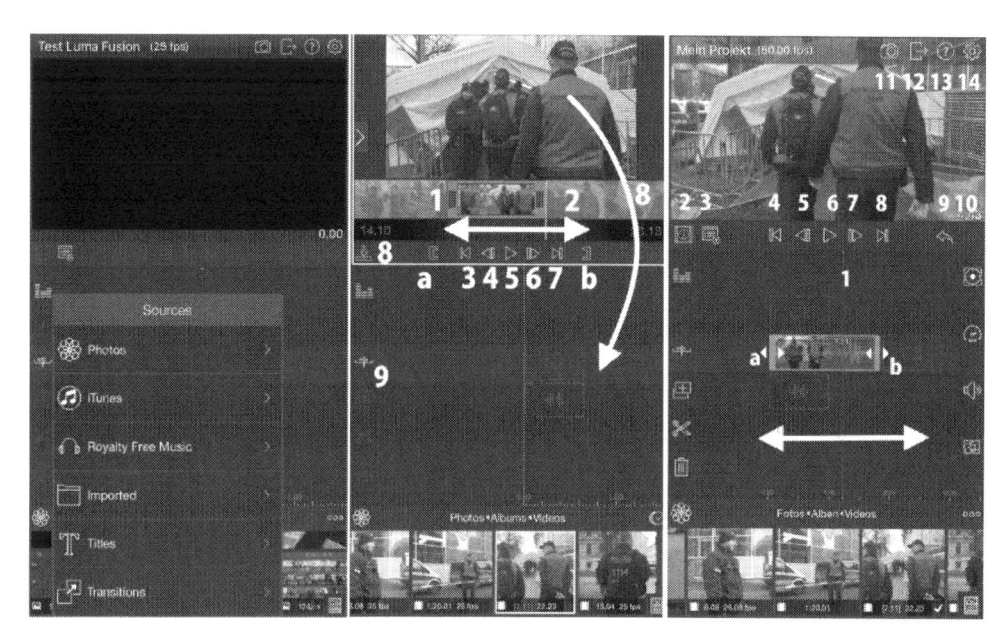

Fig. 06-05 to -07

If you select a clip in the timeline for future editing (with a simple tap), the clip will appear at the top of the preview window (fig. 06-06). When you do this for the first time, an additional window with clip details opens (fig. 06-08) that can be closed with the arrow at the side. There are two ways to select the sections that shall be opened in the timeline. You can either move the blue bars of the "In" (1) and "Out" points with drag and drop or you can move the playhead (arrow). (a) and (b) are used to fix "In" and "Out" at the correct positions. It's also possible to play the raw material clip (5). With (3) and (7) you can jump the playhead back and forth from the beginning of a clip to selected "In" and "Out" points. To precisely determine "In" and "Out" you can move the playhead a frame forward (4) or backward (6).

There are also two ways to position the finished clip in the timeline: drag and drop the preview image – it is now possible to place the clip on a video track and at different positions. If the playhead of the timeline is positioned at the end of a clip, the clip can be placed in the timeline with a simple tap on (8). It's important to decide whether clips shall be inserted (9) or shall replace already existing clips in the timeline (9 will turn blue). It appears as a blue clip in the timeline (fig. 06-07).

Navigation in the timeline is similar to the preview window. If you pinch and hold with two fingers, you can maximize or minimize the scale of the timeline. A tap on the black area of the timeline window, moves the playhead (displayed as a blue line) (1) back and forth as indicated by the arrow. (6) plays the content of the timeline. The playhead can be moved a frame backward (4) or forward (7). With (5) the playhead jumps back a crop mark and forward with (8) – several of these features are similar to a fully-fledged desktop editing program. Lifesavers are the arrows (9) and (10) which undo or redo an editing step. If you tap the preview window at the top, a new menu will be displayed at the top left: the photo icon (11) takes a snapshot. Here you can also share the film or play it to the photo gallery (12). LumaFusion tutorials can be accessed by tapping on the question mark icon (13). With the wheel icon (14) you can adjust the settings as described above. (3) reopens the project view so that you can easily switch between projects. LumaFusion automatically saves the intermediate results of the editing process; manual saving is not necessary (or even possible). The info icon on the film roll opens detailed information about the clip (fig. 06-08). This will also be displayed if material is opened for the first time in the preview window. With another tap on the info icon or the arrow (circled) you can close the information window.

A clip can easily be edited in the timeline. After the clip was selected with a tap, it can be trimmed by sliding the blue bars in the front (fig. 06-07, a) or back (b). If a clip is selected, it can be edited with the symbols at the side (fig. 06-08): it is possible to animate movement in the image (zoom, rotation etc.) (1), to change the speed for time lapses or slow motions (2), to edit the volume of the clip (3) as well as to use image filters (4).

LumaFusion offers a wide range of options to adjust colours, contrast as well as brightness of an image. The editing process starts with the selection of a preset. This will be used as a basis for adjusting single values, e.g. if an image that lacks white balance has turned blue. The authors are divided in their opinions: Bjoern´s feeling is that these LumaFusion tools are almost pushing the limits of a small mobile phone screen and its capacity to make a final evaluation of the image quality. Wytse finds that the possibilities of Luma Fusion are very helpful even on a small screen. A side note: Many of these functions related to image animation and colour corrections reappear in the photo editing app "LumaFX" that was also developed by LumaTouch.

If you tap twice on the video clip in the timeline, the same editing window will open (fig. 06-09). At the bottom of the image you can then navigate through the different editing options described below (1-4). Image animation animates a movement with the help of key frames (circled). The image can also be mirrored (1) or tilted (2) which allows you to convert a vertical format to a horizontal format. Material that is available in other formats can also be adjusted; the icons 3-6 are self-explanatory.

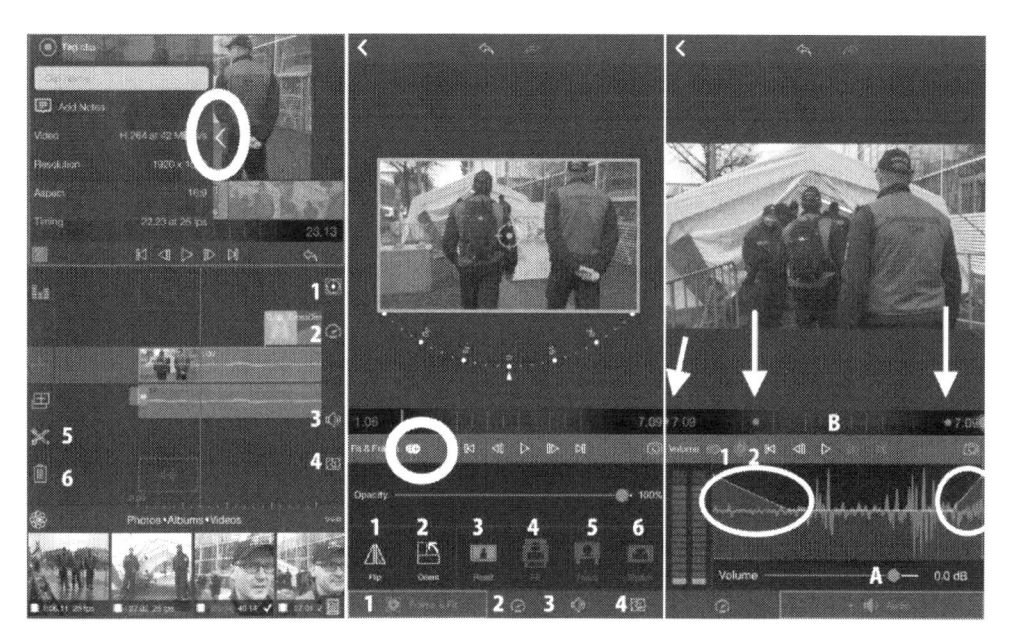

Fig. 06-08 to-10

The audio track of a video clip can also be edited precisely and exactly fitted to the frame (fig. 06-10). The volume slider (A) changes the overall volume of a clip. If you move the wheel (B) in the clip and change the volume, the program will place key frame points at the respective location (marked with arrows that indicate the new volume parameters). All key frames can either be deleted at once (1) or one by one (2). This allows you to create perfect fades, such as "to duck" a soundbite, i.e. fading it while an off-voice is translating. The same applies to simple audio tracks that are marked green in LumaFusion.

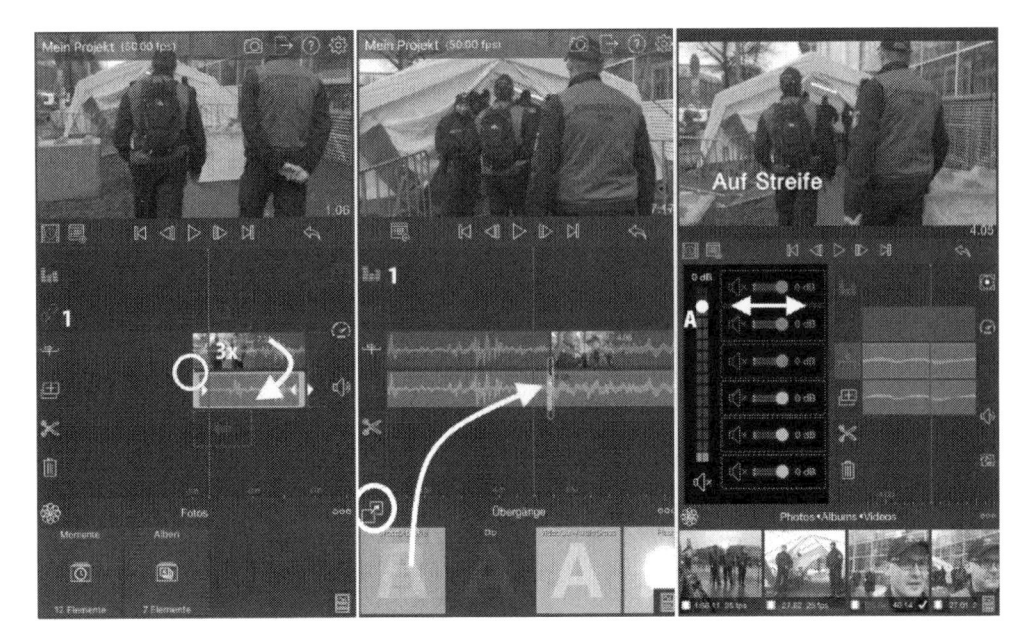

Fig. 06-11 to-13

An audio track can be imported to the timeline, e.g. from music libraries or audio programs. Splitting the audio from a video track also creates a new audio track. In LumaFusion this step is not very intuitive, but is still similar to the step that was used in Pinnacle Studio Mobile Pro: if you tap a clip not twice (for editing as described above) but three times, an audio track (fig. 06-11) is created from the clip and positioned on the next available audio track below. At the same time LumaFusion automatically turns off the audio track of the corresponding video clip. Now we have separate video and audio tracks – similar to a desktop editing program. The audio clips can now be edited, moved, levelled and so forth (with a simple or a double tap), just as described above for video clips.

It can be very helpful to edit audio and video separately if you want to mix different atmo tracks or if you want to use atmo for an image whose track is damaged or distracting. They can also be moved separately from the video track, e.g. to produce so-called "overlays": the statement of an interview guest already starts while I'm still looking at his action in the image. In a soundbite (instead of an off comment) he explains to me what he is doing. Or he might keep on talking while I'm already looking at different images of the action described. It's also possible to create transitions between audio clips.

A particularly strong feature of LumaFusion is the possibility to insert simple cross fades to sound tracks. I don't know any other smartphone program that allows this. In professional TV editing cutters generally don't insert any cross fades between the clips to create better transitions. That is now always necessary. In some cases, however, there might be an annoying "clicking" noise when one clip moves on to the next: now a cross fade is obligatory. In LumaFusion you can find it in the video output menu (fig. 06-12): first of all you need to select the icon for fades and transitions (circled) instead of the flower icon for photos and videos (icon at the bottom left above the material selection). You need to tap on the first type of fade ("cross dissolve") and move the small bar (arrow) to the transition point between the audio clips in question. Now the cross fade is already where it needs to be. LumaFusion also offers the transition type "Video Cut Audio Cross" which you can drag and drop between two adjacent video clips. As the title describes, without even creating a separate audio track, the app produces a sound transition while leaving a hard "cut" between the pictures.

A side note: if you move this type of transition to the end of a clip, a Figlende (What is that?) will be created. If you move it to the beginning, it will create a fade-in. The length can be trimmed as needed: at first you might have to maximize the scale of the timeline (see above – two fingers "pull" the timeline apart). In the next step you select the fade just like you would select a clip; then you trim it by tapping and extending one end. The clip will be automatically extended to the other direction by the identical number of images. If you want to use several cross fades, whose default length might be too short, you can change the length in the settings menu (see above). It is necessary to separate audio from video for such audio cross fades and to work with the green audio tracks: if you moved the same transition to a blue video track, you would not only create a cross fade but also a fade of two images.

In LumaFusion you should plan the distribution of tracks before you start editing. A tap on the mixer icon (1) opens an audio mixer (fig. 06-13) which makes it possible to readjust entire tracks after editing. This saves you a lot of work when you adjust single clips. Generally atmo tracks only reach 30% of the sound levels of soundbites and overvoice comments of an author. If you had to adjust each clip individually, you would need a lot of time. If all soundbites were placed on audio track 2, the audio comment of the author on audio track 3, and the atmo on track 1, the volume of the latter could be dipped (arrow). If the entire video were produced too high or too low in volume, the mixer (A) would increase the volume. But be careful: if the recording was already too low, any "noise" would increase and the piece might be broadcasted only with limitations.

Working with the audio mixer is important: a clean sound track can smooth the overall impression of the material. It is important to edit the material with "normal", i.e. medium phone volume and to listen to it with and without headphones. Only then will it be possible to determine whether the audio tracks are compatible (and also match the video).

Fig. 06-14 to-16

The possibilities of LumaFusion are almost endless. The program can do some things that a fully-fledged editing program on the computer couldn't do any better. What is impressive is the wide range of options to create titles and writing on moving images. This step also starts with the selection of the correct material source at the bottom left: instead of the flower for videos or the double squares for transitions you will now choose the letter "T" for title. Now you can choose from different title types that are used as the basis for further editing. A click on a template opens the actual window that allows you to edit the title (fig. 06-14). Now you can enter the text (1) and define the font (2), the font size (3) as well as the style and colour (4). In the preview window you can simply move the text box with a finger and you can also maximize and minimize it. In the timeline the title turns into an individual clip that can be positioned on one of the upper video tracks on top of the moving image. It will then be "stamped" onto the selected images. As any other clip you can trim the title or add transitions for fade-ins and -outs (see above).

Despite the large variety of LumaFusion it is rather unlikely that its full range of functions will ever be used. Working on a mobile phone still relies too much on fine motor skills. LumaFusion works really well on iPads, too – it's a good alternative for complex image editing. It is really great that LumaFusion offers an answer to every "problem": if an image was shot vertically, LumaFusion will convert it to a horizontal format. If the colours don't match, the program can adjust them. If the audio track of a clip is damaged, it can be replaced with another one. And since editing several video tracks is now possible, you can easily shoot quick pieces to camera that are related to news topics, add a few images of the location to the material and you will still be able to deliver broadcastable material for online use or linear TV in a very short time – and in good quality.

https://luma-touch.com/lumafusion-for-ios/

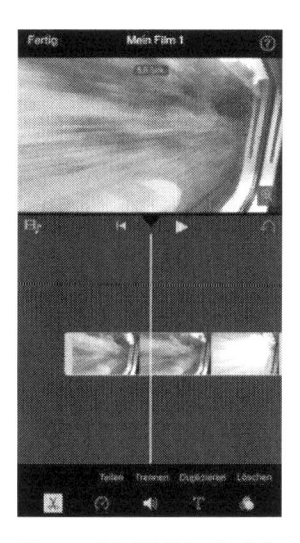

Figure 06-17 iMovie (iOs only)

iMovie is another solid program for video editing. But in comparison to LumaFusion it has one big disadvantage: it only works with just under 30 images per second (29,97 fps) and can't really be used for PAL productions. One of iMovies biggest problem is that editing is not very accurate: when you are trimming a clip, the smallest possible unit for correction is 0.1 seconds – precise and exact fitting to the frame is impossible. The transitions between clips are displayed as a fade icon even though a fade is not intended. This makes it difficult to synchronise video tracks with audio tracks that don't display any fades at the transition points. If you are mainly working for online and NTSC-providers, you should give iMovie a try and look at the pros and cons. In the end the decision is also a matter of personal preference – while some people prefer a certain editing program, others

171

swear by a different one. Unfortunately iMovie "crowds" valuable storage space with about 700 MB while LumaFusion needs less than one tenth of storage space – a further argument that speaks for the app described above.

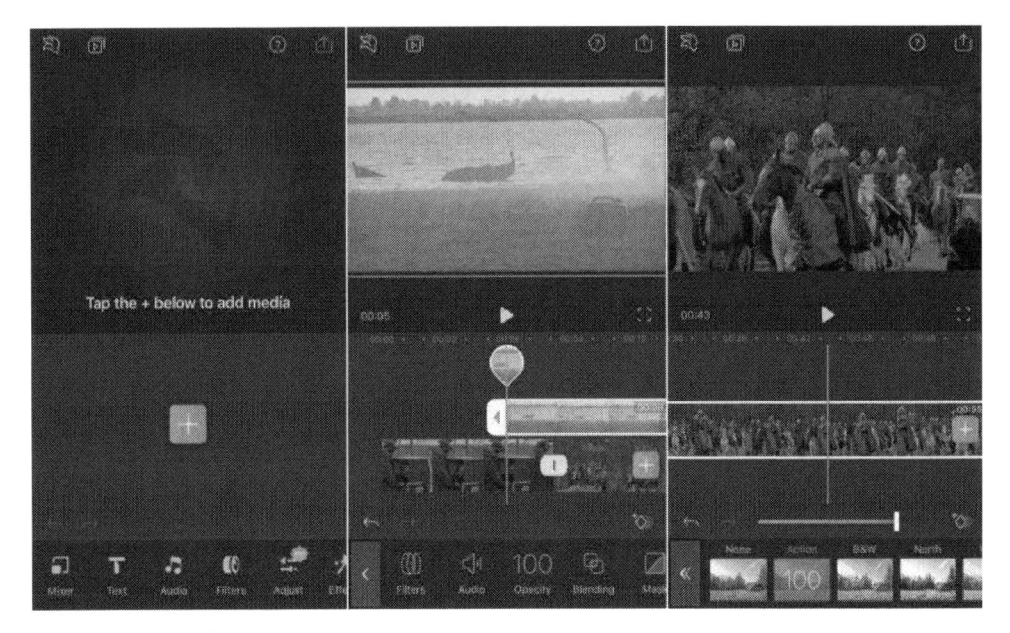

Figure 06-18 Videoleap

A solid third video editing app that might come in handy is rather new on the market: Videoleap. It offers multiple tracks of video and has a lot of very useful features. The layout is very simple. The top half of the screen is your preview window. This is where you can see what you created. The bottom half is reserved for the timeline and all the available options. To add video simply press "+". You now get a window with all your photos and videos. Select the ones you want to use and press "Add to project". The videos are not positioned on the timeline in the order you selected them. By pressing and holding them you can drag them for rearrangement.

When you want to add a second video layer simply scroll through the timeline to where you want the new video to go and press "mixer". The video will now be placed on top of the first one, but will not be full screen. By pinching with two fingers you can zoom in to make it fit the screen. When using the free version of the app you can use up to three layers of video. With the paid version you can add even more.

On the bottom of the screen you can find the options to add text, audio, filters and effects. You can also adjust the format of your project for things like square or vertical video. In the pro version you also get color correction and some extra effects. This is the biggest problem with Videoleap. If you want to take full advantage of everything in the app, you need to pay a rather steep prize: € 12,49 for a one month subscription or € 6,16 per month for one year. Or you could opt for buying the full version and pay € 159,99! This app is very good but also one of the most expensive apps on the market.

There are several other editing options on iOS available for online editing. Most notable might be the app Quik by GoPro. The app is good enough for quick and dirty editing. You can select the clips you want to use and drag them in the right order. Then add some music, titles and filters and it is ready to publish. There is no way to fine-tune what you made or make J-cuts or L-cuts. A lot of things are done automatically and that might not be what you, as a professional, want. The app uses 30 frames per second and thus the projects cannot be used for broadcast TV in PAL areas.

6.3 Editing for iPhone and Android

Figure 06-18 I Adobe Premiere Rush (Filming interface)

A new and possibly very interesting player on the market of Mobile Storytelling is Adobe with their **Adobe Premiere Rush** app. It is an app that can handle both filming and editing and is available on iOS and on desktop (an Android version is scheduled for 2019). What this means is that you can start your project on the phone and finish up on desktop.

The release that is in the market now is still struggling with some bugs but in general it works well both on the editing and on the filming side. In the latter, it gives you a lot of the controls you also find in FilmicPro. (The interface even looks a bit similar, see fig. 06-18 I) There is a square to control focus and a circle for exposure. And, just like in FilmicPro, you can manually control things like ISO, white balance and shutter speed. And in settings you can change frame rate and resolution. It is not as elaborate as FilmicPro, but it comes close.

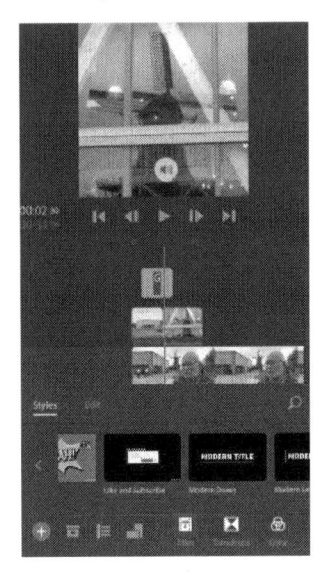

In editing (fig. 06-18 II), it is a bit limited if you are used to LumaFusion or Kinemaster, but it has a lot of useful features that come in handy if you are editing for TV or Online. You get multiple video- and audio layers. You get colour correction, tons of titles, cropping and transitions. But also an audiofilter system that allows you to (for example) filter out background noise or amplify voices. And when you are done editing, you can export in portrait, landscape or square format. The biggest question though is this: is it worth the price? To fully use all the features you will have to have a full Adobe subscription or a special Adobe Rush subscription. The latter is not that expensive but it is worth knowing that there will be a monthly bill (around 10 $) when using it. You can try the app for free because there are 3 free exports that come with the app but after that you will have to pay.

Figure 06-18 II Adobe Premiere Rush Edit Interface

6.4 Editing with Android phones

Kinemaster is an outstanding video-editing app for Android phones (fig. 06-19). It has been thoroughly developed and improved over the years and offers many important functions. A second video track is already available for some phones with certain processors (more details can be found on the developers' website). In the latest update Kinemaster also give you the abillity to edit in portrait and square video. As far as we know Kinemaster is also the only app that does not modify the frame rate of the processed material. This means: when editing with Kinemaster users can't convert to a different frame rate, but material that has been filmed with 25 fps is still available in 25 fps after editing. Other apps (such as PowerDirector) work with 30 fps. A problem is the paying method: the app is not based on a one-time fee, but the developers charge a regular subscription fee. If you use Kinemaster only every now and then, we won't recommend buying it.

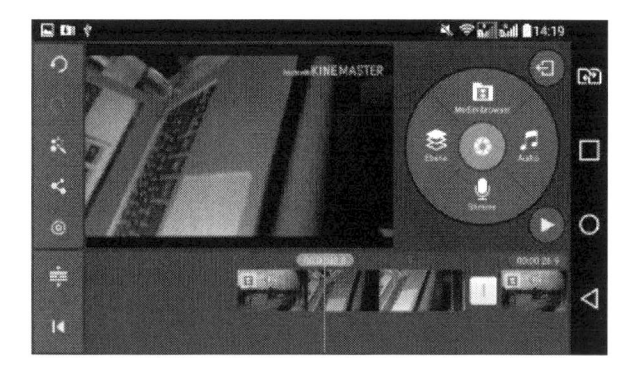

Figure 06-19

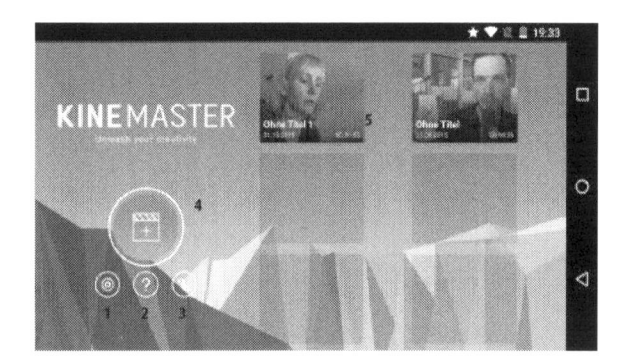

Figure 06-20

When you open Kinemaster, the project view opens – in a horizontal format (fig. 06-20): here you can change the basic settings (1), access the help section that offers short videos (2) and contact the Kinemaster support (3). The big red button (4) starts a new project, the photo bookmark (5) opens an already existing project. After a short intermediate step in which the video can be played or discarded, you get to the editing window (fig. 06-21). The timeline (2) is positioned below the large preview window (1), a wheel- or cake-like menu can be found on the right side of the preview window. Here you can record videos (3) – though we would recommend using the camera apps presented in chapter 5. In addition you can import videos (4), audios (5) and add text and other elements to the image (7). With the microphone (6) you can record the overvoice after editing. Apart from that you can play the material that you've already edited in a full screen mode (8). A tap on (9) brings you back to the project menu.

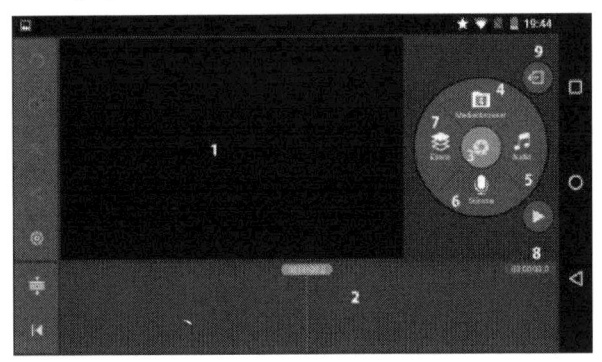

Figure 06-21

Figure 06-22

Simple clips can be imported via the media library (fig. 06-22). A simple tap transfers the respective clip to the timeline; the clip can now be edited (the edges of the clip turn red) (fig. 06-23). There are several available functions: you can rotate and mirror (2), cut and share (3). There are effects (4) as well as zoom-ins on details of the video (5), but these always involve a loss of quality. You can also change the volume of the clip (6) and use more options (scroll down). The position of the playhead (1) is important for the editing process (2). Here you can split the clip, for example. You can also trim clips: if you tap on the clip and choose the option "cut/share" (3), yellow markers appear at the beginning and end of the clip which you can use to simply change the clip length.

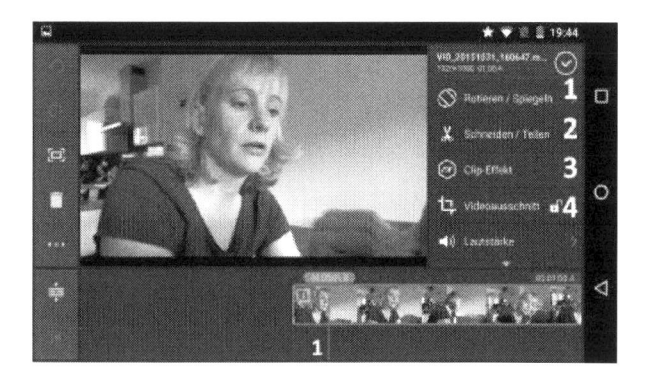

Figure 06-23

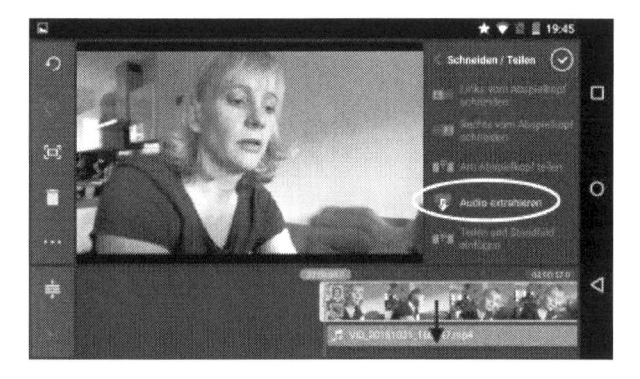

Figure 06-24

On the video track Kinemaster links moving images to sound. As in LumaFusion you can separate the audio track. In the "cut/share" menu" you'll find the option "extract audio" (fig. 06-24): the sound that is linked to the video is automatically set to "0" volume; a smaller audio track is created below the video track. You can now edit the audio track separately. Even audio fades can be manually controlled in the "Volume Envelope" menu

177

(fig. 06-25). The small pin in the bottom-left corner (circled) is also important: you can pin a clip to the timeline so that it is fixed during editing which creates, for example, asynchronism between sound and image.

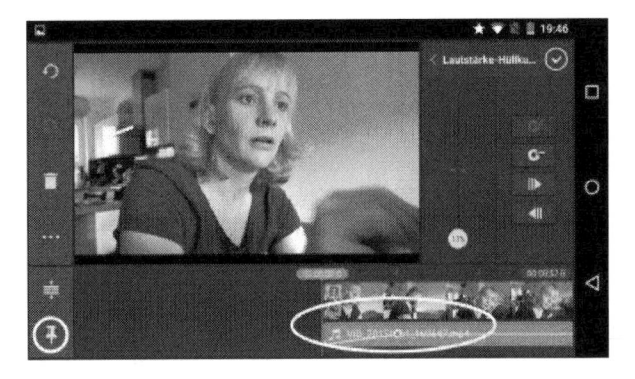

Figure 06-25

Tap the microphone to record an overvoice (see function 6 in fig. 06-21). Kinemaster makes an audio level available and accepts external sound sources such as clip-on microphones (fig. 06-26). The audio import function (see function 5 in fig. 06-21) allows you to import music that can be used in the video.

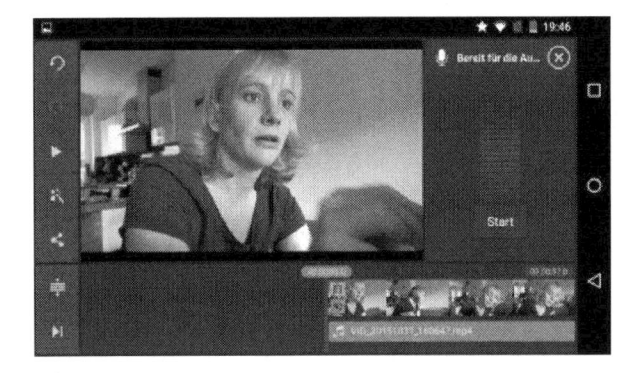

Figure 06-26

6 TV on the move: Editing

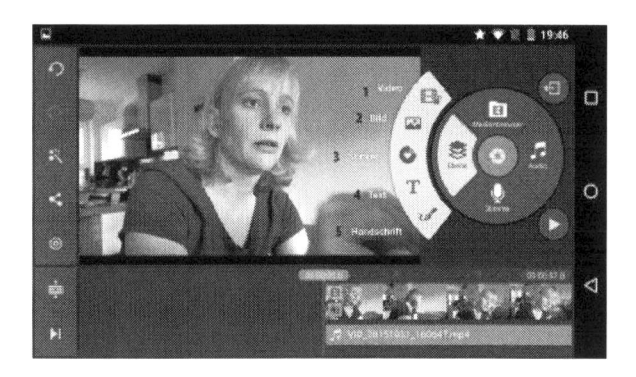

Figure 06-27

Kinemaster also offers a wide range of so-called "layer" functions (fig. 06-27). The additional video track (1) is of particular interest; yet it is only available for certain phone models (see above). A video can completely or partially overlay another video. In contrast to professional desktop editing programs the video track that is visible is not the top but the lower video track. This is a great function for editing so-called soundbite films. You can place the soundbite of the protagonist, who is continuously narrating, on the video track and consistently "illustrate" his actions with images (fig. 06-28).

Figure 06-28

Additional layer functions let you insert a photo (2), add stickers (small graphic elements) (3) as well as text and handwriting (4 and 5). The text function is relatively

179

flexible and can be used to create titles or credits (which indicate your sources) as well as to add subtitles to a video (fig. 06-29). Since the use of videos on mobile devices is increasing, this question arises: how often will we still notice the "conventional" TV sound? Many video platforms, such as AJ+-Net, have started to transport content with "captions" and don't rely on off-screen speaker texts anymore.

Figure 06-29

Transitions between video clips are managed by the "Transition" symbol (fig. 06-30). If you are a journalist who is used to editing material at a desktop computer, this function might be slightly unusual (just as with LumaFusion): irrespective of length and type of the transition this small square "dangles" in-between the clips as if these were not merging. The same applies to true hard cuts: the grey square with the simple vertical bar symbolises the most frequent transition.

6 TV on the move: Editing

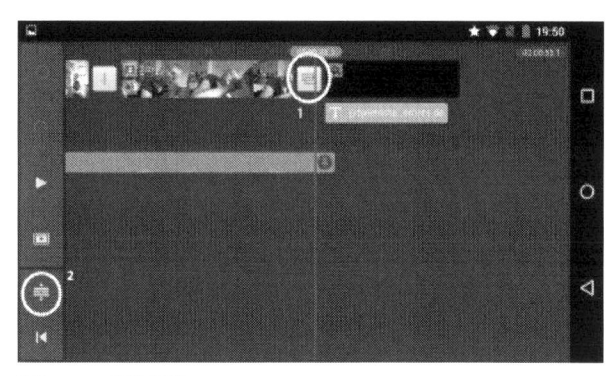

Figure 06-30

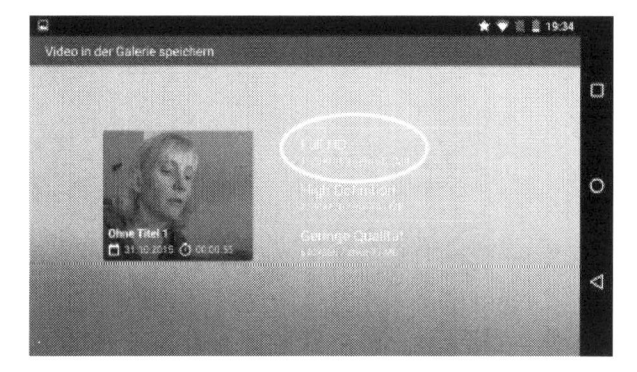

Figure 06-31

The clip will be saved to the gallery after editing (fig. 06-31) or it will be directly shared to Facebook or YouTube. If you filmed in Full HD, you should also playout your final material in Full HD. The image rate (frame rate in fps) does not change as was described above. Please make sure to not close the app during saving: Kinemaster requires the full processing power of the smartphone to produce faultless videos.

https://www.kinemaster.com/

An Android alternative to Kinemaster is PowerDirector (Android). The app is less complex and also offers fewer options. On certain phones it now offers a second video track to overlay soundbite edits. You can also edit vertical videos with the app (such as in a 9:16 format). It is also possible to extract the audio from a combined video/audio clip (by duplicating the video clip and pulling it onto an audio track). PowerDirector saves films with 29,97 fps (or 24 fps) which means that they have to be converted for TV broadcasting. This always goes along with a loss of quality. On the other hand the functions are more than satisfactory for journalism today, such as online journalism. Older Android models also work better with the less complex app than with Kinemaster. A further advantage: PowerDirector is a one-time purchase; a subscription for which you would have to pay regularly is not necessary.

Figure 06-32

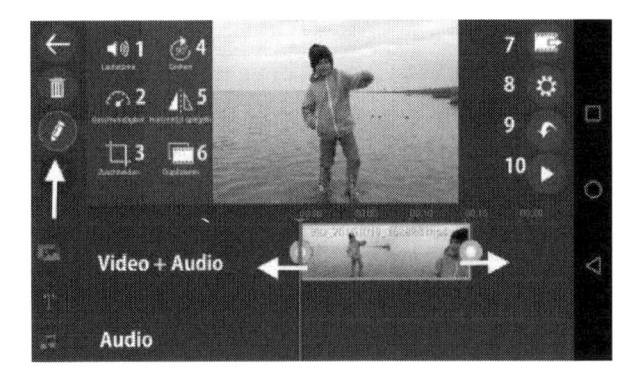

Figure 06-33

182

PowerDirector starts with a project overview (fig. 06-32). After starting a project, it displays a timeline below the preview window (fig. 06-33). It consists of a combined video and audio track, a track for text and overlays as well as a separate audio track that may record the overvoice (use "Add audio"). Tap the pen icon to edit clips. Trim clips by tapping on the green buttons at the beginning and end of a clip (white arrows). You can also adjust the volume (1) and the speed (2) of the clip, choose image details (3) and change the alignment (4). The clip can also be horizontally mirrored (5) or duplicated. A tap on the film icon with the arrow (7) "produces" the film (fig. 06-34): you can either save it to the gallery or share it on Facebook or YouTube. By tapping on the wheel icon (8) you will get to more settings. The arrow (9) brings you back to the project window, which is also the start screen of the program. The play icon (1) plays the video in full screen mode.

Figure 06-34

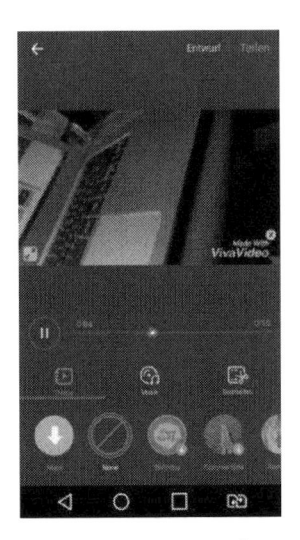

Figure 06-35 VivaVideo

VivaVideo (Android, iPhone) (fig. 06-35) is a very popular video-editing app that targets the general market. Parts of the editing process are sourced out to the cloud so that working with VivaVideo will get problematic if the data connection is bad. Editing videos in the app is very easy. There are many additional functions available. If you appreciate a professional timeline for your editing purposes, you will be disappointed. VivaVideo only records with a resolution of 640 x 368 pixels – which can't be used for TV and even results in visible quality differences if used online.

Figure 06-36 AdobeClip

Another editing option is AdobeClip (fig. 06-36): it does not (yet?) offer the variety of functions that is offered by PowerDirector or Kinemaster. In particular, the complex editing of audio is almost impossible. AdobeClip is rather strange: with the automatic compilation of scenes the surface is similar to mass-market programs. On the other hand – and this is one of its advantages – AdobeClip fits into a workflow whose final product can be edited with Adobe Premiere on a desktop computer. This may be appealing, especially if a reporter does quick and dirty edits of raw material while on the move. The material can then be used to produce a complete film in the editing process.

Many #Mojos also like the WeVideo app. However, it does not playout "full HD" (this partly depends on the phone) which means that it has to down convert good film material, i.e. it makes it worse.

6.5 Editing with Windows phones

MovieMaker is the app of choice for editing with Windows phones. It can be used vertically, just as LumaFusion for iPhones. MovieMaker differs from conventional desktop editing programs in important aspects: it's almost impossible to directly work in the timeline. You need the edit functions which each open a new window. An example: You can't simply "drag and drop" a clip. This is only possible with the menu functions "Move Left" and "Move Right" respectively. MovieMaker only provides a combined video/audio track as well as an additional audio track. Apart from that the program seems to be relatively slow.

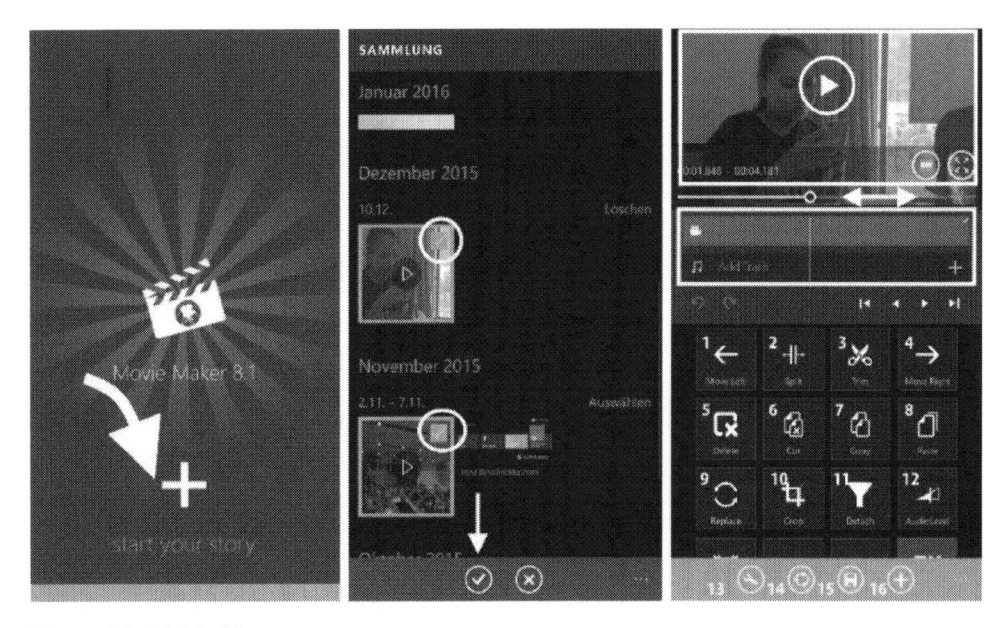

Figure 06-37, 38, 39

MovieMaker starts with the project window: "Start your story" (fig. 06-37). A tap on the plus icon opens the media library (fig. 06-38) in which you can select single clips (blue checkmark). After you've selected several clips (you can import more clips in a later step), you need to accept your selection with the white checkmark (arrow). Now the editing window opens (fig. 06-39).

The editing window of MovieMaker is divided into three main sections: on the top there is the preview window, followed by the timeline. In-between these two sections you will find the playhead (arrow). It's not possible to move the playhead, which is shown as a single line, in the timeline itself. Below the timeline you will find various editing options that take up almost half the screen. You can select a clip with a simple tap and move it to the left (1) or right (4), one clip at a time. You can split it into two clips at the playhead (2) or trim it at the edges (3). A clip can be deleted (5), cut (6), copied (7) and inserted (8). A clip can also be replaced by another clip (9) – the length and the position of the clip won't change. It's also possible to cut a section out of a clip ("crop", 10). The following function is particularly important: "Detach" (11) separates the audio track from the video clips. A new audio track is created below the video track. In addition you can also change the volume of the clip (12). In the blue bottom bar you can adjust the settings (13) that MovieMaker applies to all clips: it's possible, for example, to modify the length of still images that have been added or to turn off the volume of all clips. The "Share" icon (14) shares the film on YouTube, Instagram or other social networks. A tap on the "disc" icon (15) saves the film to the phone. And you can add further media with a tap on the "Plus icon (16).

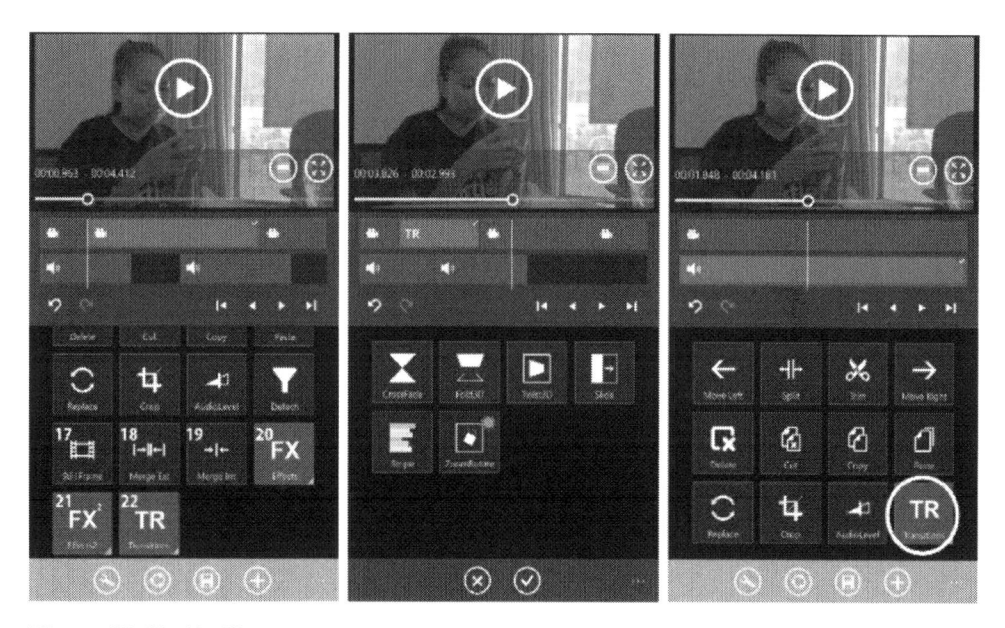

Figure 06-40, 41, 42

The options for video editing are still versatile (fig. 06-40): you can produce a still frame from a moving image clip and insert it in the timeline (17). It's also possible to merge a clip with all adjacent clips or only with the clip closest to the playhead (19). Many effects (20 and 21) are dispensable when it comes to journalistic films. With regard to transitions (22) only conventional fades may be useful. These are called "crossfade" (fig. 06-37).

A similar menu is available for audio editing: after a tap on the audio clip many functions are displayed that have already been described above (fig. 06-41). The menu item "TR" (Transitions) includes the important Fade in/Fade Out (fig. 06-42).

Figure 06-39, 40, 41

Once you've completed the editing process you can save the finished film with a tap on the disc icon. A sub-menu opens (fig. 06-40) that offers several options: you can export the audio track separately as an MP3 file or you can save the project for MovieMaker as a project file for further editing. You can send the project via Wi-Fi or – and that is important – you can save it: "Save video". The new window offers several options (fig. 06-41). Depending on the intended purpose the film can be saved in HD with the necessary image rate (25 fps for PAL). The higher the bitrate, the higher is the quality and the need for storage space. In the example the selected bitrate (15 Mbps) tends towards the lower end of the scale of useful bitrates.

Interview Mike Castellucci: Phoning it it: "Professionals still need to be able to tell a good story."

Mike Castelluci is a former broadcast journalist for WFAA in Texas and now storytelling and video news professor for Michigan State University. He created a complete 30-minute TV show for WFAA with his iPhone. The show won him two Emmy Awards. After that he made two more iPhone shows.

Twitter:@MikeCastellucci

How did you get the idea to start shooting a complete TV-show on your phone?

Do you remember a consumer grade camera called The Flip? 140 dollars with no external mic? I believe it was one of the first consumer grade HD cameras. I found myself in a creative black hole at the TV station I was working at in San Diego. I wondered if I could shoot a 2-minute package with it and make it broadcast worthy. THAT turned in to a half hour show. Fast forward a couple of years. I moved back to Dallas, Texas, and the 5th largest TV market in the country. My boss knew I did a show with a Flip. She asked if I could somehow do a 2-minute story using an iPhone. I said, "I don't know, but I'd love to give it a shot!" So, the answer to your question is – —I always tend to take something to the extreme and did it here.

What was the reaction of your employer? Did you get any support?

Obviously, the reaction from my boss after the first story was one of fascination. Then, when I presented the first few minutes of the half hour special, she was equally amazed. She, Carolyn Mungo, fully supported my efforts.

How did your interviewees respond when you arrived on the scene with your phone?

The first time I went out to do a story on my phone, the subject was visibly underwhelmed! He was an incredible artist who was visiting Dallas. He had heard that the powerhouse WFAA would be arriving to do a story with him and that he would be featured on the evening broadcast. He literally asked where the cameraperson was and where the sound person was. I told him I would be shooting on my phone and to not worry. I also told him to watch it that evening and he'd know that his effort would not be wasted. He called me 5 minutes after it aired and said: —"I get it now." He was literally the ONLY subject who I felt was underwhelmed when I showed up, at least the only one who wore their emotion on their sleeve! The vast majority of folks I do stories with seem the very opposite. They seem more comfortable, more at ease. Heck it's only me and my phone! What damage could I do?? It's also a better chance for me to create a fast relationship which is essential in my storytelling. I recently did a story on a steam train. The head of it happen to be going through cancer treatments. We spent a few hours together and at the end of the shoot she said that every TV station in the area at one time or another has done stories with her and that our time together was the most enjoyable. Then when she saw the story, she was overwhelmed.

What was the set up you used?

The first set up I used for the first story was an iPhone 5 with 16G of storage, a redi-cam holder, a tripod, a wide angle ollo-clip and a wireless mic held on to the tripod with vVelcro. I believe I did the first half hour show with that set up. In the last two half hour specials, I used a Beastgrip, wide angle, wireless mic and tripod. I also use a Rode video micro for natural sound and alternate plugging that in with the wireless mic cable.

What was your workflow like?

I learned early that I needed to keep clips short. It actually fit in to my "shoot and move" mentality anyway. I'd ask a question, let them answer, stop recording, move, then ask another question. I keep interview clips to 2 minutes or less, b-roll shots seldom exceed 30 seconds. I know that with 40 clips or so I'd have a decent 2-minute story. That's only about 4 or 5 gigs. So even with 16 gigs of storage, it hardly ever was an issue. I'd download each story to a hard drive, erase the clips on the phone and start over.

Did you run into any problems producing Phoning it in?

People always ask me what the challenges are.? I always think about it and say—there are none. I literally never can come up with problems. Time consuming would be an issue, but that comes with anything where you care about quality. I suppose one "problem" is that it's difficult maybe to shoot a football game or the moon, since they are so far away, but I look at things like that as challenges, not problems.

How do you see the future of Mobile Journalism?

It's a great question. As I've ended two of my Phoning it in specials with the statement: -"technology will change, storytelling will never change." So then you ask yourself: will it change to bigger cameras with bigger crews? I don't think so. Newsrooms will continue to get smaller. One person crews are the norm now. Workflow with a phone is good. I think the future is bright for mobile journalism. Professionals still need to be able to tell a good story. It's all anyone wants.

Any pointers for newbees in the field?

I have just finished a workshop in Southern California. I love the fact that they come away inspired. They come away inspired, I think, because the technology is not overwhelming to them. They can do it. It just takes drive and determination and the will to tell engaging, sometimes emotional stories. The very reason why Phoning it in exists.

Mike Castelluci´s Gear for "iPhoning it in"

7 TV on the move: Live Streaming

Summary

Reporting live with the smartphone creates new opportunities but also new risks. How can we stream live in a responsible way? How does the role of journalist differ from an eyewitness? Which apps are useful? What are the key issues of live streaming?

Live streams are different from any live report that we have seen on TV so far: until only recently it was impossible to create a live image without a "Satellite News Gathering" (SNG) van and a camera team. As a result many reporters were often immobile, were standing in front of barriers or on empty streets, either waiting for the protest march to arrive or having just missed it. There were a variety of reasons why it was almost impossible to make "mobile" TV, i.e. TV on the move: it's time consuming to set up SNGs and to establish a satellite connection – and once the connection is set up, it's impossible to move the vehicle, especially during a live broadcasting.

On the other hand satellite connections are more reliable – in comparison to live streams from a mobile phone. If you are streaming on the internet, interruptions are more than likely to happen. Some streams might not work at all because of bad network coverage, network overload or blockage – a scenario often observed after terror attacks. In addition there is a noticeable delay during network live streams: some apps have a delay of 20 to 60 seconds between the live moment and the time the audience actually sees it. This "latency" period is so long that it would be impossible for a reporter on location to have a conversation with the host in a studio.

Live streaming from a mobile phone opens up a new dimension for "mobile journalism": finally the bandwidths of mobile communication are good enough to both send and receive live videos from everywhere. 3G creates acceptable results; 4G (LTE) provides sender and recipient with very good live streaming quality, at least for the most part. And 5G is just around the corner, making the experience even better. There are apps that use these assets by providing good encoding software that allows user-friendly streaming. Live streaming is becoming more popular: while some apps such as Bambuser have been on the market for a long time, the first big boost was created with the introduction of Meerkat and Twitter's takeover of Periscope shortly after. Facebook Live is currently creating the next wave –

with a much bigger reach due to this feature being part of the Facebook platform. Its relevance is also higher because many journalistic platforms are going to use live streaming in the context of their Facebook appearance. Facebook has been intensively promoting live streaming, often moving live streams to the top of the timeline. With Instagram Stories, Instagram also introduced a live function for the users of the smartphone app.

"Falsehood flies, and the truth comes limping after it." This statement, which was made by the Irish satirist Jonathan Swift in the 18th century, would describe today's live streams perfectly: "live images are already traveling around the globe while traditional media is still busy putting their shoes on". And SNGs crews are still busy setting up their satellite dishes. There are 3 billion mobile phones "out there" which means that 3 billion people could theoretically do a live broadcast within seconds.

"The destroying innovation that traditional television is now confronted with" – that's how Michael Rosenblum describes live streaming apps. A few people refer to Rosenblum as the "father of video journalism". He has trained thousands of VJs worldwide and has been a consultant for media corporations. Which means: It's not a blind person who is talking about colours. Rosenblum argues that traditional media are offered an "enormous, life-changing, industry-changing opportunity". From Rosenblum's perspective the media should go after the live streams of these billions of people and use the material to curate their own services and pass them along to their audiences. During a talk at the BBC, however, he realized that the media don't see an opportunity in these "new live providers" but mainly a risk, i.e. a competition as he describes the situation in his blog "The VJ".

However, "live streaming" and "live reporting" are worlds apart as shown by many recent streams. This brings us back to Jonathan Swift and a another modification of his statement: "live streams are traveling, useful live reports lag behind." The quality of the content of many streams is lousy; some don't have any relevance from a journalistic point of view. Others pick up on current events – providing evidence that users as well as providers face new problems with regard to these new apps. If you are following an event that is developing live on location, you will almost never have the time – or keep the necessary distance – to classify and to analyse the images. And will you be able to assess – or even predict – the image that is going to develop in front of your camera? Will you be able to predict the motif that you are going to stream to the world within a matter of seconds? When 20 people were killed in a bomb attack in Bangkok in August 2015, a live Periscope stream even showed body parts – a line was crossed that was difficult to accept.

7.1 Not only an eyewitness: live streaming asks for responsibility

If journalists handle live streaming apps in a responsible way, they can be different from eyewitnesses. The boundaries, of course, are fluid and non-journalists (such as eyewitnesses) can also deal with the instrument "live streaming" in a responsible manner. From my point of view, however, journalists have to act responsibly, if they do not want to lose their credibility and the trust of their audience.

One more self-evident fact: it is ok to experiment as extensively as possible and to test boundaries. But it is also important to learn from these experiences and to draw conclusions. In Germany, the BILD newspaper as well as the online platform stern.de have been taking live streaming apps seriously, especially Periscope, and have been testing them thoroughly. "BILD" even claims to have invented its own live streaming form, the "Periscoportage". The fact that reporters of these media institutions are responsible for the following – rather problematic – examples has to be interpreted with care. Many other media outlets have not allowed themselves to make any mistakes because they neither trusted live streaming nor did they have enough confidence. They now benefit from the experiences that were made by the few pioneers.

The attacks in Paris on the night of November 13th, 2015 are considered to be one of the breakthrough moments of live streaming apps reaching a broader audience. These apps had only been available for less than a year. Within minutes after the series of attacks started dozens of live streams were online. Shots were heard, and anxious people were to be seen. There were so many eyewitnesses who streamed from downtown Paris and so many people who watched these streams that Periscope temporarily crashed – which, by the way, illustrates a problem that live streaming apps generally have during major events: since they rely on mobile networks, they are prone to interruptions.

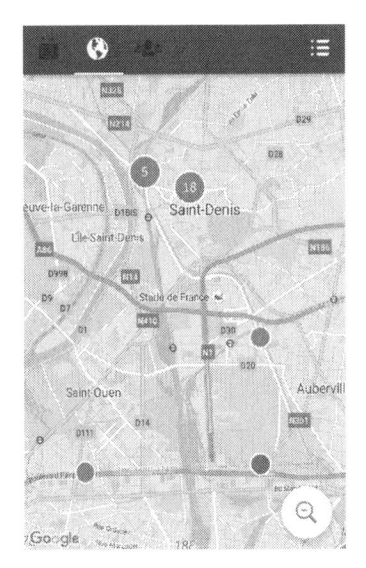

Figure 07-01 Periscope streams of the anti-terror operation in Saint Dénis.

In the days following the attacks Periscope provided many streams from Paris for which eyewitnesses and also journalists were responsible. On the morning of November 18th, a police force, supported by troops and Special Forces, searched through apartments in the Parisian district of St. Dénis. There were several exchanges of fire during which three people were killed, including one of the alleged suspects of the terrorist attacks. The world was able to follow the anti-terror operation live on Periscope (fig. 07-01): a total of 23 saved streams was available shortly after, including the live images provided by the stern reporter Philipp Weber (fig. 07-02). The blogger Stefan Niggemeier calls the stern coverage "terror porn" and quotes Weber's original words in extracts on his blog:

Figure 07-02 stern reporter Philipp Weber on Periscope.

„*Okay, something is going on here. I just follow the crowd. I'm following the people over there. I don't know what's happening.*

I don't know what's happening. I'm just following them ...

Oh oh, the police are moving forward. Police officers draw their weapons. Police officers draw their weapons. They are moving forward and ...

Police officers with drawn weapons are walking this way. We don't know what they are looking for. I'm directly behind the police officers. Directly behind the police officers who have drawn their weapons.

"The most irresponsible piece of journalism that I've seen in a long time", says Stefan Niggemeier on his blog stefan-niggemeier.de about Weber's Periscope coverage: "Here we have a journalist who – according to his own statement – doesn't know anything about the situation in which he finds himself except that it is presumably very dangerous. He doesn't only put himself in danger, but also the police whom he 'pursues'. Talking like a drunken person he keeps repeating that he is standing behind a police officer who has drawn a weapon, drawn a weapon. He does not consider for a single moment whether he's making a good choice in standing there with his mobile phone, filming and running and filming. "

This is harsh criticism: Weber primarily uses the technical possibilities but neglects, in Niggemeier's eyes, his journalistic duties – to classify, to analyse and to inform. And last but not least, he puts himself and possibly others in danger. On the other hand Weber uses a form of reporting that is new for many journalists; he as well as many others need to make their own experience first. He delivers little more content than a "mere" eyewitness – but would an eyewitness be confronted with such fierce criticism for this stream? Many viewers watched Weber's live reports. Online media such as the successful American platform Vice experience an intensive use of authentic streams, especially by young users, in which a reporter subjectively reports what he experiences.

There is one more thing to consider when live streaming in such a situation. If you are on the scene of a terror attack or a police operation and are live streaming, chances are that the terrorists are watching your stream as well. And by streaming you are also informing them on what is happening. Thus, you are providing them with information about the whereabouts of possible victims and police.

Weber is not the only person who has had such an extreme experience – which is also the topic of our interview with him at the end of this chapter. BILD has also been experimenting intensively. Their reporter Paul Ronzheimer accompanied Syrian refugees on their way to Germany and broadcasted the crossing of the Mediterranean Sea live on Periscope (fig. 07-03).

Figure 07-03 BILD reporter Paul Ronzheimer.

"We are here at the Mediterranean Sea. People panic because there seems to be a problem with the motor. It is definitely (...) Where are we now? Where are we? (...)"

A group of people, among them a journalist, is in a life-threatening situation – live on Periscope. An ethical boundary is crossed – without any doubt – and it is also crossing the lines of conventional journalistic regulations. According to the reporter 90.000 people ended up watching the stream. It is the reporter who crosses a line, who turns into an eyewitness, who lacks distance, who even becomes part of the action himself – that's what people love and want to see.

Live streaming apps lack the filter and also the post-processing which might make them particularly attractive and authentic for some users. But their content often crosses boundaries – which can cause problems as the examples above have shown. A reporter who starts a live stream should be aware that he is perceived as a journalist and that his statements are classified as credible. He is an eyewitness, too, but he is more than that. Therefore, it is always worthwhile to reflect on your personal role in live streaming: where are the (moral, legal, technical) limits? Which topics can a reporter master in a live stream? Which topics might be overwhelming? Which situations are dangerous? Which are reasonable?

7.2 The legal aspects of live streaming

Live streaming laws don't differ from laws that apply to other journalistic forms. Freedom of expression also applies to Periscope reporters; a journalist has the right to stream a police operation or a press conference – within the same framework in which conventional camera teams or newspaper reporters report. If you decide to send your personal experience live into the world by simply tapping an icon on your smartphone, you should consider the limitations of journalistic work first. They apply to all reports alike – but they may be more easily forgotten in the heat of the "live moment".

Live Streaming – What is allowed and what isn't

Personal right: personal image rights

➡ Ask people for permission!

Exceptions: people of public interest, gatherings, "add-ons"

Property right: stadium, concert venue, office building

➡ Ask organizer / owner.

Copyright: theatre, cinema, music performance

➡ Ask copyright owner for permission.

Broadcasting law: regular journalistic content?

➡ Broadcasting licence required.

Personal rights also apply to Facebook and Periscope. Above all it's the personal image right that counts: if you are broadcasting live images of people, you will always need their permission. If kids are involved, you will need the parents' permission. Exceptions are people of public interest, such as politicians, as well as people who are participating in public gatherings or who are simple "add-ons" by coincidence. If you are taking images secretly without the filmed person noticing what you are doing, you will still be violating their personal rights. This especially applies to streams that are broadcasted from an apartment or from another private space. A case that is particularly problematic is the filming of naked or defenceless (e.g. drunk people or people injured in an accident) people without permission. Periscope, for example, excludes "overtly pornographic or sexual" as well as "brutal" content. If there is an accident or a catastrophic event, first responders such as fire fighters or the crew of an ambulance should either be non-recognisable when being filmed or should be asked for their permission.

Property rights also limit live streaming: museums, sports clubs or organisers of concerts may regularise filming and photography. They want to avoid that expensive sports rights are losing value so they don't allow live streams of Bundesliga matches broadcasted by the audience. Such limitations are often defined in the General Terms and Conditions that a football fan agrees to when purchasing the ticket. With regard to copyright law organisers of sports events don't have any legal means against live streaming – in contrast to movie theatres or theatre stages: if the film was of artistic value, a live stream would be a violation of the copyright law. The copyright owner would have to agree to a Facebook live stream from the opening night of a theatre play at the local theatre.

And this is not meant as a joke: live streaming can also be seen as licensed "broadcasting". So you should make yourself aware of the situation in your country. The German situation for example is this: According to the Rundfunkstaatsvertrag / Interstate Broadcasting Agreement (§ 2 as well as § 20 articles 1 and 3) a broadcasting license is obligatory not only for conventional stations such as ARD, ZDF or RTL. Under certain conditions this rule also applies to internet providers ("telemedia"). Providers of content will need a broadcasting license if they reach more than 500 people at the same time. This applies to streaming apps. In addition the content would have to be journalistic and editorial (§ 2 section 3 no. 4 RstV) which may apply to a live coverage, but not to a cat video. A broadcasting license will also be required if the streaming takes place according to a regular broadcasting schedule, for example every Wednesday after a parliamentary session. Anyone who streams an event every now and then and does not provide a broadcast that runs on a schedule, does not need a license. Another criterion for a licence is whether a provider broadcasts in a linear way – this does not apply to live streaming, but to clips that are saved on YouTube or Vimeo since these videos are always available (different: live streams to YouTube, see chapter 7.4). Germany´s tabloid newspaper BILD has just been sued by government agencies for its live streams: According to court papers, BILD is violating German broadcasting laws with its regular live streams on social media platforms.

The significance of live streaming from the perspective of media law is a frequently discussed topic. I'm pretty sure that from a legal point of view several of the streaming stars that are offering radio have never heard of a broadcasting license, let alone have applied for it. The relevant Interstate Broadcasting Agreement is not old but it almost seems to be antiquated when it comes to the topic of live streaming. Another topic that's going to be interesting: the political debate of modifications of the Interstate Broadcasting Agreement which currently regulates ARD, RTL and other linear stations, but gives more or less free rein to Netflix, Facebook or individual stream producers.

7.3 Content-related live streaming tips and tricks

Live streaming is more than simple "live broadcasting". As a part of social media many live streaming apps are designed for dialogue – communication, a conversation with the audience who participates via text messages, asks questions and makes suggestions. This mainly applies to Facebook Live or Periscope. Anyone who streams on a regular basis can build a large followership, i.e. an audience who regularly watches streams.

Comments are not always nice and friendly: a live streamer also has to put up with criticism. In my opinion it is important to show a reaction to critical comments and questions. I've made the best experiences by simply being authentic. If I do not know the answer to a question, I will say so. If I don't agree, I will say so, too. Users are often surprised – nowadays many people are not used to criticism being handled openly. Foul-mouthed comments by trolls are an exception: I will only respond to them if they require a correction or ask for a classification because they are racist or offensive. Such comments can be deleted later on; the author can be blocked. It might be wise to have a social media editor on standby to monitor the broadcasting quality during the live stream and edit comments where necessary.

Timing is important: if you want to stream a press conference, you shouldn't be online too early since this would eat up battery power and data volume. And you would also loose many viewers during the time in which nothing happens. In the timelines of Facebook, Periscope or Twitter your video would not stay at the top of the newsfeed. Once the actual event starts at the podium, only half the people would be still watching – while your stream has already moved to the invisible bottom of the feed. If the stream is too short, though, people will have a hard time finding it: it is worthwhile to keep an eye on the number of viewers and to be online for four or five minutes at least. It might also be helpful to announce a stream in a Tweet or a Facebook post. Here is an example:

"Online in 20 minutes from the @hsv press conference on @periscopetv, channel: @bjoernsta."

What's your story morning glory? Many streams on Periscope and Facebook are irrelevant from a journalistic point of view: the majority of streams feature young men who are chatting away – some of them are really successful because they see live streaming as a channel of communication and not only as a broadcasting means. Anyone who wants to live stream journalistic content should know the story: what is the content of the stream? The title should derive from the content and should be similar to a good headline: concise, precise, and comprehensible. It should also work on social media such as Twitter. There are many apps that post a Tweet to turn the viewers' attention to the stream. It's also important to follow the rules of Twitter when naming the stream and, more importantly, to use hashtags and Twitter handles (@).

A promise made is a promise kept: during the stream the story still needs to be coherent. The event may be unfolding in front of the smartphone lens. Then it is important to distinguish between what is important and what isn't. It might be helpful to switch the location in order to get a better view of the event – or to avoid any scenes that should not appear in a stream (e.g. injured or maybe even dead people that could be identifiable). If the event doesn't speak for itself or if it's necessary to bridge gaps, it will be helpful if the reporter is well prepared, can contribute background information and a classification as well as an analysis of the event. An interview that has been scheduled prior to the live stream can be helpful and provide important information.

You are not a chatterbox, but a reporter: a good reporter on location is doing what he is supposed to do according to his job title: he "brings back", he reports on what he is experiencing on location. A reporter is a good reporter when he doesn't simply recount what the audience sees, but when he describes additional impressions: what does he or she hear? What does he smell, feel, maybe even taste? Many reporters who worry that they might not be able to speak without notes for a long period of time, need to remember to describe their sensory impressions. This is not limited to the visual sense. If the stream is longer, it will be helpful to summarise and provide context repeatedly: where is the reporter? What has happened so far? Because many viewers might discover the stream with a delay and don't really know which event they are suddenly following live on their smartphone.

Some broadcasters seem to forget what they are supposed to do when they are going live for an online platform. When going live on TV or radio they are used to telling the story, but when they go live on Facebook, they just press 'go live' and leave everything else to the viewers. They just show what's happening without providing any context. This will hurt your company! People expect to see quality reporting in your live streams as much as they would expect it on other broadcasting channels.

The lingua franca of Periscope is English: but this should not prevent anyone from streaming in French, German, Spanish, Dutch or any other language. However, authors need to be aware that the audience is potentially larger when streaming in English. When you need to make a language decision, it is the relevance of the event that offers the necessary clues. If, for example, a political event takes place on a regional (or even federal) level in Germany, a German stream will reach more viewers. If the event is of above-regional significance (such as a G20 summit or a plane crash), a stream in English that can be used internationally will be likely to attract more viewers. If you have a big followership in the German-speaking countries – especially on Facebook – you might still be able to stream in German.

7 tips for a good live stream

1. Timing: start your stream with the event; if necessary, make previous announcements
2. Title: comprehensible, concise, precise – and designed for Twitter and other social media use
3. Be prepared: gather important information for the analysis; if necessary schedule an interview
4. Choose the language on the basis of the relevance of the event and the target group
5. Report: describe sensual impressions, take all senses into consideration
6. Information: summarise the events repeatedly; viewers might tune in later
7. Image content: if nothing happens, switch the location

7.4 It's not just the content that matters

If you are streaming live, you need to pay attention to your data volume. Apps such as Periscope or Facebook Live transmit moving images with a good resolution: Periscope, for example, streams with a resolution of 640 x 360 pixels which needs 400 to 500 kilobytes per second – live streaming burns up data volume. So it might be worthwhile to check your mobile plan and add to your data volume.

Network coverage is also important: 3G produces a stream that is more or less shake- and failure-free; 4G would be even better. If you realize that your network coverage is limited, you will be better off to put your energy into good video recordings that can be uploaded later on. It might be helpful to use Wi-Fi or a mobile hotspot that uses a different mobile network. It might also be a good idea to walk a couple of steps: if you are inside a building, move towards the window, for example. So-called "speed checker" apps check the quality of the connection before you start the stream. But the status bar of your phone also provides information about the signal strength.

If you are using Facebook Live, Periscope and other apps you should enable your GPS location. Only then will it be possible for apps to display your stream on the map of available streams. And only then can it be discovered by people who are interested in your content. Otherwise personal streams would not be displayed as in the example of the anti-terror operation in St. Dénis (see 7.1.)

Vertical or horizontal? Image alignment is a question that also plays a role in live streaming – we've already discussed this topic in chapter 5 (TV on the move). When Meerkat and Periscope launched, they were designed to only stream vertically. This decision was based on the knowledge that people usually follow streams on mobile phones and that many users wouldn't rotate their phones. Meanwhile though, most apps (among them are Periscope, Birdplane, Bambuser or LiveInFive) also offer horizontal streams. The advantage: it is easier to re-play them in a traditional horizontal format (such as on linear TV). Apart from that more surroundings are visible which can be especially important for live streams of developing events. On the other hand vertical streams also have a lot of positive aspects: if you are planning a personality show, for example, the vertical format might be more useful (that's why it is also called "portrait" format). Facebook Live's solution is a compromise; it streams in a square format (at least when streamed from the original Facebook App; this will be different if you are using director apps, see chapter 7.12).

A steady hand is worth the trouble: the image leaves a better, more professional impression. It might make sense to work with a partner: while one reporter is holding the phone, the other one speaks. Here, the hand-held tripod is a good option. A fixed tripod creates a very static live coverage. Live streaming relies on the reporter's movements. The movements take the viewers along – if possible – and guide them through the experience or event. If you produce a stream all by yourself, you might want to use a tripod (if necessary this can be a small magnetic tripod placed on the top of the car or on a street sign) so that you can act in front of the camera. It is important that the events in the background are still recognizable.

Streaming in the middle of the night is difficult. A small headlamp can illuminate the reporter at least. If you don't have one available, you can look for streetlights, shop windows or emergency vehicles that emit a little bit of light. But in this situation it will be almost impossible to see any events that are happening in the background. That's why a good story is important. If you can provide a good story and use words to explain the events hidden in the darkness, you will still be able to produce an interesting stream.

The sound quality also plays an important role in live streaming. If you are streaming from a quiet room, you will be able to achieve acceptable results with the built-in microphone. But anyone who is reporting "on location" or interviews a guest will quickly reach his limits. If the stream is designed for the sound of the reporter, you should use an external lavaliere microphone (see chapter 3.2.). If it were the original audio on location that is more important, a directional microphone would achieve better results. It might be difficult to monitor the audio quality because live streaming apps don't offer the option to listen to your audio whilst streaming live. To check whether your microphone is working properly use one of the audio apps we discussed in one of the previous chapters. If the sound is ok there, it will probably be ok in the streaming app as well. If it is not, your viewers will probably point that out to you. This may be dull, but to the point: it's not what you say, but how you say it – even in live streams.

A useful tip:

If the live stream is interrupted due to a bad connection, it's impossible to resume it – the stream has to be re-started. This means that the viewers have to rediscover this new stream – losing viewers is inevitable. That's why you should always check network coverage before you start a stream, especially if you are moving and switch from one network to another during the broadcast (e.g. from a Wi-Fi network to an LTE network). In addition I also save the stream title and description by selecting and copying title and description. If there is an interruption, I can quickly paste the information and start a new broadcast without a long delay.

Live streaming: tips and tricks

1. Charge your phone and pack an external battery
2. Turn on your GPS
3. Check the quality of the network, use Wi-Fi or look for a different location if necessary
4. Check light, look for headlamps or other light sources if necessary
5. Use an external microphone, otherwise: travel light!
6. Frequent high latency: allow for delays!
7. Copy the title and description of your stream and save it temporarily

7.5 Live streaming apps: Periscope

Periscope (iOs and Android) is currently one of the most popular live streaming apps. The instrument of observation used by submarines is part of the Twitter corporation and is closely linked to the services provided by Twitter. For a short time it was possible to use Periscope without a Twitter account, but it is now directly linked to the platform so that you can now direct followers to your personal stream. In addition a Periscope screenshot is always added to the Tweet. This gets attention and looks nice. Many users started using Periscope once it was directly linked to Twitter. German media such as BILD or stern.de experimented with Periscope. But this shall not hide the fact that the number of Periscope users is still extremely small – streaming in the app is not a big event: it's still an exception if the audience number reaches a four-digit number.

Periscope starts with a list of active and completed streams (fig. 07-04). You can change the display in the top menu: next to the start page (1) you can order active and saved streams on a map based on the location (2) or you can display them in a list format (3). Popular Periscopers can be accessed with a tap on the people icon (4). This menu item at the top right corner also includes your personal profile with your followers and subscribed channels. If you want to start a stream, you will have to tap on the red camera icon at the bottom right (arrow). Before you start recording, you can name the stream in the following window (fig. 07-05). You can also define various features: enable the location (1) and determine that only those users that you are following are allowed to send messages during the Periscope stream (2). The Twitter icon (3) is important: if activated, a Tweet that includes the stream title appears in your Twitter stream. That's why it is important to use hashtags and the Twitter handle correctly in the title (see above). At the top of the screen you can decide whether the stream is publicly available or only visible to a selected number of users (5). The red button starts the live stream if the quality of connection is sufficient.

During the live stream (fig. 07-06) the names of the people watching the stream are displayed at the bottom left (1). So are their messages and questions. Again: Periscope is a communication platform (as are many other streaming apps) – if you want to stream successfully, you should respond to comments whenever possible. These comments are saved and can later be viewed in the recording. At the bottom right you can see the current number of viewers. If this shows a significant increase during the stream or the composition of viewer changes considerably, it might be worthwhile to summarize the previous events or to give a short classification of what has happened: from where do you stream? What is the reason for the stream? You can stop the stream with a tap on the red button (3) and you can switch between front and rear camera with a tap on the camera icon (4). This can be useful during a stream: viewers like to see both the event as well as the commenting journalist during a Periscope or other live stream. This conveys authenticity which becomes more important in social media. You can access the options menu with a tap on the arrow icon (5).

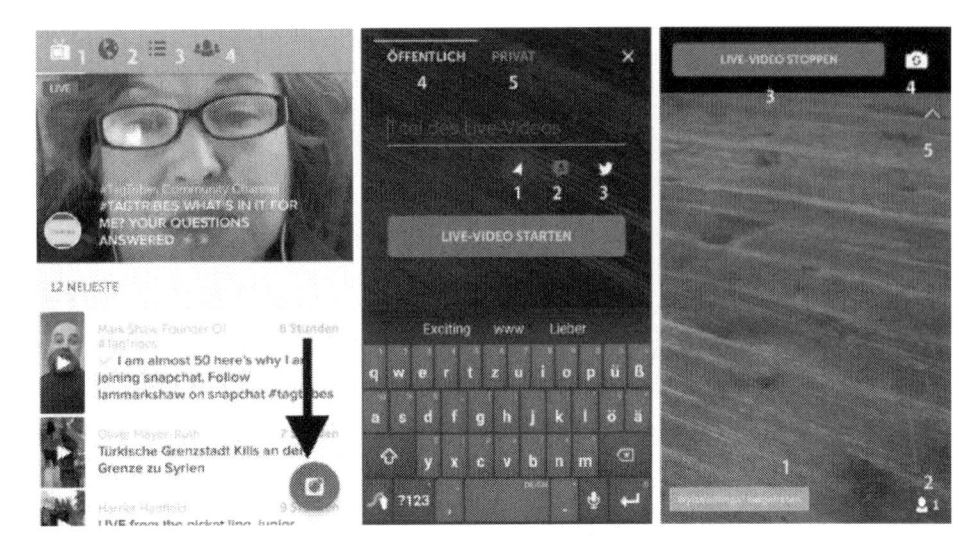

Figure 07-04, 05, 06

Figure 07-07

After a stream is completed, Periscope displays the average viewing length as well as the overall length of the stream (fig. 07-07). The author can also decide whether he wants to save the stream or delete it right away (with a tap on the three dots (circled) that opens the respective menu). With the launch of Facebook Live Periscope abandoned its strategy to make videos available for 24 hours only – in theory videos are now indefinitely available.

208

An interesting bonus is that you get some stats from your live session. You can see how many people have watched it and even who watched it. If you want to measure what works and what doesn't, this might come in handy.

7.6 Live streaming apps: The rise and fall of Meerkat

Meerkat was the most successful live streaming app for a few days when it was launched in February 2015, right before the digital conference SxSW (South by Southwest). The digital Bohemian world embraced this new, glamorous opportunity to communicate live with the world and to report their personal experiences. There were already a couple of live streaming apps on the market, such as Bambuser, but the breakthrough of Meerkat was based on the following features: a simple, yet well-designed, clearly-arranged interface, a focus on the app without the need for desktop registration and the orientation towards mobile and social use: from the smartphone to the smartphone. Part of Meerkat's success was the use of Twitter data: the app accessed the short messaging service to find out who follows whom – and it transferred the data to its own app. Twitter punished this as a "violation of the terms of use" and blocked Meerkat's access. But only a couple of days later Twitter bought Periscope and added their own live streaming service to the Twitter portfolio. On October 4th, 2016 Meerkat withdrew its live streaming app from the stores. It now focuses on "Houseparty" streaming, a chat among friends, which is not very appealing for journalistic use. The app exemplifies how a hyped app quickly turns into a flop – and it also shows that the market for smartphone apps is short-lived. Meerkat's fate also shows that it doesn't make much sense to depend on only one app. Because if the app disappears, so do your followers and – if the worst comes to the worst – your journalistic existence.

7.7 Live streaming apps: Facebook Live

Figure 07-08 A live stream in the mobile Facebook app

Facebook Live is Periscope's biggest competitor – after the end of Meerkat: Until recently the "live" function (fig. 07-08) was only available on Facebook to selected stars and starlets under the name of "Mentions". At the end of 2015 Facebook first opened it up to all verified profiles (marked with the blue check mark) and later on to all users. Facebook has been pushing live streaming extremely and plays streams to many timelines. Meanwhile a live stream map is also available that allows users to search for streams based on location – similar to Periscope. However, there are some signs that Facebook is now stepping away from the live streaming hype again and looking for the next big thing, Apparently the number of viewers on Facebook Live have been declining rapidly. But even if Facebook doesn't push live videos as strongly as they did in the past, Facebook Live is still a very useful tool.

Facebook expands its services increasingly to a "second internet": they make everything available in your personal timeline – articles published in popular newspapers, "instant articles" as well as live streams. This is Facebook's biggest opportunity – and a risk for any existing live streaming service: with Facebook Live streams are directly distributed to an already existing, maybe even a large group of followers that have already subscribed to the content of a sender. Live streams now join photos, films and texts. The unknown variable

7 TV on the move: Live Streaming

though is Facebook´s algorithm: While they were formerly pushing live video, they know seem to step away from it.

A Facebook stream remains in your personal timeline – a function that also forced Periscope to make streams available continuously and not delete them after 24 hours.

The usage of Facebook Live is similar to the live streaming apps described above. In the main Facebook app an additional live stream icon (circled) is displayed in the "post" menu (fig. 07-09). In this menu you can already define who is going to be able to watch the stream: will the stream be publicly available, i.e. will all users be able to watch it? Will it only be available to friends or only for personal use (1)? The last option might be helpful for a test run: if you are not really sure whether, for example, the sound setting is correct, you should first stream "privately". This is not a random example: neither Facebook Live nor any other live streaming service supports listening to your own sound whilst being live. You can already name and describe your stream in this first window (2).

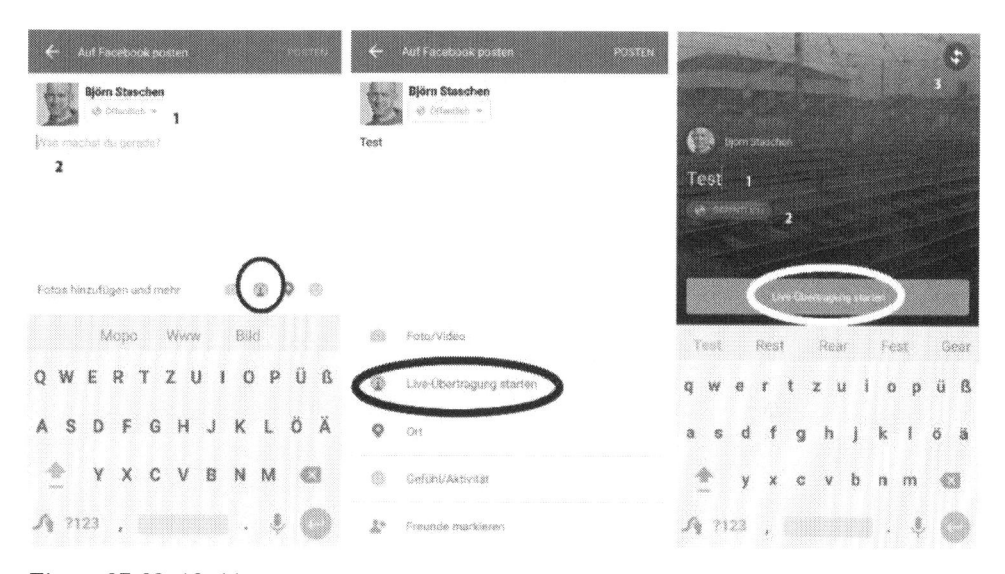

Figure 07-09, 10, 11

If you tap on the live icon, the posting screen will change (fig. 07-10). In the bottom area the selectable options are now larger – as is the live streaming icon. You can still edit addressee, title and description in the posting window. A tap on "Start live broadcast" now opens the live window (fig. 07-11), though the live broadcast hasn't started yet. Here you can also edit title and description (1) as well as addressee (2). You can now choose which

211

camera you want to use (front or back) and you can also switch between these two during the live stream. Choose a filter or mask or select the pencil for writing on your screen while you are going live. also switch between these two during the live stream. The actual live broadcast starts with a tap on the "Start live broadcast" button (circled) which will turn blue if the quality of connection is good enough.

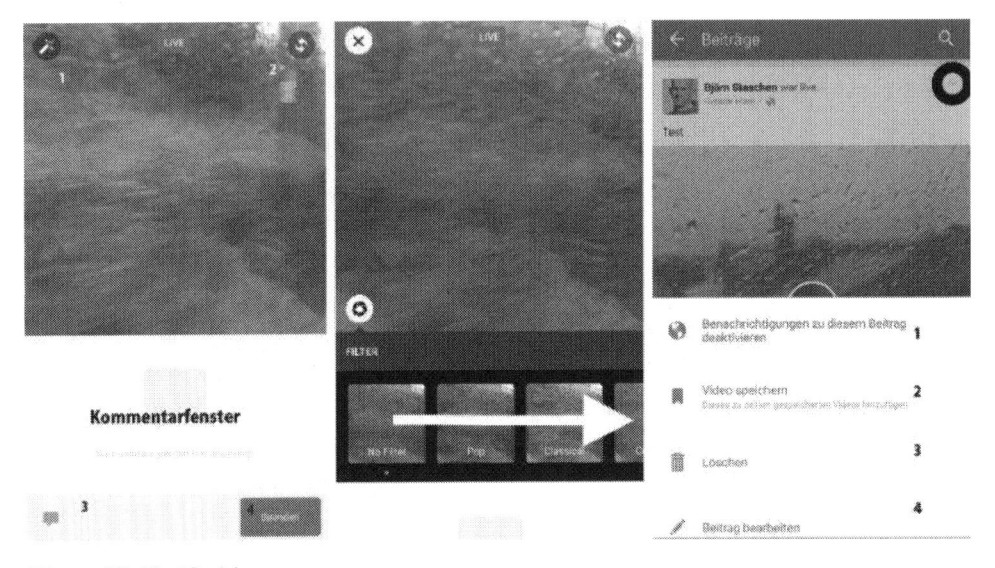

Figure 07-12, 13, 14

Only now does the Facebook live broadcast start: the colour of the menu changes from blue to red (fig. 07-12). Viewer comments and questions are displayed at the bottom of the window (3). With the arrows (2) switch between front and rear camera. With the magic wand (1) you can choose different filters (scroll) which tint the image (fig. 07-13). The red button (4) stops the broadcast.

After the live broadcast is completed the video recording appears in the timeline (fig. 07-14). As any other post it can be edited with a tap on the arrow menu (circled): you can deactivate post-related notifications (1) or you can save the video to your phone (2). The last option is useful if you want to upload your video to other channels, such as YouTube. You can delete the post (3) or edit the text of the post at a later step (4): this might be useful since the Facebook smartphone app does not recognize tags (links to other Facebook users via the @ symbol) which can be added later at the desktop computer. In this way you can call the protagonists' attention to the stream at a later step and invite them to share the recording which in turn will increase its reach.

At the end of a broadcast you again get some stats that might be useful for evaluation. It even gives you some statistics on when people started watching and when they left. You can thus find out what works for your target audience and what doesn't.

Other main social networks like Snapchat and Instagram have taken up livestreaming as well with similar options and features.

7.8 Live streaming apps: Instagram

After Periscope and Facebook ventured into the live streaming world, Instagram didn´t think twice: The platform also added a live streaming feature. While Instagram has not become a popular platform for live streams so far, if compared to Facebook or Periscope, it is still good to know that it offers a livestreaming option. That might be especially relevant if you have the majority of your followers on Instagram.

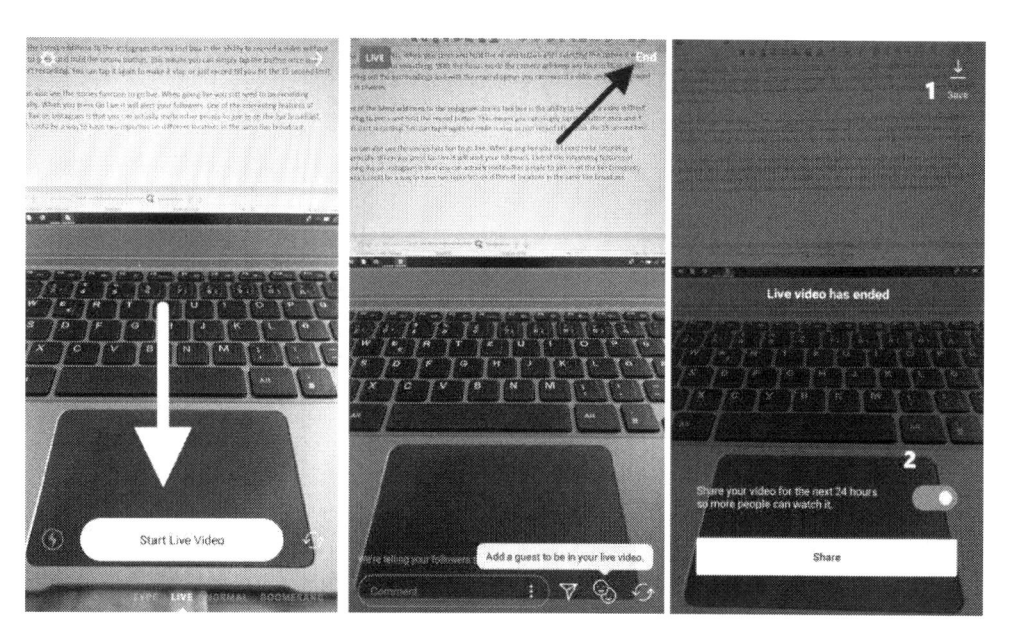

Figure 07-15, 16, 17

213

To go live, start a story by pressing your profile picture on the far left of the Instagram mobile app. You will still be recording vertically. Choose the "LIVE" option (fig. 07-15). To start the live video, simply press the button on the bottom of the screen. Instagram will alert your followers and you will go live instantly: there is no need to name the stream as other platforms require you to do. One of the interesting features of going live on Instagram is that you can actually invite other people to join the live broadcast. Now you could even have two reporters at different locations in the same live broadcast (fig. 07-16). To end the broadcast, press "END" in the top right corner. You can save the video to your camera roll (fig. 07-17, 1) and decide whether you want to share it with your followers as a post as well. Then the video will not self-delete after 24 hours.

7.9 Live streaming apps: YouTube

Live streaming within your personal YouTube channel has its advantages: on the one hand streams are available as recordings after completion. They can be edited, named and deleted. If your personal YouTube channel is already popular and is used frequently because it offers good content, the stream will make a positive contribution to your personal "media brand". It's not hidden on a fixed, but only infrequently used live streaming platform, but it is part of an already popular service provider.

Before you start you first live stream on your YouTube channel, the channel needs to be activated for live broadcastings. This is possible on the condition that your personal YouTube account is verified – a process that can be carried out with the help of a verification code that is sent to your mobile phone. In addition, the channel needs to be in "good condition". This means: anyone who repeatedly violates copyright regulations or any other YouTube usage guidelines won't be able to activate his account for live streams. The activation itself can only be realised on a desktop computer and might take up to 24 hours. A spontaneous first live stream is therefore not possible – live streaming on YouTube requires preparation.

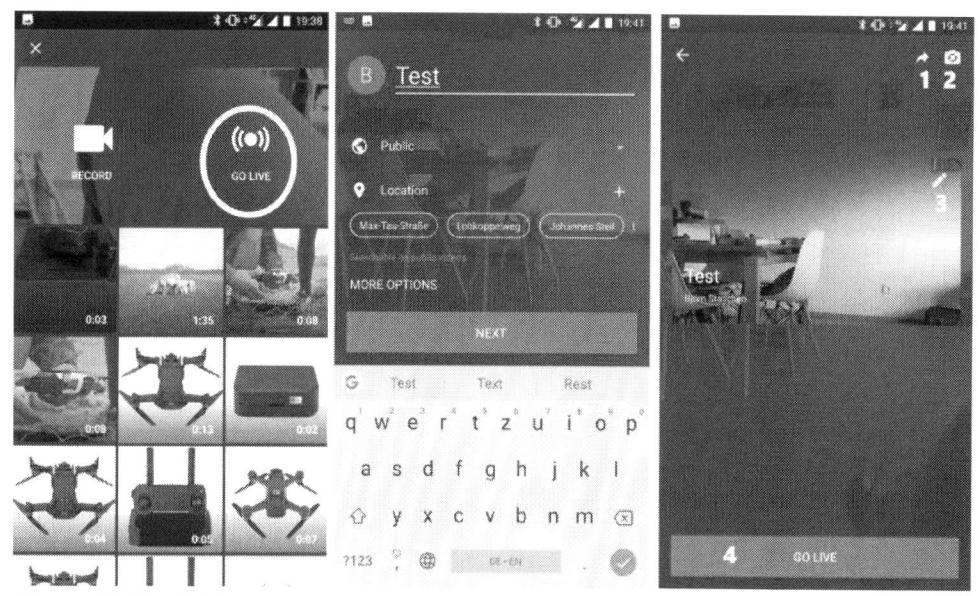

Figure 07-18, 19, 20

Before March 2018 third party apps (like LiveIn5) were necessary to stream live to your YouTube channel. The apps are still available on the playstore but lack features compared to YouTube's own live streaming feature incorporated into its mobile app: Simply press the camera button on the top, then "Go Live" (fig. 07-18). You are required to name the stream (fig. 07-19) and decide whether to stream publicly or only to followers who know the link to follow your stream – a feature that could be interesting for training purposes, for example. You can also add the location of your stream. Once you have pressed "Next" you can share a link to your stream (fig. 07-20, 1), change between front and back camera (2) or go back to naming your stream (3). If you are ready, go live (4)!

Figure 07-21, 22

YouTube asks you to hold your phone horizontally before you start streaming. The streaming window (fig. 07-21) looks similar to other platforms. You can change between front and back camera (1), add comments (2), use different filters even for a live stream (3, see also fig. 07-22) and share a link to social platforms as well as mute the microphone (4, see also fig. 07-23).

Figure 07-23, 24

Once you have ended the broadcast, YouTube will process your video in order to add it to your YouTube channel. You can delete by pressing the three menu buttons marked by the arrow (fig. 07-24). Unfortunately, YouTube doesn´t allow you to save a stream directly to your camera roll in order to use it for other products.

7.10 Additional live streaming apps for professional users

The live streaming market is a fierce battleground: The big players have crushed early platforms like Meerkat (see chapter 7.6). Another very popular app has seized existence as recently as 2018: Bambuser was on the market for a much longer time period than Periscope, Facebook and others: the first apps were developed by a Swedish company as early as 2007 and they were available for a big number of platforms (Android and iOs as well as Symbian or Windows Mobile). Bambuser was free for single users; companies needed to pay a fee that is based on the number of channels and the frequency of usage. Bambuser didn´t claim to be a social network, even though it featured a couple of social functions: for example, viewers could send comments to the person broadcasting the stream. During a Bambuser stream it was also possible to simultaneously use other social networks such as Twitter or similar services.

Bambuser was aimed at experts as well as non-professionals; and this again was both an opportunity and a risk. Amateur streamers as well as broadcasting stations were roaming the platform. Some people had a critical opinion about this: the app didn´t do justice to anyone. It was a hybrid of social streaming platforms and a professional tool for journalists to produce a good quality live stream that could immediately be used for linear TV. After nearly 11 years, the Bambuser company pulled the plug and stopped the Bambuser service. They also closed down the iOs live streaming platform "Birdplane" wihich was aimes at a broader audience. The company is now focussing on a professional platform developed in the last couple of years called "Iris".

Figure 07-25 Live streaming app "Iris"

Iris (iOs and Android) (fig. 07-25) is a Bambuser version that mainly addresses professional users. The Danish broadcasting service, for example, signed a contract with Bambuser to equip a four-digit number of journalists with Iris. The news agency Associated Press (AP) is also using Iris for live streams. Iris offers reliable live streaming in a quality that can be used for linear TV. But the usage of Iris is only possible with an infrastructure consisting of Bambuser servers that are located in the station itself.

More solutions that don't address individual users and can't be installed without a bigger investment will be presented in chapter 7.13.

Figure 07-26 Live streaming app "Livestream"

Livestream for iOs and Android (fig. 07-26) has been on the market since 2007. The Livestream app has been refined over the years. As of today it is simpler to use than in the past, but it's still more complicated than Periscope or Facebook Live. Livestream sends streams to its own platform. That's why it can also offer solutions for individual users. But the focus is on hardware solutions (including soft- and hardware based multiple camera streaming tools). Livestream has contracts with several professional sports leagues as well as concert organizers, mainly based in the USA, and it broadcasts bigger events on a regular basis. Livestream launched the pocketsize camera "Mevo". It records a 4K image in which you can selectively zoom and pan with the help of the app. This is how you can use the camera to produce a live stream (also for other platforms such as Facebook) that resembles a multi camera production.

https://getmevo.com/

Figure 07-27 Live streaming app IBM Cloud Stream (formerly "Ustream")

IBM Cloud Video, formerly known as Ustream (fig. 07-27), was also founded in 2007 which means that it preceded Periscope and Meerkat. The founders wanted to give US military personnel an opportunity to communicate with their families at home. Politicians such as Barack Obama or Hillary Clinton or the singer Tori Adams also used Ustream for live videos. At the beginning of 2016 IBM bought the company with the aim to integrate Ustream into IBM's video cloud service. Whether this step has any consequences for individual users and what these may look like is currently unknown. Right now NASA and US educational institutions use Ustream for training videos – the focus is not on journalistic services.

http://www.ustream.tv/

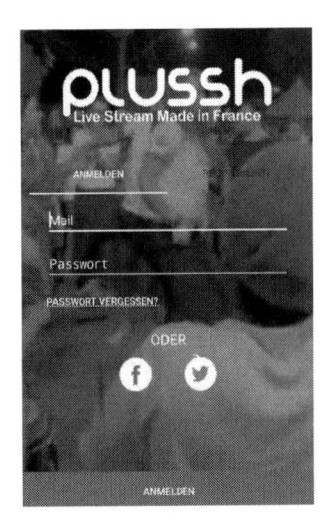

Figure 07-28 Live streaming app "plussh"

A fairly recent addition to the live streaming family is the French app „plussh" (fig. 07-28). It offers several usage alternatives – it's free for individual users, but it also offers bundles for corporations (starting at € 250 per month). Corporations can stream to their own sites and they can also display their corporate logo instead of the plussh symbol. Plussh praises its high image resolution and the streams in a square format. It was developed by three former journalists who worked for French media outlets which might explain the inclusion of the above-mentioned features. Plussh, however, does not offer an adaptive bit rate that adjusts the quality of the stream and the connection. But the app indicates the quality of the stream on a speedometer-like instrument so that users can adjust the settings for image resolution (which reaches up to Full HD 1920 x 1080 as of now) and bit rate. The app has great potential, but market penetration is really low.

7.11 Non-journalistic live streaming apps

The market for live streaming apps is exploding: more and more providers and platforms launch their services because on the one hand mobile networks are getting more powerful. On the other hand the cost of mobile data volume used extensively in live streaming is decreasing. In addition to the above-mentioned services that either address journalistic as well as non-journalistic users (Periscope, Meerkat) or that focuses on more professional target groups (Bambuser, streams to YouTube) there are also services that don't transport any journalistic content whatsoever. However, their user groups are so big that they could be used as "hunting grounds" for potential new target groups.

Figure 07-29 Live streaming app "YouNow"

YouNow (Android, iOs) (fig. 07-29) has been extremely popular with younger target groups – this is where many teenagers feel at home. In 2015, 70 per cent of its users were younger than 24 years; roughly 100 million streams have been made available on YouNow each months. The result: a daily average of 150,000 streams. This number is obviously higher than the number generated by Periscope and Meerkat together – the majority of streams, however, is more or less irrelevant from a journalistic point of view. The hashtag #sleepingsquad leads the audience to sleeping teenagers. The platforms funds itself by asking users to pay a voluntary fee for streams that they like – the money was previously deposited. Child welfare institutions complain that age verification is missing and the protection of minors is permanently violated. So far YouNow hasn't been of interest for mobile journalism. But due to its large user community the app is a phenomenon that demonstrates the potential of live streaming apps.

Eyetok (iOs, Android) (fig. 07-30) has been launched only recently. At the Mobile World in Barcelona in 2015 the app attracted many supporters and friends. Eyetok's special features: users can re-stream any stream that they like. With directional arrows the users can ask the author to pan in a certain direction or to show specific content. So far the app only has had a niche existence. But the Spanish developers now joined forces with the "Shoulderpod" inventors (see chapter 3.5.) which could be an indication of their future

221

goals – maybe Eyetok also plans to offer professional streams with journalistic content, at least to some extent.

Figure 07-30 Live streaming app "Eyetok"

https://www.eyetok.com/

7.12 Live streaming with several image sources

There are several apps available that let you produce a complete show. They can make use of several smartphones that are logged into to same Wi-Fi network as image sources, for example. Apart from that these systems also allow the use of titles ("lower thirds"), e.g. for identifying conversational partners, or videos to play within your live show. Some of these apps are expensive, but all of them can send live streams to various platforms, such as to Facebook or YouTube. The following apps are available on the market: Teradek, Wirecast and SwitcherStudio. They are mainly aimed at streams to Facebook. Yet Periscope recently decided to allow streams from external (so-called "third party") apps – an interesting step with regard to the competition with Facebook.

7 TV on the move: Live Streaming

A question that still remains unanswered: how successful can a Facebook live stream that was produced with a lot of effort involving several cameras and play-in videos actually be? Let's remember that Periscope and Facebook streams are mainly consumed on mobile devices. It makes sense, of course, to follow some professional rules. But using "the language of television" to create a show with an (inaccessible) host, a studio debate and videos without adapting it to the Facebook environment contradicts – at least from my point of view – our knowledge that social media asks for its own language. It's the dialogue that is important in Facebook Live, Periscope and the remaining services – how would a host react to a comment if he still had to fulfil his "traditional role" as a studio host? Apart from that we also learned that the audience appreciates the authentic behind-the-scenes look – they already know what a studio looks like. That's why the apps that are presented here give the opportunity to produce a show on the go that will then be aired on linear TV. They could also trigger new formats – an elaborately produced multiple camera stream that works on social media and that is not a simple 1:1 transfer from traditional television to social media.

One example of how it could work is the Christmas show produced on iPhones for Omrop Fryslan in the Netherlands. We connected three iPhones, used an iPad as a switching board and added a fourth camera. In this 'show' we had a host interviewing people from our regular TV programs to talk about the highlights of the past year. Being very aware of the different type of interaction expected on Facebook we added a gaming element. Viewers could win a Christmas sweater or hat if they interacted with the video. Between the interviews a 'wheel of fortune' decided who got the hat and sweater. It made people feel involved in what was going on. The news show we produced was partly serious, but also had a less serious element that got people involved.

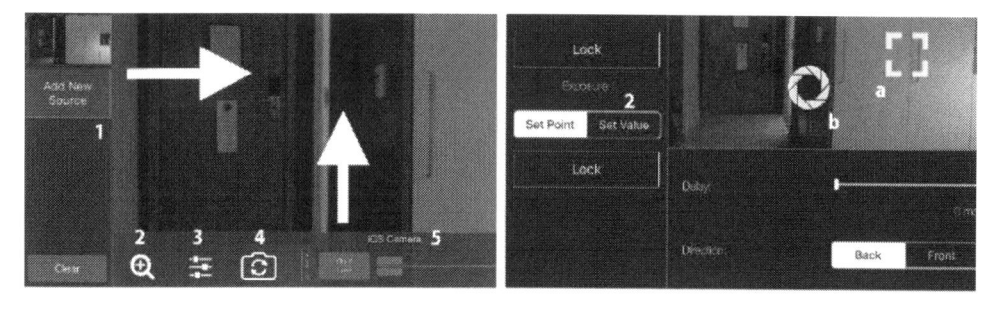

Figure 07-31, 32

"Live Air" by Teradek (iOs only) is available for free but keep in mind that the functionality is limited if you do not want to pay for anything. The app (which we will present here as an example for other apps) has a large functional scope. It streams to YouTube or Periscope, among others. But in its smartphone app Teradek had to turn off Facebook support since the company is not an official Facebook partner. You can still stream to Facebook when you use a different camera and just use the iPhone as a director. The iPad can still be used as a camera for on Facebook. "Swipe" menus can be rolled in from three sides (arrows) into the camera window (fig. 07-31). Here you can select different sources (1) such as other iPhones, previously recorded videos and fade-ins. The bottom menu includes a zoom (which is not recommended because of quality loss), further camera settings (3), the switch between front and rear camera (4) as well as the audio level. The basic app settings can be adjusted with a tap on the wheel icon (6).

Teradek allows extensive manual camera control (fig. 07-32): the focus (1) can either be set with the reticule (a) to a fixed point or it can be set manually. The same applies to exposure (2) and the exposure reticle (b). White balance (3) and tint (4) can also be manually defined. Depending on the situation it might be useful to rely on automatic correction for once, especially if the streams are longer. One of Teradek's strengths is how it deals with audio content: each image source also provides audio content that can be switched on or off or that can be levelled in a separate mixer and separate from the image.

User comments, however, can only be followed with limitations: this is why the stream should be followed on a second device so that the dialogue with the audience can be maintained. A wobbly-free Teradek stream strongly relies on a good router. In addition image sources (iPhones) should have power supply, such as via a USB extension cord. In general more equipment will be needed on location than it is common for #Mojo purposes.

https://teradek.com/collections/live-air-family

7.13 Professional solutions with separate hardware

All of the live streaming apps presented above have a problem: the success of a broadcasting depends on the quality of the mobile or internet connection (if Wi-Fi is used). In chapter 3 I already mentioned a couple of tricks about how to transmit data if the mobile connection is bad. That's where I also mentioned Speedify – an app that combines a mobile connection with a Wi-Fi connection. This so-called "bundling" guarantees a two-way data transportation. The broadcast is more secure and less prone to network fluctuation. In addition the "bundling" of two separate connections that are each not strong enough on their own can help to reach the desired goal – better safe than sorry. There are several companies that have been taking advantage of this "bundling" to improve video live streaming – TV-like quality and broadcasting with less outages. With the help of a hard- or software encoder the video image is converted into a stream of data which is sent to a server via two separate channels. The server then puts the image back together.

The guarantee of successful broadcasting is higher; latency is lower: nowadays the applications are so powerful that they can bundle up to 8 LTE mobile connections and, if necessary, additional Wi-Fi connections. The risk of stream failure is now much lower and latency is much shorter: the applications now achieve a latency of less than 2 seconds so that live conversations between the host in the studio and the reporter on location are possible. But the servers that are needed cost money. So does the hardware as well as the license for using the software encoder. That's why this technology is not profitable for a single mobile journalist but only for large broadcasting corporations who are willing to make investments. Right now a broadcasting unit such as a receiver set starts at a price point of € 8,000 and goes up to € 12,000. Some providers even ask for more than € 20,000.

The number of providers is growing continuously: worldwide there are about half a dozen companies. The biggest ones are LiveU from Israel with a high market share in Europe as well as Dejero from Canada which focuses on customers on the US-American market, but also on customers in Great Britain. Further providers are AviWest (based in Brittany/France), TVU or Comrex (both USA).

Figure 07-33 LiveU – Eight mobile connections on the back. Photo: LiveU

All companies offer so-called live backpacks (fig. 07-33) that combine up to ten mobile data sets. They achieve a data transfer rate of up to 8 megabytes per second. Apart from that there are smaller units that consist of four or two data sets. These can be directly attached to a camera to transfer live images. In addition all companies are now also offering apps (fig. 07-34, fig. 07-35) that can bundle Wi-Fi and mobile connections as described above. This makes live streams in broadcasting quality and with a latency of only two seconds possible. Live conversations are now almost possible. These apps are free for Android and iPhone, but they don't work without the expensive servers as receivers.

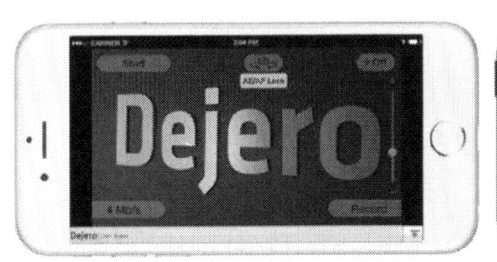

Figure 07-34, 35 The Dejero app. Photo: Dejero (left); The LiveU app. Photo: LiveU (right)

Additional Resources

Links

Maya Kosoff, "How to use YouNow app". Business Insider Germany. Accessed February 20th, 2016.http://www.businessinsider.de/how-to-use-younow-app-2015-11?r=US&IR=T.

Periscope "Gemeinschaftsrichtlinien". Accessed February 8th, 2016.https://www.periscope.tv/content

Frauke Schobelt, "Live auf der Flucht mit Periscope und Twitter". WundV Online. Accessed February 8th, 2016.http://www.wuv.de/medien/live_auf_der_flucht_mit_periscope_und_tw

Jörg Breithut, "Meerkat vs. Periscope: Das können die neuen Livestreaming-Apps". Accessed February 9th, 2016.http://www.spiegel.de/netzwelt/apps/meerkat-versus-periscope-livestreaming-apps-im-vergleich-a-1025738.htmlitter

Stefan Niggemeier, "Ich steh direkt hinter den Polizisten mit gezogener Waffe: Der Terror-Porno des Stern." stefan-niggemeier.de. Accessed February 8th, 2016.http://www.stefan-niggemeier.de/blog/22247/ich-steh-direkt-hinter-den-polizisten-mit-gezogener-waffe-der-terror-porno-des-stern/

Michael Rosenblum, "Reflections on Live Streaming with The BBC". The VJ. Accessed February 6th, 2016.https://www.thevj.com/vjworld/reflections-on-live-streaming-with-the-bbc/

Interview with Philipp Weber: Livestreaming: "Thorough preparation is everything."

Philipp Weber is a freelance editor, reporter and video journalist working for stern.de (the online edition of the German magazine "Stern"), ARD and other media. He studied journalism at the "Hamburg Media School" as well as "Theatre and Media Studies" in Bayreuth. Philipp Weber is one of the few journalists in Germany who started to experiment with live streams early on. His broadcasts from Paris and Brussels after the terror attacks, in 2015 and 2016 were one of the most watched live streams in Germany and Europe.

Twitter:@PhilippWeber

When and in which situation did you start live streaming?

I produced my first live stream when I was in Greece – at the height of the financial crisis. The daily withdrawal limit for Greeks was set to 60 Euro at that time. I live streamed the lines that formed in front of the ATMs and then I proved that for me as a German it was possible to withdraw 100 Euro – in contrast to the Greeks. That's when I used Periscope for the first time.

Why is live streaming so interesting for the online edition of a print magazine?

Live streaming enables us for the first time to compete with the big TV stations not only with regard to written content but also with regard to moving images: apps such as

Periscope or Facebook Live make it possible to report with a video about current events such as the terror attacks in Paris and Brussels quickly. Because we carry the necessary equipment in our pockets that ARD, ZDF, BBC and others have to bring along in their enormous OB vans. I'm exaggerating of course, but to some extent it's still true.

Why do live images even matter for you?

Moving images generally play a big role on websites such as stern.de. Moving image has been one of the biggest trends over the past years and the trend still continues. This becomes visible when looking at the number of users, our personal habits and the fact that we see so many people watching videos in the subway on our way to work. And now for the first time we have the possibility to report live with moving images – a big opportunity for online platforms that want and need to be faster than their printed editions.

You also did a live stream after the attacks in Paris. Your stream about the police raids in the Saint Dénis area was criticised. Would you describe the situation in which you streamed?

The situation – which strange enough generated one of the largest number of Periscope users in Germany – unfolded a couple of days after the Paris attacks when the police were looking for the Hintermänner of the attacks in Saint Dénis, a suburb of Paris. There was a large barricaded area. During the operation I noticed that the police also controlled a street at a distance from the barrier. I ran after them, along with about 100 other journalists, but – and this is really important to mention – I neither interfered with the police nor did I cross any barriers. On the contrary: I simply ran after them and captured the work of the police live with my phone. But you have to look at this stream in the context of 15 additional streams that I produced in Paris: at the night club Bataclan, in front of the church of Notre-Dame during the memorial service, at the Place de la République during the moment of silence. Periscope as a tool can be used to capture authenticity. This reminded me of early live reports on the radio. But now we don't only listen live, we also see live images. In Saint Dénis I was able to capture the uncertainty of the police in a very authentic manner. You can criticize the stream, for sure. But you could also say: this was authentic. What is really important though and I think everyone should know this: You never throw your journalistic principles out the window. I can only speak for myself when I say that I didn't throw them out the window in this situation. I authentically followed a police operation. In my opinion this was appropriate from a journalistic point of view. Apparently, it was also interesting to many people.

How big is the journalistic challenge in such a live situation?

I think that this is definitely a very challenging situation. A good stream finds the right balance between creating an authentic feeling of being close to the action and keeping a healthy journalistic distance. From a technical viewpoint it is possible to be online and in the thick of it in less than 20 seconds, but that's not the point: to keep your journalistic distance and ability to reflect, you need to be mentally prepared – in writing, if at all possible. I always add a small memo pad to my equipment on which I write down any relevant information related to the current situation. Thorough preparation is everything, for live streams as well as for any other journalistic form. If you think all you have to do is pressing the broadcast button and have done with it, you will fail.

Preparation is one aspect. But how do you see a live situation in which you broadcast all by yourself and don't have anyone who supports you or edits your work – as would be the case if you were writing an article?

Here's an important tip: don't do a live stream all by yourself because there's always the risk of missing important aspects. Technically, my colleagues at home in the newsroom – which is in my case the online platform stern.de in Hamburg – should monitor the stream. In my opinion it would be fascinating to add some type of "supervisor" to live streaming apps who can engage in a stream when necessary. I also recommend having a second mobile phone on hand so people can call you if in doubt. Another option could be to be on a phone to stay connected to the newsroom during a live stream.

When you are doing a live stream you don't have anyone who directs you and looks at the quality of the image and the content – correct?

Correct. It's really difficult to take all different levels into consideration at the same time. That's why preparation is so important: you have to know the facts, a combination of agency reports and your own investigation on location – which is a very normal journalistic task. But then you also have to film; maybe you will do a live interview with people. You need to react to comments from the audience that watches your stream and look out for trolls that might make questionable comments. This has already happened to me. And you always need to pay attention to your technology – is the battery still charged, is the network still stable?

What do you think: will live streaming become more important for journalistic online platforms like yours?

I think that it's going to become more important because many aspects in journalism are closely related to the technical possibilities that are available– even if you might refuse to accept this. A print brand that enters the online market can suddenly make use of options that have previously been available only to conventional TV stations. Live streaming is important, too, and it's going to play a role in the future. But on the other hand it is pretty obvious that 3 years from now a site such as stern.de is not going to exclusively stream videos. And I'm not sure whether an app like Periscope is the end of the rope/line. At the beginning there was an app called Meerkat which hardly anyone is talking about anymore. And now Facebook is entering the live streaming market with force.

A few more practical questions: how do you name your stream?

I usually choose a relatively practical/precise title: What is it all about? Then I often add a hashtag which identifies the stream as a journalistic report/work. Because nowadays everyone can do a live stream. I often use the hashtag "Stern" or "Stern-Reporter" so that people know that I'm streaming as a journalist and not as a private individual.

What are your recommendations for live streaming equipment?

As little as possible. These three items are very important for my work: the first item that I always use is a mount. There's a big difference between holding a phone with your hands only or with a mount. The quality is much better, too, because it is less shaky. If you are really crazy, you could also film "normal" videos with a conventional video camera or DSLR and mount your mobile phone on top of the camera to do a live stream. I've done that several times and it works quite well. But in the end all you need is a small mount. I always use the Shoulderpod (see chapter 3.5.), but you can also use a selfie stick. The second item I recommend is an external battery because it's hard to believe how much battery power is needed for live streaming: bigger is better than smaller; with a snap-hook you can attach the Powerbank to your pants or backpack in no time. The third item is related to sound: I play safe and almost always use an external microphone (see chapter 3.3.). I know that the sound quality of mobile phones is not that bad, but as soon as I leave a closed room I don't trust the internal phone microphones anymore

Which microphones do you use for a live stream?

When I know that I'm the one who is going to speak and who is in the focus, I'm relying on a lavaliere microphone, e.g. the Rode-Smartlav+. Long before the actual stream I hide the cable underneath my shirt so that I can attach it any time. Apart from that I also use a directional Rode microphone. It works really well in interview situations. Periscope or Facebook Live don't really focus on a technical quality that is absolutely perfect. And yet: if my audience doesn't understand what I'm saying, I will receive complaints in the comments sections within seconds: "speak up" or "too much noise". People will be more forgiving if the image is bad, but less so if it is the sound that is bad.

What's your experience: is it possible to use Periscope material after a live stream for additional films/reports?

After the stream the use of the material is rather limited. You can insert the material into a report and label it with a fade-in that says "From the live stream". This can add variety to a conventional report – if the live footage is really good or authentic. It's also possible to put together a "Best of" of different streams or to link the unedited streams in a later step. The latter is not really ideal since most streams are relatively long. It is important to label the stream as a Periscope of Facebook Live post. Only then will the viewer understand that he is watching a live stream whose quality might be not as good.

Philipp Weber's equipment: Samsung Galaxy S5, Shoulderpod S1 with R1 Pro mount, Rode Videomic with windscreen and TRRS-TRS adapter, Rode Smartlav+ clip-on microphone and EasyAcc-replacement battery with snap hook.

8 Digital Storytelling on the Move
Summary

Using the advantages of the smartphone: edit photos and moving images, animate texts and combine different media with each other

Smartphones can do more than conventional means of production. So far we have mainly demonstrated how smartphones can be used to shoot videos that have broadcasting standards, i.e. how smartphones can take over the work of a TV camera. We described how a smartphone makes good sound recordings, i.e. how smartphones can take over the work of a sound recording device (Flashplayer etc.). Despite all restrictions it is still obvious that a good part of current journalistic work for radio, television and online can be done with a smartphone.

However, the smartphone shows its real strengths when it comes to further processing: smartphones are powerhouses of digital storytelling. A large number of different apps allow you to edit, combine and merge media content to create new meaningful units. Here the smartphone does much more than a TV camera, radio recorder or photo camera. Philipp Bromwell, a reporter at the Irish station RTÉ (see interview at the end of chapter 5), sees combined forms of digital storytelling as the biggest opportunity of the smartphone, especially for social media. For several years he has been producing "traditional television" with a smartphone but is increasingly shifting his focus to new forms of "digital storytelling". Here the journalistic results of smartphones are not merely "as good as", but also better than conventional means of productions – with all their limitations.

The demands placed on videos for social media differed considerably from those of conventional television. (Some of them might work equally well on linear TV if we didn't always rely on our "conventional" forms). Generally, they are shorter (often only 30 seconds long), they work without sound, they rely on text overlays (because during mobile usage people often don't listen to the sound), and they benefit even more from strong images and emotions. Birgit Klumpp, who has been very successful developing new web videos for Tagesschau and Tagesthemen, put together her most important rules for videos in social media. And since she used Twitter to do this, the list is incredibly concise and precise.

Rules for web videos

1. Start with your strongest image if the story allows it.
2. Use text overlays (but don't forget good audio quality!).
3. Where is your eye? This is where the text should be placed.
4. Less (text) is better.
5. Writing in black is too contrasty – white and smaller is better.
6. Look for the detail and the unusual aspect.
7. Insert a strong and surprising image every 20 seconds.
8. The first 15 seconds of the video should really stand out. If not, people move on.

Figure 08-01 Connor McNamara: Multimedia game report via PicPlayPost

It's the story that counts: with all the possibilities that smartphones offer for digital storytelling, no one should lose sight of the content. The possibilities are endless, but not always necessary or appropriate. The most important question: Which story are you going to tell? If the "How you tell the story" (the apps and possibilities you use) supports this story, you are making the right decision. If the "How" is more confusing or distracting, your decision is wrong. Here are two "best practice" examples: the BBC sports reporter Connor McNamara developed a new version of football reports from the British "Premier League".

In the app "PicPlayPost" (see 8.3.) he combines game statistics, important scenes and player pictures as well as a short, filmed piece to camera that accompanies the game – all of which are simultaneously visible. He produces the short video on his smartphone and shares it on Twitter (fig. 08-01) right after the game – a great way of providing a quick overview of the match. The content perfectly matches the selected form.

The journalist Eva Schulz (fig. 08-02) has been equally successful. She publishes great explanatory stories using her Snapchat name "hurraeva": after the attacks in Paris, for example, she visited the Molenbeek district of Brussels. During the presidential elections in Austria in 2016 she questioned the candidates, explained survey results and analysed the outcome of the election (fig. 08-03). Her step-by-step explanations and analyses are a perfect fit for the medium Snapchat.

Figure 08-02, 03 Eva Schulz on Snapchat (left); videos explaining the election in Austria (right).

There are countless apps that can be used to edit images, text and sound. In the following we're going to give you our favourite examples of the best and simplest options to tell stories digitally. Some of you might miss an app; others won't find our suggestions worth mentioning. Which is only normal since working methods are different. It is worthwhile to keep up with the release of new programs in the app stores and to regularly read in forums and on Twitter about apps that make new forms possible.

8.1 Post-processing of photos

Smartphones are good cameras: with manual camera control it is possible to get great images. IPhone apps such as ProCamera, Camera+, VSCO Camera or "Manual" are a big help and complement the built-in camera app. Similar functions for Android phones are offered by ProShot, CameraFV5, Open Camera or "Manual Camera". The Windows phone is already equipped with a generic camera app that offers advanced manual control.

Smartphones also offer great tools and programs for photo editing. The app market offers a large variety of options. That's why we'll only mention a few, very popular apps or apps that are particularly suitable for journalists.

Snapseed is available on all platforms (Android, iOs, Windows). The app is free and was bought by Google in 2012 – takeover price: unknown. The app is equipped with many helpful functions that make it possible to edit images in just a few steps – often with excellent results. The app takes getting used to but is very hands-on and adapted to smartphone use: with the pencil icon in the bottom right corner you can open the menu that offers a wide range of editing options (fig. 08-04). Moving your finger up and down changes the various editing options; moving left and right decreases or increases the relevant values respectively (fig. 08-05).

With Snapseed you can fine-tune brightness, contrast, saturation and colour values, among others (1). Now you can "pimp" every photo: a little more contrast, saturation and ambience often make a big difference. In addition the app can crop photos freely or to pre-set formats (square, 4:3) (2). It also transforms them (3): the two-dimensional image can be rotated or tilted. Small areas in which brightness, saturation and contrast can be modified may be "selectively adjusted" (4) – to slightly brighten underexposed image segments, for example. Snapseed can place vignettes at the edge of the screen (5), sharpen and accentuate image details (structures, lines) (6). A very helpful function is image rotation (fig. 08-06) – if, for example, the horizon is not straight (7) (which happens to the best of us, right?). Image sections can be adjusted (8) and even repaired (9) with a finger (brush) as the app calculates a correction from surrounding pixels (9). Further down (scroll up) Snapseed offers a large number of filters, some of which are great (10). With the latest updates Snapseed can also be used to write text on images, making the creation of so-called "quote cards" really easy (see fig. 8.10). With recent updates, Snapseed also introduced titles to put on pictures, and more filters for quick alterations.

8 Digital Storytelling on the Move

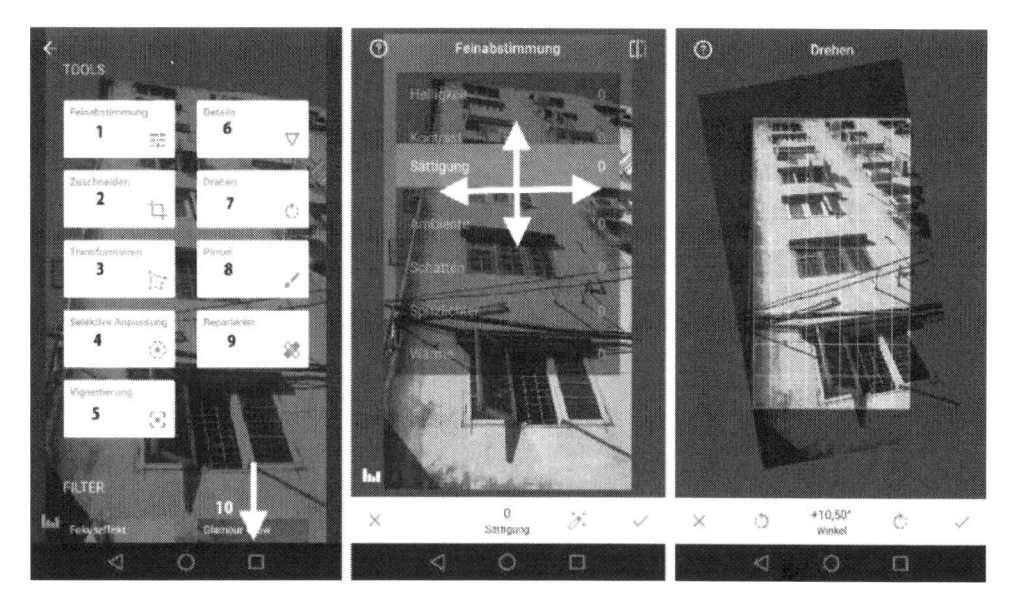

Figure 08-04, 05, 06

In addition to Snapseed there are other professional image editing programs. Adobe makes "Lightroom" available for Android and iPhone – for free. The idea is that "Lightroom" users will start editing an image on the smartphone and finish it with the paid desktop software "Photoshop" – which is "Lightroom's" big brother. The range of functions is large, and the quality is excellent – it is a very good option (fig. 08-07).

Figure 08-07 Adobe Lightroom

237

Figure 08-08, 09 VSCO (left); Instagram (right)

The app VSCO (Android and iPhone) is also popular. It offers a large number of editing options and filters, some of which can be purchased (fig. 08-08). The filters make it possible to realistically imitate the look of different photography styles with "conventional" cameras (such as DSLR). Originally, the "Visual Supply Company" (VSCO) made money by developing filters and pre-sets for programs such as Adobe Lightroom or Aperture. Since the company started to develop its own apps, it has been already referred to as "the next Instagram" because it is also a photo community.

The Instagram app also offers many possibilities to edit an image (fig. 08-09). However, it limits the format to a square – a characteristic feature of Instagram. Instagram is much more than a photo platform: the number of videos is rapidly increasing, as is the number of media outlets that use Instagram as an important distribution channel. Texts that accompany photos are becoming more and more important: some people think that Instagram could be an alternative to Facebook for publishing journalistic content that consists of text and image. Apart from that, many people swear by Photogene (iOs).

8.2 Bringing photos to life

An image is worth a thousand words – this is common knowledge. But after being edited with the smartphone, an image can do so much more: it can tell a story, reveal research results and methods. And it may not only speak to one's eyes, but also to one's ears. For this purpose, there are several apps in which images can be linked to other carriers of information.

So-called "quote cards", for example, are popular on Twitter. Quote cards are photos (often photos of protagonists) that transport quotes at the same time ((fig. 08-10). On the one hand, quote and author are graphically appealing and visible at first glance. On the other hand, quote cards are a good instrument to transport more than the 140 characters that are allowed on Twitter, especially with regard to longer quotes. I created the example presented here with the free app "Photosuite" on an Android phone within a few minutes. Photosuite is a comprehensive image editor that also edits graphic elements. Other apps that can apply text to images with just a few clicks are Phonto (Android), Wordswag (iOs & Android), Textgram (Android), Typic (iOs), Over (iOS & Android) or the Snapseed app presented in chapter 8.1. Xcerpt (Android), for example, is an app that creates "quote cards" from text passages that have been read and copied to the clipboard.

Figure 08-10 An example of a quote card, created with PhotoSuite for Android ("Failure is part of the craft.")

Several photos can be combined with so-called "grid"-programs. A nice example is the Twitter service offered by Nick Sutton (BBC) and Philipp Bromwell (RTÉ) who tweet front pages of daily newspapers from Great Britain and Northern Ireland on a daily basis. For this purpose Philipp Bromwell uses the app "Diptic" (iOs and Android), but other apps such as

Photo Grid, PicGrid and the like work equally well. They are so flexible that they can create different formats with different combinations. With "Diptic" you can also move and colour single frames. PicPlayPost (see 8.3.) can also create these photo collages as well as the free app Layout (from the Instagram company).

http://www.dipticapp.com/

Figure 08-11 Diptic

The "Thinglink" app lets you experience a photo. With small bookmarks you can add different forms of content to an image. These bookmarks link to information (descriptions, links). The viewer can touch the different parts of the image (with the finger on a smartphone, with the mouse on a computer) and access the information. Thinglink is useful if you want to describe the content of an image in more detail. An example is the group picture of refugees taken at the beach of Kos: hidden behind each Thinglink tag is the personal escape story of one of the people portrayed in the image. In addition, there are many Thinglinks on the web that bring structure to so-called "I-spy-images", such as the photo of the "Mobile Journalism" equipment (fig. 08-12). Recently, Thinglink activated its services for 360-degree photos and videos – an exciting option for digital storytellers (see chapter 9).

https://www.thinglink.com/

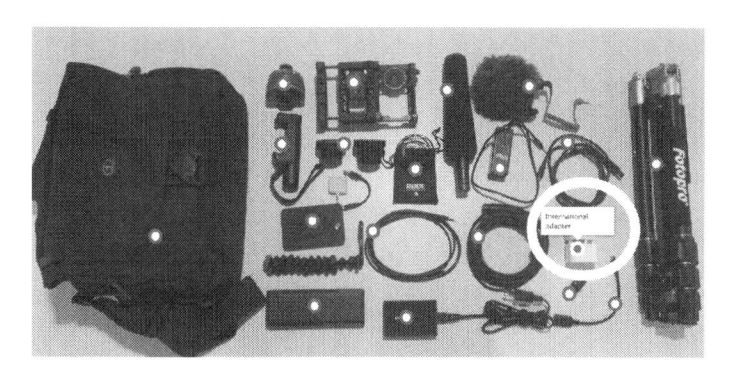

Figure 08-12 Thinglink explains what you can see: one piece of information per tag (circled).

"Thinglink for your ears" is produced by the Jamsnap app (iOs only): photos can be tagged with links to audio recordings. Jamsnap is not only a journalistic service: there are many amateur jamsnappers out there. But the service still serves journalistic purposes. Here are a couple of examples: the photo of the press conference with three speakers whose key messages are linked to audio files that can be accessed via a tag in the photo. The photo of the ship launching ceremony in which the most decisive moment (bottle meets nose of ship) as well as a short piece-to-camera for classification is linked. Or the demonstration with VoxPops by three participants that can be seen in the photo.

Using Jamsnap is intuitive and simple: a new post starts with a photo (fig. 08-13). This can either be taken with the app itself (1) or it can be downloaded from the gallery (2). In addition, Jamsnap also provides a flash (3). The front camera can also be used. You can then place one or more audio files (see arrow) on the finished photo (fig. 08-14). You can record these either with the app or you can insert them from cloud storage such as Dropbox or from audio paste. Jamsnaps can be directly played to Facebook, Twitter or Tumblr (circled) (fig. 08-15). A name is assigned to the snap during the upload (1); the publication on the Jamsnap site can be selected (2). The snap will be published with a tap on the "share" button (3).

Figure 08-13, 14, 15 Jamsnap

An app similar to Jamsnap for iOs is also available for Android and Windows: it is called Foundbite. The main difference between these two apps is that Foundbite links several photos to a single audio while Jamsnap (as demonstrated above) links a single photo to several audios. Foundbite is not just a journalistic service: it is also possible to directly link image and audio segments to Twitter and Facebook. Possible examples: shots taken of a protest march could be combined with a central piece of an ambient sound bite; images from a bakery with a short interview in which the baker explains the most important steps (visible in the photos) in the bread making process – or your own report of a meeting with an inspiring person who can be seen in the photos.

Foundbite also starts with the selection of the photos: they can either be downloaded from the gallery or directly taken with the app. Now a window opens in which an audio track can be recorded that accompanies the photo (fig. 08-16). The track can be "trimmed" (i.e. shortened at the beginning and end) in another step. You can also add more images. During the upload (fig. 08-17) the user can decide whether he wants to add geotags (1) to the Foundbite, he can also name the photo-image combination (2) and link its publication to Facebook (3) or Twitter (4) during the upload (5). In the main menu (1) (fig. 08-18) it is then possible to search published Foundbites for locations (2). You can also directly communicate with members (3) and edit your personal profile including your Foundbites (4). Modify the basis settings and access the help section with a tap on the three little dots (5).

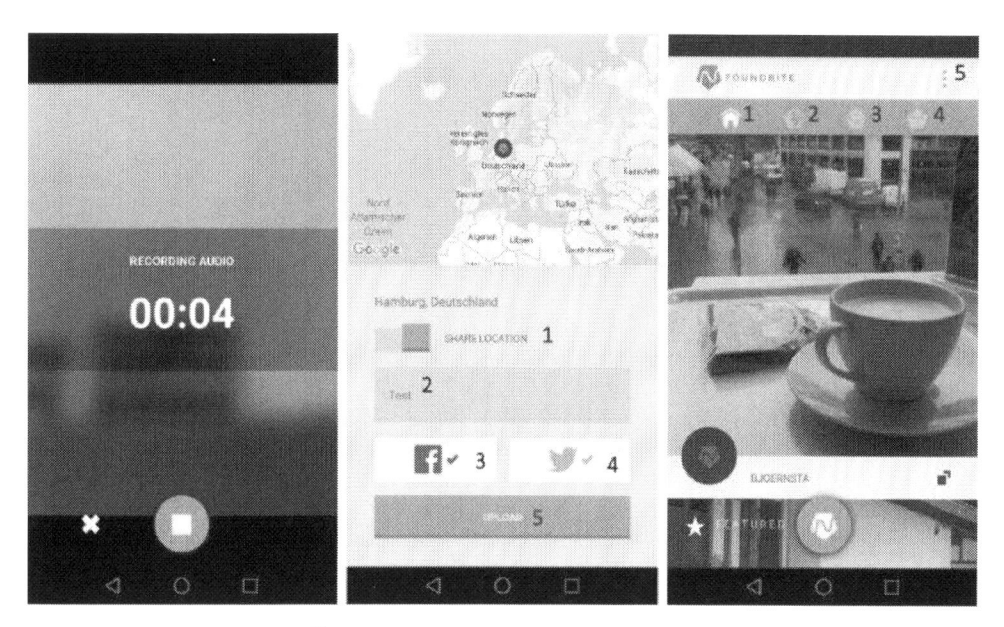

Figure 08-16, 17, 18 Foundbite

8.3 How to combine audio, image and video

The PicPlayPost app is a great tool to use the strengths of your smartphone. We've already mentioned the Premier League reports by Connor McNamara above (fig. 08-01) for which he combines audio, photo and video material with the app. PicPlayPost is available for all platforms (iOs, Windows, Android), which is another bonus feature. The app can produce small, snappy miniatures – such as the short piece-to-camera of the reporter from a house fire, combined with a map that shows the exact location of the fire (screenshot of Google maps or another map program) as well as photos of fire-fighting operations that

PicPlayPost uses to create a slideshow. Another idea: a survey among passers-by combined with graphical elements of a current opinion poll or the sports report. PicPlayPost can produce several formats (16:9, 4:3 or the square format for Instagram etc.).

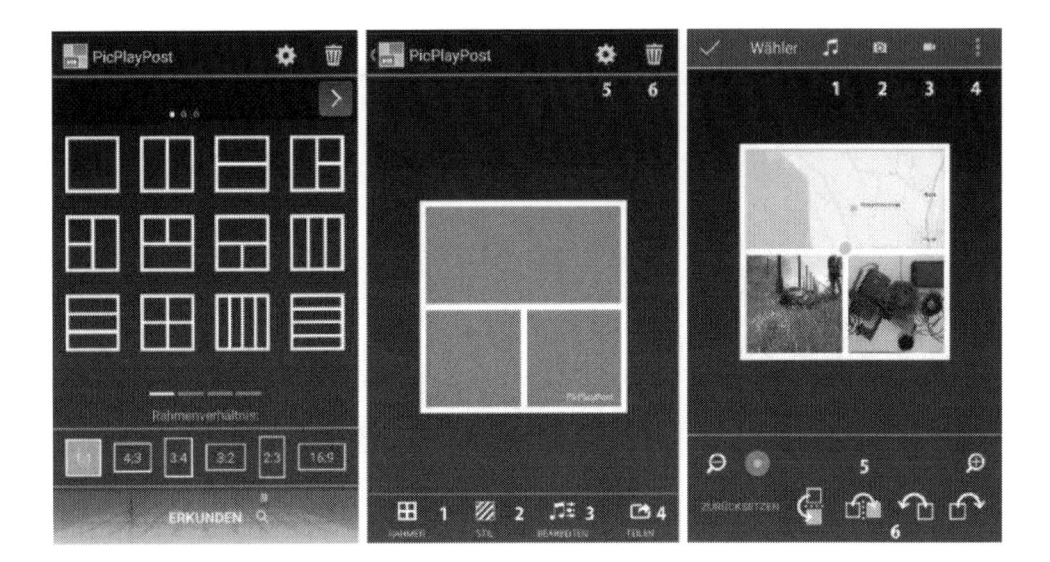

Figure 08-19, 20, 21 PicPlayPost

PicPlayPost starts with the selection of the frame (fig. 08-19). Now you need to decide how many forms of media you want to combine and how you plan to arrange them. At the bottom you can select the frame format – ranging from a square format to 4:3 and 16:9. The selected frame opens after selection (fig. 08-20) and can now be edited. With a tap on the menu option "frame" (1) you get back to the frame selections. It is also possible to edit the style of the frame (3) as well as the audio options. At the bottom you can now share your finished piece (4). Further settings, such as the help menu, can be accessed with a tap on the settings wheel. In addition, you can purchase a paid extension of the app; watermarks (the "PicPlayPost" writing in the finished products) and advertising disappear. Photos, videos and audio files can be inserted into the frames by simply tapping in a box. A new window opens (fig. 08-21) in which you can add audio (1), photos (2) or videos (3). With a tap on the menu items (4) you may also add a slide show, a gif-sequence from Giphy or a YouTube video. You can also delete any medium that you've added. Their size can be

8 Digital Storytelling on the Move

changed via the slider (5). To move a medium to another window, tap on the menu items at the bottom of the page (6).

Further settings customize the multimedia artwork. If you want to change the "style", you need to open the corresponding menu (fig. 08-22). Here you can define the frame (1), the rounding of the corners (2) as well as colours. You can also define audio and video details (fig. 08-23), for example whether videos in different frames should only start one after the other (1). Audio can be faded out (2) and the volume of video (3) and music (3) can be defined. It is possible to directly play the finished product to different platforms (fig. 08-24), such as Instagram, Facebook, YouTube or Tumblr. It is also possible to save the multimedia combo as a video or gif to the gallery of your phone.

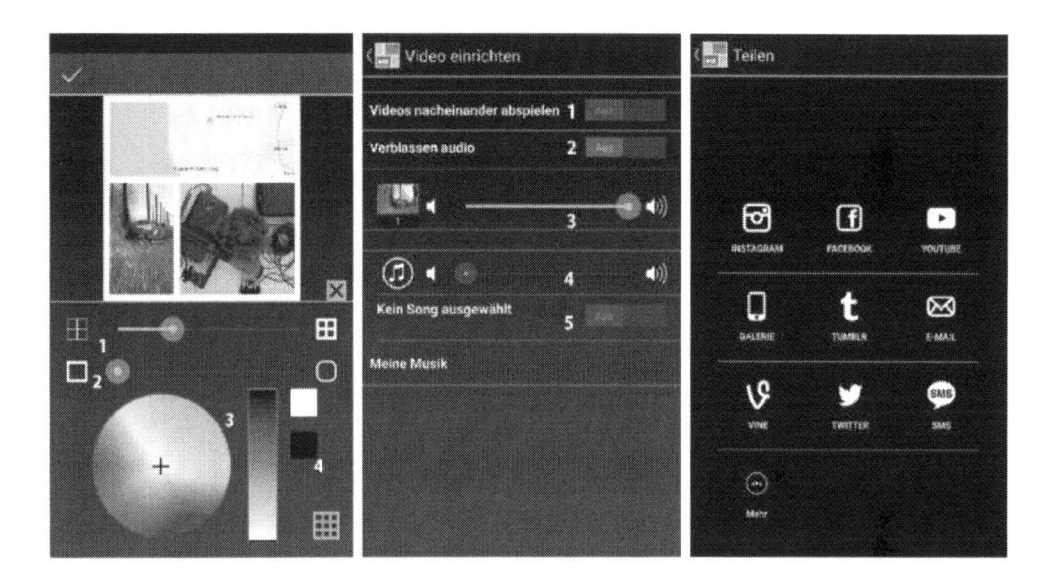

Figure 08-22, 23, 24

The "Legend" app animates text for videos – which is the perfect solution for short video titles, opening and closing credits or text overlays. Legend offers many different types of fonts and animations, colour palettes and play out options. The app uses a coloured background or a photo as a background. Legend is a paid app and is currently available for iOs and Android.

Legend starts with the text (fig. 08-25): it is important to define the line break at the correct position with the enter key. If the line breaks are random, the bold statement that you had in mind might be less meaningful. You can choose the background in the selections below the preview window: a photo can be taken with the app (1) or imported from the gallery (2). You can also search for an image on Flickr (4) or completely discard the project (5). The animation starts with a tap on the "play button" (3) after the text input is final.

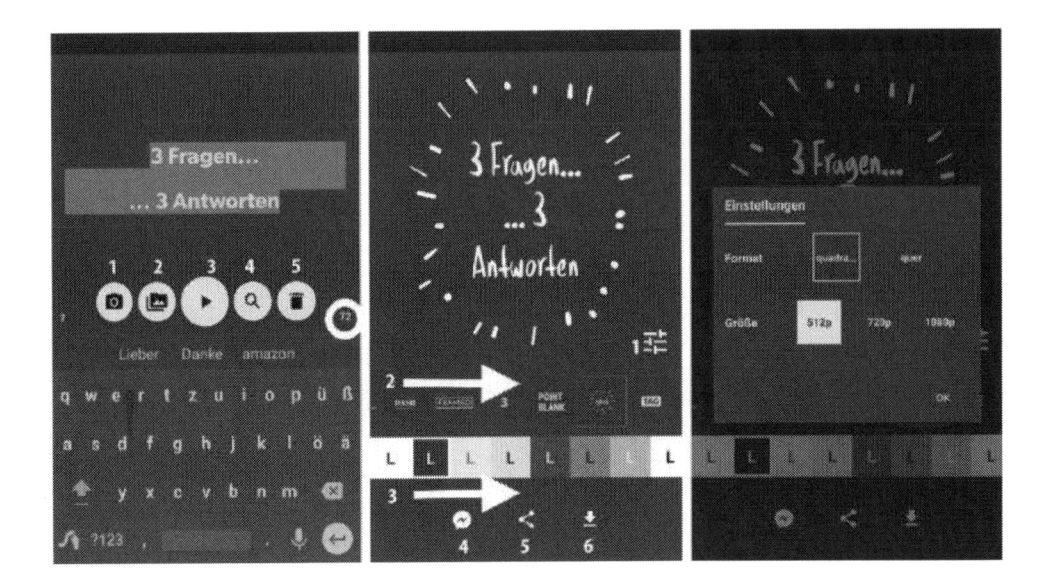

Figure 08-25, 26, 27

Legend produces the selected preview: this makes the job easier since the desired effects become immediately visible (fig. 08-26). Legend is a great app to test and play with the effects. To select different animation patterns tap the top menu bar (2) that offers many scrollable options. Various colour palettes can be selected below (3); these are also scrollable. (3) sends the animation to Facebook as a GIF. It can be shared (4) as a video or GIF animation with several apps – or it can be saved to the gallery of the phone (5). The menu sliders (1) access important app settings (fig. 08-27). Here you can set the resolution: 1080p stands for the classic HD TV resolution in 1920 x 1080 pixels which is the typical landscape format while a square animation is perfect for Instagram.

While Legend only works with a motionless background, the "Gravie" app (iOs only) also positions text on videos. And it is capable of so much more: it is possible to produce a complete short film – from the recording and rough editing to the music in the background. I wouldn't recommend it, though, since the apps presented in chapter 6 offer many more possibilities and options for video editing.

Figure 08-28, 29, 30

A new Gravie project starts with a tap on the "plus" icon. In a first step you can chose a title template. Then the camera window opens (fig. 08-28) in which videos can be recorded. With a simple click you choose between front and rear camera (1) and turn on the flash (2). You can also define the duration/length (3) before you start recording: if you want to always capture 3-second-long sequences, you will need to select "3"; the camera will always stop automatically. The recording starts with a tap on the red button (4). However, Gravie uses the generic camera – with all its problems during video production: it's impossible to set focus and aperture to a fixed value. That's why I recommend using the camera apps presented in chapter 5 for video recording. These can be imported to the app via (5). The selection takes getting used to: you either import the complete video or "record" it in parts by pressing the "record" button. This replaces the positioning of in and out markers known from editing programs. In this way it is also possible to group several video sequences in the window.

Once the video sequence is created, different title overlays can be added (fig. 08-29): you need to use the keypad (1) to add text. Effects are added via (3). A tap on the garbage bin discards the project (4). Gravie display the changes in a timeline to which music can also be imported. With a tap on the settings wheel (5) the fine-tuning of important video settings

247

such as the quality of the export or a fade in/out in black or white is possible. The placement of the title in the video can be defined with a tap on the symbol (2). A new window opens (fig. 08-30) in which in (1) and out marks (2) of the overlays can be adjusted. The title may span the entire video (3) or from crop mark to crop mark (4).

Figure 08-31

Gravie also solves one of the biggest problems of videos for social media: since users watch most videos on their mobile phones, they often don't notice the audio track. The subway is noisy. Not everyone has got headphones on hand. When I go on a shoot, my goal is usually a "conventional" film for linear TV. This was also the case when I met Mike Smithson in 2016 right before the referendum on the British Brexit. He is in charge of one of the most read-blogs about political betting. I used the images from his shoot for a report in the special broadcast on the German TV channel ARD. But first I created a short version with Gravie without audio and shared it on Twitter (fig. 08-31). In this way, material can be used several times without an additional shoot and too much extra effort.

Another app that adds animated text to pictures is Mayu. The downside: Texts are limited to 40 characters, the pictures need to be cropped to square format whereas adding text to video is not an option. The upside: Mayu is free while Legend and Gravie are paid apps.

Another interesting option is Wizibel (iOS-only). This app will have the greatest appeal for radio journalists. In the app you can insert audio from any of the audio editing apps and it will display a wave pattern as you play it out. As a background to the wave pattern you can add pictures (stills). Besides you can change the way the wave pattern looks by changing style and colour. After the edit you can export it as a video. This is an interesting way of making a radio report more appealing for distribution on social media.

The Vont app also adds text to video. The iOs-app is less convenient than Gravie, but offers a big advantage: Vont can import and use personal font types. If you produce videos for larger media corporations, you can easily integrate any "Corporate Design" guidelines when creating the title and text overlays.

http://www.phon.to/vont

Quik (iOs & Android) is another app that combines video, photos and sound. Originally, the paid app was called "Replay" until it was taken over by GoPro. Since then it's been available for free. Like Legend (see above) Quik offers various design themes in which you can combine different types of media. Quick is particularly useful for quickly producing a video on the go that looks complicated but only takes up little time for production.

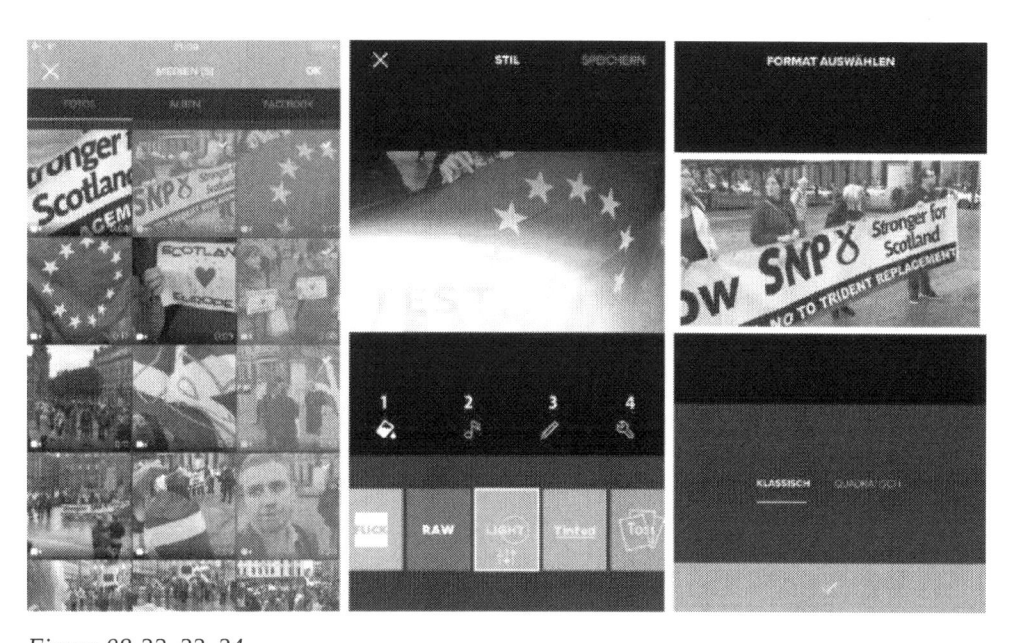

Figure 08-32, 33, 34

Quik starts with an overview in which you can watch selected videos, create your own or manage videos that were produced previously. The "create" menu opens the media selection (fig. 08-32). Here you can choose both photos as well as videos for later animation – Quik asks for a minimum of five elements. The selection determines the order in which the element will later be used in the film. After the selection the user confirms with "OK" and gets to the actual editing menu (fig. 08-33). Here you can select a design (1) or edit or change the music (2). The pen (3) opens a menu for editing details: where is the "important area" of a photo that you want to zoom in on? Do you want a text or an image overlay? The video format (landscape or square) can be set with a click on the tool icon (fig. 08-34). You can directly share your finished Quik-video from the app to Instagram, Facebook or Twitter. It is also possible to save the video to the camera roll for further editing or for an upload from the app.

https://quik.gopro.com

There are several apps that offer a similar service, such as a Storyo: the app combines and animates photos to music and text in predefined designs. With the app you can produce successful video extremely fast. The results might not be aired on linear, traditional TV, but have the potential to be successful on social media. At a seminar with students of the Henri-Nannen-School I was asked whether I see such videos as journalistic products. I usually consider myself a purist, using music and effects only if their use seems to be reasonable. On the other hand, the apps presented here create impressive results produced on location and in a short period of time. This can be beneficial to "mobile reporting". In the end it's always the story that counts and image and sound need to support it.

8.4 Snapchat

Snapshat is positioned somewhere between hype and mystery – at least from the viewpoint of German media. 35 % of German teenagers use Snapchat (according to a study of the teenager magazine Bravo). This puts the app in fourth place, following Whatsapp, YouTube and Instagram, but used more frequently than Facebook! With the exception of Eva Schulz (hurraeva) or Richard Gutjahr (gutjahr) German journalists are not considered as successful Snapchat users. The ZDF show heute+ has started their first Snapchat attempts in May 2016. "funk", a young program of ARD and ZDF, has recently started its own, news-oriented Snapchat channel, called "hochkant".

In contrast to that media corporations in the United States have been using Snapchat intensively. It is striking fact that online media are much more successful with their Snapchat products than traditional media: 54 % of US Snapchat users at the age of 13 to 24 use Buzzfeed frequently (according to a survey among 1117 users for the "Snapchat Report" of the research institute "futurescape", see "Additional Resources" at the end of the chapter), while only 24 % of Snapchat millennials like to use CNN, for example.

Snapchat is an important channel to reach younger media users. In Philipp Steuer's book "Snap Me If You Can", which can be downloaded for free (and which is a good manual for Snapchat offering many tips and tricks), the author writes: "Snapchat is perceived by the public as especially young and cool. While on Facebook you can now even be friends with your own grandma, but from the start Snapchat has been targeting the younger audience with its mobile-first strategy." "Mobile first" means that Snapchat is exclusively designed for smartphone use – in contrast to Facebook, for example. Steuer identified more differences between the two platforms: "In contrast to Facebook or Twitter Snapchat is a much more intimate network in which users feel safer and less observed. (...) In addition Snapchat is a network full of attention. Each photo/video is deliberately clicked on by the users and does not disappear in the crowded timelines – another difference to other networks. This makes Snapchat particularly interesting for companies and brands." However, a survey of the US magazine "Variety" revealed that more than 30% of Snapchat users use the network mainly because their parents are not on Snapchat. And let's be honest: doesn't traditional media resemble "the parents"? What does this mean for the success of media brands on Snapchat?

Snapchat is a channel with its own language and functions. Snapchat relies on communication within groups of friends: Snapchat message ("snaps") can be sent to an individual or to several friends. You can also post snaps to your own "story", which is your present life story, your daily diary. Only your followers can watch your story. Finding new snappers is not very easy: a conventional search function as offered by Twitter is missing. There are no hashtags and no timelines flooded with content as on Facebook. In this respect, it is rather difficult to get new followers: users need to know the exact Snapchat name or "Snapcode" (the square, yellow, individual Snapchat icon of each user) to follow a Snapper.

Snaps are self-destroying: Snapchat messages are only visible for a short time. The length of a snap appearing on the recipient's mobile phone is set by the sender – it ranges between one and ten seconds. Recipients can watch it a second time (however, the number of replays is limited). If the recipient doesn't take a screenshot, the snaps will disappear once and for all. The same applies to the content of your personal "story": it's available for 24 hours only and will be deleted afterwards.

Snapchat loves the vertical format – which is also a peculiarity. The app combines short videos and photos with drawings and texts. For me, Snapchat is a lot of fun because I can draw with the app and can send and receive small works of art. However, Snapchat is extremely short-lived. And journalists will have to develop their own language and a special way of storytelling to use Snapchat successfully. After all, a Snapchat story is made up of single bits and pieces that form a story, but whose order cannot be changed. A snap in a story cannot be modified or exchanged in retrospect. For these reasons it is worthwhile to plan a Snapstory, to consider the order and form in which thoughts will be presented – unless a current event unfolds in front of your own eyes or lens so that there is simply no time for planning.

Snapchat takes time – snapping "in passing" while also shooting good TV videos and editing a film suitable for TV will hardly be possible. Due to the special language and specifications of Snapchat (and its vertical format) the finished material cannot be used more than once. If you snap about a current, evolving event, you will have to concentrate on it, too – at least that's my opinion.

Good examples of Snapstories are created by Eva Schulz (@hurraeva) mentioned above. Her snaps work well and are very successful. She even got a nomination for the Grimme Online Award 2016 for here snaps because Eva Schulz understands and speaks the language of Snapchat. She uses short and concise pieces of information that build upon each other as well as all types of media: videos, from the Moolenbeek district in Brussels, for example, the home of the Paris terrorists. She shows street life and gives impressions. But her stories are also very personalized – Eva is often visible when she reports. That makes her snaps authentic which is also important for being successful on Snapchat. She also offers a creative way of viewer orientation by providing little animations made of pre-cut paper symbols, for example, which she used during the elections in Austria in the spring of 2016.

A good Snapchat story…

… is well planned: short pieces of information build upon each other

… is not longer than two to three minutes

… is highly personalized and authentic

… uses video, photos and graphic elements in a creative and humorous way

… is created on location

… cannot be edited later, but can only be deleted

… self-destroys after 24 hours

… can be saved and posted as a video to YouTube, Facebook or another platform.

Snapchat starts with the recording window (fig. 08-35 – what you see here is the Android app – Snapchat for iOS differs in a few details): forget everything that you've heard about camera and editing apps – Snapchat is completely different. The only similarity is the lightning symbol (1) which switches the flash on or off, even in Snapchat. The Snapchat symbol (2) takes you to the friends / followers menu and to the profile setting (see fig. 08-38). You can switch between front and rear camera with a tap on the camera icon (3) or with a quick double click on the screen. If you tap on the square (4), you will get to an overview of all conversations (a swipe to the right fulfils the same function). Stories of other users as well as the discovery and live offers curated by Snapchat can be accessed with a tap on the three lines (6) or a swipe to the left.

The actual editing of a snap starts with the capture button (5): to take a video, hold the capture button down; to take a photo, simply tap it. If you focus on your face (or another person's face) on the screen, you will activate face recognition. Now you can add masks and distortions, which is presumably less interesting from a journalistic point of view, but a lot of fun. Only recently #Mojo-colleague Yusuf Omar (yusufomarsa) used the masks in a meaningful way in a Snapchat report about victims of abuse in India: with the masks he made the faces of his interview partners unrecognizable and anonymous.

Figure 08-35, 36, 37 Snapchat1

The finished recording can be edited in a next step (fig. 08-36). Emojis and other symbols can be be added with a tap on the stylized sheet (2), a tap on the "T" (3) adds text. All in all, there are three ways of writing text on an image or video (in the grey bar, freestyle, aligned left or centred) – by simply tapping the "T" once, twice or three times. The text can then be moved with drag and drop. With the pencil (4) you can draw on the image. You can choose a colour from the colour palette for both the text and the drawing function. Hold down on the colour palette for a larger selection. The small stopwatch (5) is used to set how long users are allowed to watch the snap (1 to 10 seconds). A tap on the arrow (6) saves a snap to the gallery of your phone. With the "plus" icon (7) the snap will be added to your personal story and will then be visible to all users for 24 hours. If you want to send a snap to only one person or to several people, you need to tap the big arrow (8). Anyone who swipes horizontally can add colour filters, temperature, speed or images to the respective geographic position (fig. 08-37).

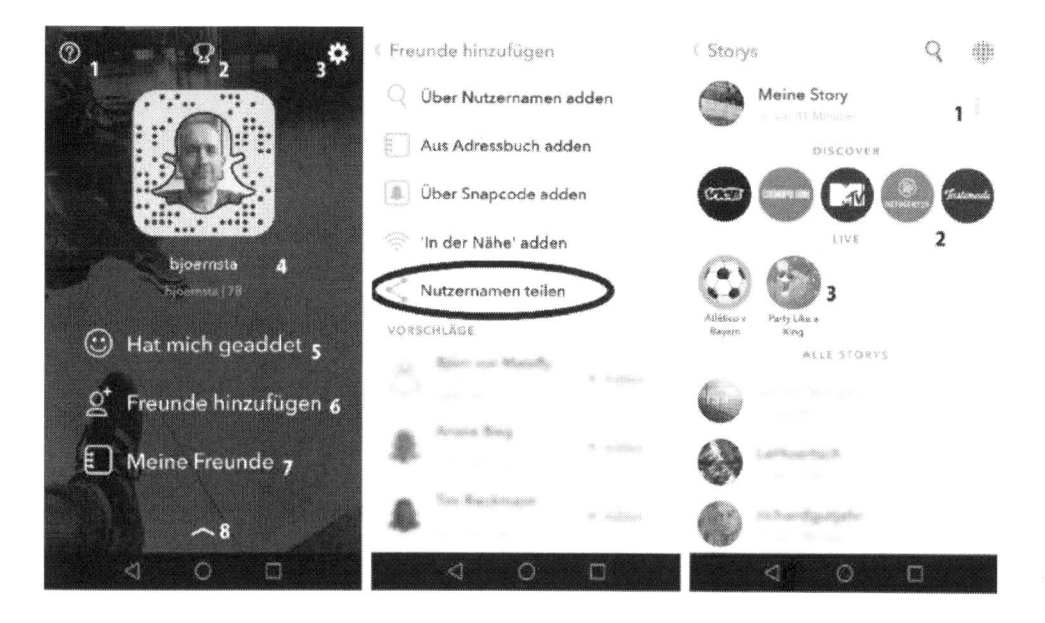

Figure 08-38, 39, 40

Additionally, Snapchat provides an overview of your friends (fig. 08-38) – friends who have added you recently (5) and your list of friends (7). You can add new friends with (6) but only if you know their exact Snapchat name (or the yellow "Snapcode"). The question mark (1) offers help to new users. Snapchat is also a game and promise trophies for certain activities (2). Important settings can be adjusted via the wheel icon (3), such as notification settings or who is allowed to view your story or to contact you on Snapchat. It is important to build your followership: your personal snapcode opens with a simple touch. You can take a new profile image (a series of four shots) or share it with a tap on the "share" icon. Snapchat then generates a link that can be used on Twitter, for example. The same link can be requested by opening the menu "add friends" (6) (fig. 08-39) – by clicking "Share user name" (circled).

Your own story is managed in the discover menu (fig. 08-40). Here you do not only find curated snaps by media providers (2) and from live events (4), but also the stories of people you follow. In addition, your own story opens with a tap on the three dots (1). You can delete it entirely or only in parts or you can download it as a video to share it on YouTube, for example. In this way, Snapstories become "immortal" even though Snapchat deletes them after 24 hours. Recently, Snapchat added the option to save snaps and to incorporate them later in stories as well as to post photos and videos from the gallery. This makes the app a little bit more flexible and the production of linear stories a little easier.

8.5 Instastories

"Instastories" are very similar and still very different compared to S: in the summer of 2016 Instagram launched its product that competes with Snapchat. According to Instagram over 250 million people use it every day. And some of the biggest news companies in the world are amongst the most popular users. Companies like CNN and BBC (fig. 08-41) are using the platform to promote the stories they publish on their website. Occasionally they even have productions that are made especially for Instagram Stories. The Dutch broadcaster Omroep Fryslan publishes a daily weather Instastory (fig. 08-42). But it is not just news. Big companies and organizations also use the platform for promotional purposes, like NASA, for example (fig. 08-43).

In a lot of ways Instagramstories looks like Snapchat. It is a vertical platform that is made for consumption on mobile. Just like in Snapchat, your followers can check out your story for 24 hours before it will disappear again. The stories of the people you follow are displayed on the top of the screen.

Figure 08-41, 42, 43

The advantage of Instastories in comparison to Snapchat: the stories are not the only service that Instagram offers. Anyone who already has a working account with many followers, can offer an attractive storytelling format to their audience. Apart from that, the Instagram community is older (and broader) than the Snapchat community. Its focus is on aesthetic images as well as content-rich services which the success of BBC and CNN videos, for example, demonstrates.

The disadvantage of Instastories in comparison to Snapchat: While Instastories has added more filters and other features, it still remains a slower ship to sail the multimedia storytelling seas, way behind the cooler and hipper Snapchat. And as the audience of Instastories is older – if you really want to reach young audiences, Snapchat might still be the channel you want to try, especially in Anglo-American markets.

To make your own Instastory, press your profile image on the top left (fig. 08-44, circled). Now a new menu will open displaying all the options you have to create content in your Instagram Story (fig. 08-45). The first one (1) is the newest addition to the platform. It allows you to type. After typing your message, you can change the way it looks by pressing the oval button that says "modern" on the top of the screen. After that press ">". Now you can add another layer of text, draw or add a sticker.

257

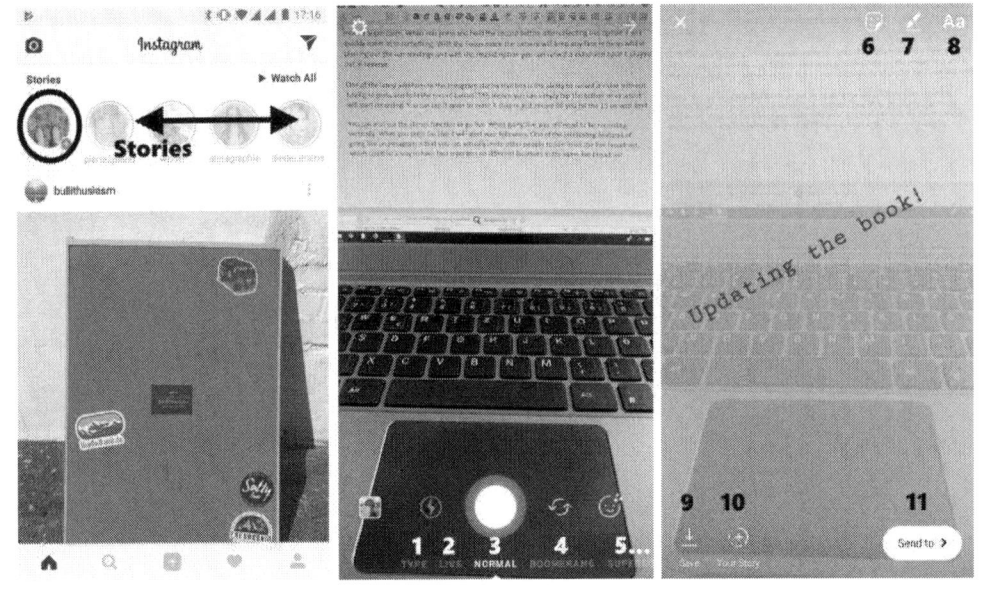

Figure 08-44, 45, 46

In the same way you can go live (2, see chapter 7.8), add pictures and videos (by tapping the thumbnail picture on the bottom left) or shoot material using the built-in camera function (3). To this material (fig. 08-46) you can add stickers (6), drawing (7) or text (8). You can also use filters to obscure someone's features (for anonymous sources), for example. Another possibility is to import recorded videos or photos from your phone to add to your story. Remember that these videos are going to be vertical, even if you shot them horizontally.

You can also record within the app with some other special effects. First there is the so-called Boomerang (4) which makes a tiny little time-lapse video that moves back and forth. Second you can make a Superzoom (5). When you press and hold the record button after selecting this option, it will quickly zoom in to something. With the Focus mode the camera will keep any face in focus while blurring out the surroundings. With the rewind option you can record a video and have it played out in reverse.

One of the latest additions to the Instagramstories tool box is the ability to record a video without having to press and hold the record button. This means you can simply tap the button once and it will start recording. You can tap it again to make it stop or just record till you hit the 15 second limit.

If you´ve finished working on a part of your story, press "your story" (10) on the bottom left to add this slide /video to your story. You can also directly send it to a friend (11) or save it to your camera roll to use in another program (9) – these options are very similar to Snapchat.

8.6 Instagram TV (IGTV)

In the ongoing struggle for audience, Instagram launched a new platform in the beginning of 2018: Instagram TV (or IGTV). It is a vertical video platform for videos up to an hour long. By targeting an audience that wants to watch longer videos it is in direct competition with Youtube. But by going for vertical video it is also offering something different. It is trying to grab the attention of people who do not want to turn their phone horizontally when watching something. The platform comes with its own app (IGTV), but with limited functionality. You can only use it to upload something from your Camera Roll and then change the cover picture. There are no editing tools in the app. If you want to edit a vertical video you will have to use one of the edting apps that are available for your phone (for example LumaFusion, Adobe Rush or Kinemaster, see chapter 6).

8.7 Digital Storytelling Apps

Digital storytellers were hopeful when storytelling apps were released that allow the combination of photos, videos and text elements within a single scrollable article. These apps are useful when you are on the move because you can quickly combine videos, photos and text to create a story without any major editing. The different story parts are told by a medium that fits the content. An example: the story of an impoverished former football professional starts with a photo of an apartment, scarcely furnished. The text briefly tells his story which is followed by a video sound bite. In the video he briefly recounts the moment in which he realized his downfall. A text section follows that lists his most important milestones since his retirement from professional football. There is also a photo of the guy as a professional player and an additional statement in the video in which he remembers better times. Since photos, text and video can be combined, it is possible to use video clips without long editing – a quick way to tell stories that can be adjusted to the respective layout of each platform. Storytelling apps can be consumed with both the smartphone and on desktop computers – this is also an advantage.

But storytelling apps have not really prevailed: it may be possible that the competition from all-encompassing platforms such as Facebook and Instagram are too strong. These platforms, too, allow the combination of photos and videos with text. It might also be possible that not many consumers are looking for these journalistic forms. In addition, the user grants some of his rights to photos and videos to the platform operator – which means that the stories won't support his or her own website but a third-party platform. At a time when Wordpress can be used to quickly build a simple blog and to add content on the go, the concept of storytelling apps might not have much of a chance. This is why Storehouse, the pioneer of storytelling apps and the winner of the Apple design award in 2014, quit its service in 2016.

At the moment Facebook is experimenting with "Canvas" and a new form of storytelling that combines photos, videos, and text in a linear story that can be scrolled. So far Canvas can only be used by corporate, but not by personal accounts. It remains to be seen whether Canvas gives storytelling a new boost or whether it confirms the shadowy existence of this form. With "Moments" Twitter offers the possibility to combine several Tweets at a desktop computer to create small stories (with the possibility of different media).

Nowadays, a whole range of storytelling apps is made available – at the Mobile World Congress 2016 in Barcelona two young developers from Sir Lanka, for example, presented their "Kawoo" project (only available for iOs). Here users can design stories in collaboration – so-called "collaborative storytelling". At the same show two British programmers presented their "Doko" project in which content can be placed on different pages, similar to a magazine. The consumer can now scroll and flip through the pages.

After the cancelation of the "Storehouse" the star of all storytelling apps is now the "Steller" app. Initially, it was only available for iOS, but now also offers a version for Android phones. In contrast to Storehouse, which relied on a traditional, clean scroll design, Steller continued to improve and is now increasingly offering several graphic and font templates. In addition, Steller stories are told over several pages that a user can flip through: an image (with a title), video or text. Steller can also be used with a Twitter or Facebook account. It starts with an overview of your own and other stories. You can start your own story with the selection of the pen icon at the bottom right. At first, the window for the design selection opens (fig. 08- 47). The templates differ with regard to font types and sizes, arrangement, colours and design elements. After the selection of the design you can now create different pages (fig. 08-48) – a title page as seen in our example with a title and subline, or text board, image boards, or pages with videos. The layout icon (1) opens the selection. To add a page, tap the plus icon (2); to change the order of pages, tap the square icon (3). A story can be stored invisible to others for further editing (4) or published so that others can see it (5). Before the publication you can press and hold the title page for a preview of the finished story (fig. 08-49).

Figure 08-47, 48, 49

The selection of Adobe apps on iOS is also interesting. Several of them can help you tell a multimedia story online. In "Adobe Spark Page" you can quickly create a story consisting of pictures, videos and text. You can also add buttons, photo grids and 'glideshows' (slideshows that glide) to make it look like an instant website. In "Adobe Spark Post" you can create posts for all mayor social platforms combining images, text and a large number of different layouts. You need an Adobe account to use these apps, but registration is fairly easy and free. A similar experience is offered by Microsoft's "Sway" (iOS and Android). If you have a Microsoft account, you can use the Sway app to build multimedia stories on the go.

Additional Resources

Links

Steuer, Philipp. Snap Me If You Can. Ein Buch für alle, die Snapchat endlich verstehen wollen. Eigenverlag. Available for free at http://snapmeifyoucan.net/.

Let's snap! BRAVO präsentiert neue Daten zur mobilen Mediennutzung der Jugendlichen. Accessed May 12th, 2016. http://www.bauermedia.com/presse/newsroom/artikel/lets-snap-bravo-praesentiert-neue-daten-zur-mobilen-mediennutzung-der-jugendlichen/controller/2016/4/25/

How Traditional Media Companies Successfully Innovate On Snapchat. Accessed May 12th, 2016. http://www.futurescape.tv/media-innovation/how-traditional-media-companies-are-successfully-innovating-on-snapchat/

Vellinga, Wytse. Mobile Storytelling: Tell Your Story. Anytime, Anywhere. Accessed May, 14th 2016. http://mobile-storytelling.com/?page_id=10

Interview Sumaiya Omar, Hashtag Our Stories: "Reality is the new quality."

Sumaiya Omar is a founder of the HashTagOurStories movement, setup to help people all over the world to tell their own stories through mobile journalism. Together with her husband Yusuf Omar she travels the world to teach how to use the MoJo tools. She is thus rapidly setting up a network of international storytellers that publish stories / content without the help of traditional broadcasters and publishers.

Twitter:@snap_sumaiya

How did you get involved in the whole Mobile Journalism movement?

I was a banker for 6 years in South Africa, involved in product management and online strategy. My husband, Yusuf, was a correspondent for a TV station at the time, already experimenting with mobile journalism. I was often behind the mobile camera, shooting everything from protests in Johannesburg to the pilgrimage in Saudi Arabia. It takes two to Mojo. I also studied how mega influencers and celebrities were telling stories on platforms like Snapchat and I helped newsrooms work out how to use the same technologies to do better journalism.

How did you come up with the Hashtagourstories concept?

Hashtag Our Stories was born from a lack of diversity in the media industry. Diversity of the voices being listened to and of the journalists themselves. From Brexit to Trump, some of the biggest trends were missed, partly because news companies have become disconnected from real people and real voices on the ground. We create shows, by training communities on the fringes of society, those that are not being heard by traditional media, to tell their own stories, in their own voices, using mobile phones.

What is the purpose of Hashtagourstories?

Explore, Empower, Engage. Explore new technologies, formats and ways of storytelling. Empower people to use the device that is within their reach, to tell their stories and create a more diverse media landscape. Engage our audiences with impactful, constructive shows, using the voices of people. Our goal is to create shows in every language, by mobiles and for mobile devices.

You travel the world for these stories –, is there a big difference in the way the mobile phone helps the journalists to tell their stories?

The mobile phone has allowed journalism to become faster, more cost effective, intimate and diverse. With the democratisation of media and the dominance of social platforms, mobile phones allow journalists to report from anywhere, with the ability to go live with the tap of a button. It cuts out the need to have multiple cameras and people on the ground. This has been fundamental in cutting costs in a tough economic media landscape. It is also far more discreet and less invasive than a large broadcast camera, which allows people to feel more comfortable to share difficult stories, in the most intimate way.

The accessibility, intimacy and cost effectiveness of the mobile phone means that everyone with a mobile phone and a story to tell can share their stories. As journalists, this means we have access to more voices and more perspectives than ever before, which lends itself to more diverse narratives. Different countries have very different cultures around mobile phone filming. Germans, for example, tend to worry about privacy and dignity more than other places. We've found South African authorities and police to be quite hostile to our mobile journalism presence. Recently, a police officer there threatened to arrest me for filming. In America, everyone wants to be on camera!

What are the biggest problems they mobile journalists have to deal with?

Data access is still the biggest challenge. In India, for example, just 20% of the population are online. But it's still the biggest Facebook market on earth already! I'm in Palestine this week, where 3G has just been rolled out. The world is changing fast!

How important is the mobile phone for storytelling on a budget?

Mojo was a cost cutting exercise in 2008 when the recession hithit, and newsrooms needed to cut back. Today it's far more than that. It's the fastest, more intimate, more real and raw way to get stories. Reality is the new quality.

What response you get on those stories?

Our social media channels, where all our videos live, are growing in followers by 20% a month. We've found that stories produced on mobiles actually perform better for mobile users, because every consideration is for mobile optimization. When producing on a mobile, you start thinking about how the content is consumed on a mobile.

How do you see the future of MoJo and of Hashtagourstories?

From news gathering to publishing, the greatest competitive advantage is now a diversity of news, views and stories, of people. Mobile journalism allows us to do this, in the most cost effective and intimate way. More cameras, more angles, more perspectives, more truth. The future is not MoJos running around shooting stories, but using advanced AI to aggregate and verify user generated content from all over the world.

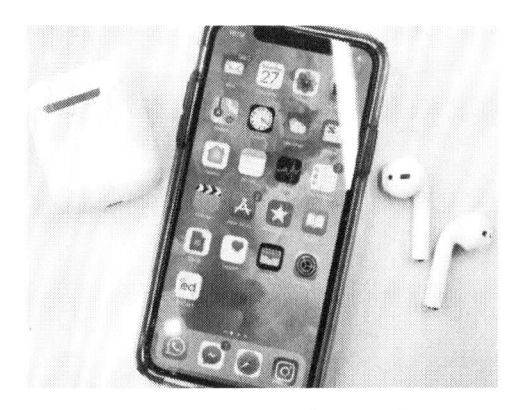

Simplistic - Sumaiya Omar´s Gear für "Hastag Our Stories".

9 360 degrees – Being on the move in all directions

Summary

Credibility, "showing the whole picture": shooting, editing, and publishing 360-degree videos. Which apps and which technology do you need for mobile production on the move? How does 360 degree storytelling work?

The usage of 360-degree material in journalism is still in its infancy. Until recently, omnidirectional photos and videos were neither produced nor could they be consumed in a tolerable quality. But this has changed rapidly: 360-degree cameras that shoot really good photos and acceptable videos are now available for less than 400 Euros. The products on the market are now aimed towards the broad masses of consumers and not towards specialised media. "360 degrees" has started its market growth from the bottom, starting with the customers and their photos of birthday parties, weddings and family vacations. The images are consumed on mobile phones that some people attach to "cardboards" or other frames for a better perception of the spatial impression. They also consume them with VR-glasses such as the "Oculus Rift", "Samsung 360 Gear" or "HTC Vive". Cardboards and VR-glasses narrow the visual field and reinforce the impression of being able to dive into and move around in another world – the "immersion" effect.

The game industry perfected immersion. Many gaming enthusiasts use glasses to dive into virtual reality (VR). "VR" offers more than 360-degree video (and much more than 360-degree photo): in a virtual room the user can move around freely – he can touch objects and lift them up (depending on the programming) – in short: he can interact. It is hard to predict, but it is highly unlikely that the use of VR-glasses will become a mass phenomenon. The use on moving smartphones, however, is already attracting an increasing number of users. 360 degree can easily be used where people are already consuming their news content (which is on the phone). In the 360-degree room, however, the viewer is tied to the position of the camera – he only sees the room from the position of the camera. He can look around in the image and he can also zoom in if there is a quality loss, but he cannot move around.

There are first attempts and projects in the area of VR-journalism – virtual scenarios that convey content: the "Wall Street Journal", for example, simulated a rollercoaster ride that illustrates the ups and downs of the stock market index NASDAQ. The US regional newspaper "Des Moines Register" did a VR-portrait of family life in Iowa in the past, present and future while the New York Times magazine programmed a tour of street art in Manhattan. But this is not what we want to talk about here: these projects don't have a lot to do with "mobile journalism". They are more an example of day- and week-long on-screen programming work.

360-degree videos are not virtual realities but the real, filmed image of our world – in a panoramic view, a filmed sphere in 360 degrees, horizontal and vertical, something like an image or video ball that can be looked at from within. This can be produced with little effort, on the move and mobile: you can take photos with the help of the corresponding app on the mobile phone and videos with small add-on cameras. Although the technical means have been available and also affordable for a while, many professional media outlets have not started to use 360-degree videos (and photos) for their purposes yet.

There are a few good examples by Ryot News: with "Welcome to Aleppo" the US-American start-up produced a 360-degree video from the Syrian city Aleppo and the streets that had been destroyed by war. A young woman's voice narrates the most recent history of the city. However, the handling of the archive material that Ryot integrated in the 360-degree video is slightly problematic since it destroys the immersion. The Dutch journalist Sander van Hoorn also took us to Aleppo with a 360-degree walk through the destroyed city.

Recently, the Huffington Post bought Ryot with the goal to equip all Huffington Post offices worldwide with 360-degree journalism – an indicator of how much the number of 360-degree videos in journalism is going to increase. Vice portrayed the "March of Millions" on December 13th, 2014 in Washington during which tens of thousands of people demanded that the police should disclose their mistakes during operations and take responsibility for them. The website Hongkongunrest.com is also impressive: it portrays the pro-democracy protests in Hong Kong in 2014 in 360 degree. The German BILD, which also pioneered in live streaming, sent their crisis reporter Paul Ronzheimer with a 360-degree camera on a refugee boat in the Mediterranean – the material conveys very intensively the cramped situation on the boat and the dangers of the passage.

The Guardian also worked on interesting experiments with 360-degree video – the very minimal project "6x9", for example, gives a view into a prison isolating cell. The audio effect of the Guardian project is also very impressive. It's usually an Achilles' heel of 360-degree video because the market for spherical sound is developing very slowly. This makes storytelling in 360 degree difficult: it is possible for the viewer to always change his viewpoint without any audio guidance that can be spatially perceived.

360-degree videos provide additional benefit. In my opinion, they are not going to replace linear television and online videos in the near future. But they can help to fulfil an important function in journalism: to cross borders. People are getting an immersive, intense insight into a world that would otherwise be closed to them – because it is not accessible to everyone (such as the control cabin of a port crane or group housing for refugees), because it is too dangerous (such as a war or crisis zone) or because there are social borders (such as apartments of people who are living in poverty).

Showing the full picture: many media are confronted with a credibility debate: "fake news" is what they hear and critics repeatedly question whether media shows "the full picture" – literally on television and online. But this question is also valid – metaphorically – for radio and print media. In fact, journalism is a selective process – to separate the important from the unimportant, to consider facts that are necessary for the report and to leave out redundant information. This selection is subject to certain objective criteria, such as the criteria of news value. A journalist who works thoroughly selects the defined criteria in a transparent way that is comprehensible for his audience. But there will always be areas for criticism regarding this selective process.

When after the attacks on the French satire magazine "Charlie Hebdo" hundreds of thousands demonstrated in Paris for tolerance and against terror, dozens of politicians also made their way to Paris. They also marched, but not at the head of the main demonstration as was suggested by initial reports and photos. The politicians met in a closed off side street and formed a separate protest march – due to security reasons. This was only shown in later reports. Here and in many other situations 360-degree images could make the creation process of a report more transparent: the audience can see with their own eyes what it really looks like on location – how much the work of journalists was restricted, for example, during President Obama's visit to the Hannover Messe in 2016. In a 360-degree video the viewer would not only see the waving Obama, but also the crowd of journalists penned behind the security barriers.

360-degree videos (and photos) can contribute to transparency and help media and their content to achieve more credibility. In addition, it also offers an opportunity to make journalistic content available to new target groups, such as gaming users. This group has already appreciated the equipment and the immersive reception situation. Yet, the use of VR and 360-degree image in journalism needs to happen in a responsible manner. The effect of a well-done immersion can be much stronger than that of a conventional video. This bears risks and opportunities at the same time: it is presumed that the danger of manipulating an audience is significantly higher in 360 degree / VR than it is in linear television. Michael Madary and Thomas K. Metziger developed an initial code of conduct for VR (see "Additional Resources" at the end of this chapter). This is what they have to say with regard to the journalistic use of VR: "We should not give the illusion that immersive journalism will tell the whole story about a complex situation."

There are also many practical questions that need to be answered, in particular with regard to the structure of 360-degree videos, the storytelling, the red thread as well as the use of audio. But there are many arguments speaking for a closer evaluation of both the opportunities as well as the limitations of 360-degree videos. In other words: to test the technology in different situations and scenarios. This is easy because the required technology is inexpensive (if you refrain from using complex multiple camera constructions and if you can accept a lower image quality) and Facebook and YouTube already provide 360-degree players on the internet (if not provided for the website by your own media corporation). Yes, 360 degree is also a hype. But the new medium has the potential to find a permanent place in the journalistic landscape – at least in some areas.

9.1 360 Degree – With an App

A single app is more than enough: without any additional hardware you can now produce a 360-degree photo. A spontaneous 360-degree photo is now possible whenever there is a relevant topic or location. You will need several minutes for the production and the lighting situation needs to be well-balanced so that all parts of the 360-degree photo are visible. Android, iOS and Windows offer the respective apps. For Android, for example, the generic camera app of certain phones that offers the "Photo Sphere" mode already helps to create 360-degree images. The app "Panorama 360" (fig. 09-01) also delivers good results: it starts with a few informative boards before users log in with their Facebook or Google+ account or e-mail address. A test version is also available without a login. The results are acceptable, but not really breath-taking.

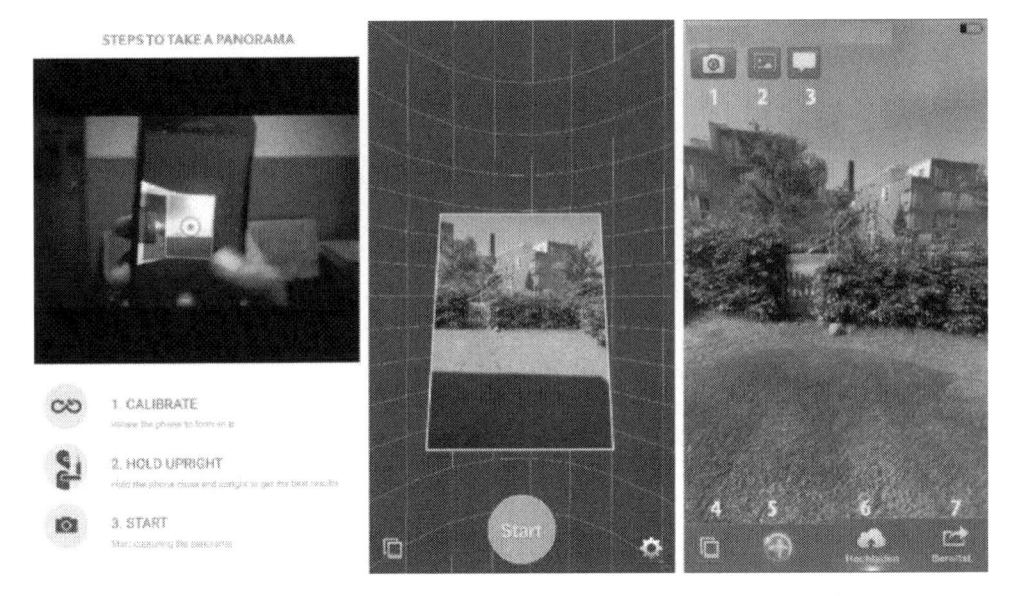

Figure 09-01, 02, 03

In addition, the apps "Photosynth" (also available for Windows phones) and "360 Panorama" (iOS only) also offer good results. For the recording "360 Panorama" displays a grey-black grid on which the partial images can be placed one by one (fig. 09-02). The app places most photos around the vertical axis for the panoramic view; the ground and sky fill relatively quickly. The finished panorama can be viewed in the app (fig. 09-03). A new image is captured with a tap on the camera icon (1). The photo icon switches between the different representations – the 360-degree view and the stereographic, compressed panorama image (very impressive). You can add a title with the speech bubble (3). The image series (4) opens the overview of the 360-degree panoramas that were already taken and whose representation can be varied with the arrow icons (5). You can upload the images to the platform of the app (6), make them available for email distribution or for usage in your own gallery (7).

The images can be published on their platforms that also support the view of 360-degree photos. On the one hand, the apps themselves offer such platforms to which you can then link from Twitter or Facebook. But Facebook itself also presents 360-degree photos (in certain formats). Additionally, the app Thinglink (see chapter 8.2.) offers the possibility to upload 360-degree photos and to add text and audio notes.

9.2 360 Degree – With a Camera

360-degree cameras record panorama videos – with a simple touch of a button. In addition, they also deliver photos with a much better quality than the above-mentioned apps. The reason? They don't "stitch together" dozens of photos but they piece together two to four shots taken by very wide-angle lenses that harmonize with each other. Over the past two to three years the cameras have become much smaller and better. The first models offer a resolution of 2K (or even 4K) for less than 500 Euro – the market shows a rapid development. Since this book describes "mobile journalism" we will concentrate on the smaller, less expensive cameras that can be controlled with a smartphone and whose material can be directly published to different platforms via a smartphone. There's no limit: the construction with six action cameras whose shots can be put together at a later stage is only the beginning. At the top it is Nokia's Ozo camera for approx. 60,000 US Dollars that completes the segment.

The driving forces behind the development of 360-degree cameras are right now the smartphone producers who expand their product portfolio. At the "Mobile World Congress" in Barcelona in 2016 both LG as well as Samsung presented their 360-degree cameras. The LG360Cam (fig. 09-04) is very similar to the Theta S, a camera launched by the camera manufacturer Ricoh that a few German news media outlets used for their first attempts with 360-degree videos. Two fisheye lenses portray a 360-degree sphere that is directly "stitched" into the camera itself. This results in a fast and easy production of the videos. Both cameras provide a good photo resolution. The video quality, however, ranges between Full HD and 2K – in relation to the entire sphere. Since only parts can be seen if played on the smartphone, the VR-glasses or a desktop computer (depending on the player, a 40 degree detail of the 360-degree sphere), the visible resolution is reduced to significantly less than HD. This is still acceptable for mobile use. In this respect, the cameras work well in short projects that add to a program. However, the material produced is not good enough for the perfect immersion with VR-glasses.

Figure 09-04, 05 LG360 Cam (left); Samsung Gear 360 (right)

A slightly better solution is offered by the Samsung-Gear-360 camera (fig. 09-05) with 3840 x 1920 pixels. When it launched, however, it could only be used with Samsung mobile phones. The manufacturer has promised a roll-out to other models. There are several other cameras that were partly supported by crowdfunding campaigns. One of them is the Giroptic 360Cam: it doesn't produce a real 360-degree sphere but leaves out an area on the ground. However, this is often unnecessary anyway since this is where the camera is usually mounted to a tripod. Further models are the 360Fly camera, the slightly bigger ALLiecam, whose manufacturer does business in the home surveillance industry, as well as more expensive models by Kodak (the combination of two action cameras with subsequent stitching). The "insta360 Nano Compact Mini" camera can be directly attached to the iPhone and produces at least a 3K sphere.

A very well working system was developped around the "Insta360" brand: The cameras allow livestreaming with certain apps and offer easy stitching on the phone. There are Insta-models that directly connect to and sit on your iPhone via lightning adapter. There is another version that connects via USB to Android models. Insta seems to have understood best the demands of a smartphone driven market for instant 360 spheres while developing models with a quality as is in most cases satisfying even for quick, professional use.

Most cameras have problems with the audio recording: Theta S or LG360Cam record audio one-dimensional so that the audio impression does not support the spatial perception of the image. And it neither supports the viewer's orientation through sound in a 360-degree sphere. The Samsung-Gear-360 is equipped with two microphones, but only manages stereo recordings without any spatial effect. Sennheiser is currently developing a small full-sphere / ambisonic microphone that can record spatial sound impressions and the latest Theta camera, the Theta V, has four microphones for a more realistic 360 audio recording.

The second problem for 360-degree audio, however, is playback: if you consume short informative content in 360 degree on your mobile phone, you will often not hear any audio at all. And if you do, I would assume that you don't have your expensive headphone on hand that would be able to play back 360-degree audio – if, and only if, the player in use would support spatial sound. In addition, not all players support spherical audio codecs that can be transported in the common video containers (such as the MP4 format). Sennheiser has recently developped a relatively affordable solution to capture 360 audio with its Ambeo Smart Headset (see chapter 3.3).

9.3 360 Degree: Filming and Storytelling

How to tell a story in 360 degree is a hotly debated topic. "What's your story?" As always, good content sells itself: images that a user would otherwise not be able to experience (from war or crisis zones, for example) are frequently requested. 360-degree actions videos of action sports topics are popular. The NDR evening show Das!, for example, invited a kite surfer to surf through Icelandic icebergs. At the NDR we also made several attempts to provide a "behind-the-scenes"-look of our daily media business: What does the studio look like? How do we create a news show? This is what users are interested in. Since in today's journalism 360-degree videos from "mobile production" are mainly consumed on smartphones and not with 360-degree glasses and complex equipment, the length should also be carefully considered. Many producers have made positive experiences with shorter films that are not longer than three minutes.

Despite the complex production process, ARTE made a seven minute video that features an Arctic documentation by the German-Canadian filmmaker Thomas Wallner (polarsea360.com). At his Canadian company "Deep Inc", Wallner has been working on storytelling in 360-degree for a long time. He developed his own player that allows the panoramic view whenever landscapes, scenes, and images are visible. When a protagonist is speaking (in Wallner's Arctic documentary an Inuit, for example), Wallner dismisses the 360-degree impression and directs the viewer closer to the protagonist – in a conventional way. This is an interesting approach that guides the viewer within a 360-degree experience although the immersive impression is disrupted from time to time.

Thomas Wallner talked about the difficulties of the film shootings at a panel discussion: he and his team set up the camera and then quickly went into hiding since there is no "behind the camera" when it comes to 360-degree videos. From a technical point of view this is only possible because most cameras can be operated remotely or simply with a touch of a button (and then: hide!). Sarah Redohl, who has been working on several 360-degree projects at the Missouri School of Journalism, sees this as a dilemma: Is it appropriate for the crew to hide – or should a team be visible to make the filming conditions transparent? Sarah Jones, who teaches journalism at the Coventry University in Great Britain, has also worked intensively with VR. In her opinion, a reporter who is visible in an image and who explains the content of the said image does not only disrupt the immersive experience, but is a distraction – the reporter deprives the 360-degree video of its core, i.e. of the immersive experience that results in the viewer being alone in an unfamiliar environment.

Without a reporter in the image it's going to be difficult to guide the viewers: where should they look? Will it be possible to communicate content if each viewer looks around freely? Maybe they miss important developments in the image because they are looking in the "wrong" direction. Above, I described the approach taken by Ryot News – protagonists report out of the off in the form of an original sound bite. This might work in calm, documentary-style sections. In other cases, audio can be ignored (at least with regard to productions with "smaller" cameras) as a guiding element, as described above. So far spherical sound has neither been recorded nor reproduced satisfactorily.

Special characteristics of 360-degree films

1. Location of the camera – rather fixed, rarely moving
2. Duration of shot – long (often 30 seconds and more)
3. Cut sequence – rather calm, only a few cuts
4. Overall length – rather short, up to 3 minutes
5. Material from the archives – not recommended since it disrupts the immersive impression

The position of the camera plays an important role: something must be "visible" in all directions. Ideally, the full 360-degree sphere contains information that contributes to the content of the film. This is why the camera is usually positioned in the middle of the action, and not with the back to the wall or at the plot periphery (fig. 09-06). In addition, the camera remains in that set-up for a longer time period. It won't happen often that a reporter will hold the camera in his hand and move around. If the reporter was moving, there wouldn't be enough time for the viewer to move in the image. The walking motion would also result in an extremely unsteady image. For the viewer, this is almost unbearable since he doesn't see this "shaky image" from a safe distance on TV. Instead the viewer has entered a completely new world and is now moving around in the same unsteady environment as the camera.

Figure 09-06 Small camera with omnidirectional view: The Ricoh Theta S does not look like a camera but sees everything.

The privacy of the people in the image needs particular attention at a 360-degree film shooting. Now it's no longer a team with conventional TV equipment that films in a single direction. This also means that people cannot only take notice of the filming, but they could oppose it where necessary or leave the setting completely. The 360-degree film is created with a camera that is not recognized as such by many people, but which records them in every corner of the room or place. In this respect, journalists should carefully consider how close uninvolved parties are allowed to get and whether they need to be informed about the journalists' work.

The length of a shot also differs from "traditional" non-immersive film: In order for a viewer to be able to look around an image and see all the details in 360 degree, the scene needs to be shown for a long time – for at least 30 seconds in the majority of cases. This is why a 360-degree video can be characterised by a calm cutting sequence – a three-minute clip might only feature five to eight different shots. In addition, a 360-degree film will usually not use any archive material because the change would destroy the immersive impression.

9.4 Publishing 360 Degree

The editing of 360-degree videos generally takes place in the apps that come with the camera. The Theta S (fig. 09-07) offers, for example, the option to publish material directly from the app to the Theta-platform from where the video can be shared to Facebook or Twitter. The "Samsung 360 Gear" offers a similar service. However, you might be better off to publish your filmed material directly on your own platforms or channels, such as YouTube or Facebook. In order to do that, you need to download the material from the camera and edit it frequently.

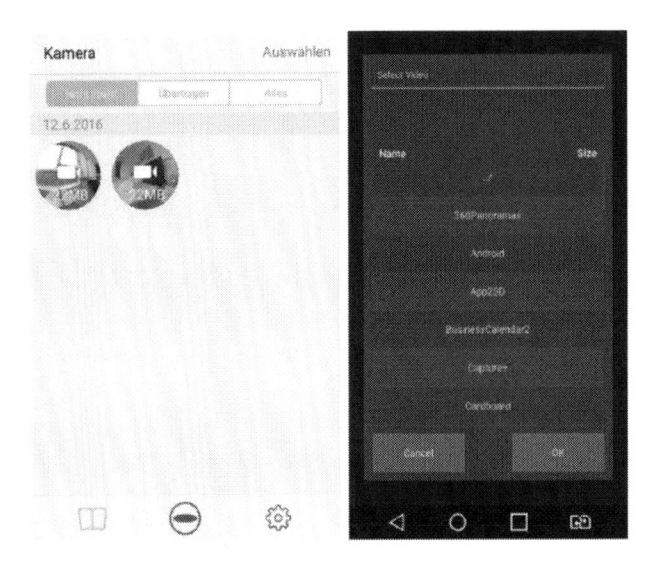

Figure 09-07, 08

During the download from the camera the material is often converted so that it can be played out in the MP4 format that many editing programs and players understand. Further editing can be carried out with many programs, such as Premiere Pro, which provides good features for 360-degree videos. Windows MovieMaker can also cut spherical MP4-material even though its representation is distorted during editing. If you only want to add an audio track to the video, Movie Maker is more than sufficient. After the editing process the material will be uploaded to a video portal – but not all platforms can be used.

360-degree videos need a player that can communicate the spherical impression, i.e. a player that "understands" the 360-degree image. These players are integrated into YouTube,

Vimeo and Facebook. During the upload it is crucial to add the relevant metadata to the 360-degree videos which function like a door key. If an MP4-file is equipped with this door key, YouTube, Vimeo and Facebook know that their player needs to represent the video in 360 degree. After you've completed the editing process, you need to add the metadata once to the MP4-file. On the desktop computer this is provided by the free app "360 Video Metadata".

The editing of 360-degree videos on the smartphone itself, however, is still in its infancy. But it is possible to completely edit a video on the smartphone: after the video was filmed with the 360-degree camera, it is transferred to the smartphone. It is then converted with an app and saved to the photo gallery. Now you can edit it, with "PowerDirector", for example (see chapter 6.3.) or Kinemaster. The finished film will be played out once again and metadata needs to be added. On Android and iPhone models you can download the app "Vrfix" which was programmed by Paul Gailey – a dedicated "Mobile Journalist". However, this program is still rather complicated and needs improvement (fig. 09-08).

Additional Resources

Vice. "Marsch den Millionen". Accessed June, 10th 2016:https://news.vice.com/article/chris-milk-spike-jonze-and-vice-news-bring-the-first-ever-virtual-reality-newscast-to-sundance

BILD. 360-Grad-Video von einem Flüchtlingsboot im Mittelmeer. Accessed June, 10th 2016:http://www.bild.de/politik/ausland/fluechtlingskrise/das-dramatische-360-grad-video-von-der-fluechtlingsrettung-44571444.bild.html

Ryot News. "Welcome to Aleppo". Accessed June, 10th 2016: https://www.youtube.com/watch?v=Nxxb_7wzvJI

Immersiv.ly. "Hongkong Unrest". Accessed June, 10th 2016: http://www.hongkongunrest.com

Wall Street Journal. "Is the Nasdaq in another Bubble?" Accessed June, 10th 2016:http://graphics.wsj.com/3d-nasdaq/

New York Times Mag. "Walking News York". Accessed June, 10th 2016:http://vrse.com/watch/nyt-mag-vr-walking-new-york/

Des Moines Register. „"Harvest of change". Accessed June, 10th 2016:http://www.desmoinesregister.com/pages/interactives/harvest-of-change/

The Guardian. "6 x 9: A Virtual Experience of Solitary Confinement". Accessed June, 10th 2016:http://www.theguardian.com/world/ng-interactive/2016/apr/27/6x9-a-virtual-experience-of-solitary-confinement

Migielicz, Geri & Zacharia, Janine. Stanford Journalism Program's guide to using virtual reality for storytelling — dos & don'ts. Accessed Septembre, 4th, 2016.https://medium.com/@StanfordJournalism/stanford-journalism-programs-guide-to-using-virtual-reality-for-storytelling-dos-don-ts-f6ca15c7ef3c#.1hzen8v6p

Madary, Michael & Metziger, Thomas K. "Real Virtuality: A Code of Ethical Conduct. Recommendations for Good Scientific Practice and the Consumers of VR-Technology". In: Frontiers in Robotics and AI. Accessed October, 26th, 2016:http://journal.frontiersin.org/article/10.3389/frobt.2016.00003/full#

Interview with Martin Heller: 360 Degrees - "The viewer gets more autonomy."

> Martin Heller works as a journalist and reporter in Berlin. He is the founder of "IntoVR", a company that develops 360 degree and VR-formats. He also manages video innovation for the WeltN24 media group at the Axel Springer Publishing House. He started the Welt VJ team and co-developed new formats for "mobile journalism".(Picture © Martin Heller / IntoVR.de)
>
> Twitter:@Ma_Heller

Why are 360-degree videos and VR even interesting in journalism?

VR is becoming more important in the future. For journalisms it is always better to be on the "inside" and not on the "outside". More and more people will have VR-glasses at home – it's hard for me to say whether this will happen in a year, in three years or in five years. They are going to consume more and more content on these glasses: games, entertainment, communication. Journalistic content can't be missing: journalism needs to be present on all platforms of distribution. The word "empathy machine" – an expression that has been quoted far too frequently – is really true: people get closer to the stories because they are practically part of the stories. It is possible for us to take people to places where they might not be otherwise. That's my point of view. We also want to tell stories about people, but it's always the location that is absolutely crucial. Watching 360-degree content on your phone or desktop computer is fun and a good introduction to the form. This already impresses many people, but the medium only develops its full potential on the VR-glasses.

Will 360 degree help the media in the debates about credibility and authenticity, keyword: "fake news" or "Lügenpresse"?

Definitely. I think I'm sure that VR will be able to increase credibility in journalism and it actually does so. The audience repeatedly reacts by telling us: "It's great that we can also see the other side." This is similar to live streaming: 360 degree is also a very honest medium because we show the complete picture in its full entirety. As journalists, we are withdrawing from the scene: we decide the position and the standpoint of the viewer, but it's up to the viewer to decide what he actually looks at and how long he looks at something. This means that we direct the view much less than in conventional stories. The viewer gets more autonomy / self-responsibility.

What does it mean for storytelling if we direct the viewer less? How can we structure and narrate stories if our viewers are more or less able to look everywhere?

On the one hand, the viewers need a lot more time. A cut can't be three or five seconds long; it needs to be 12 to 30 seconds long. This also means: we need to think more carefully about the location of the image; we need to plan much more precisely. A 360-degree shot could be compared to a theatre, for example. Here you plan the stage setting, you open and close the curtain and have a different stage setting afterwards. I can't direct the viewer's attention with camera work or cuts, but only by selecting locations and organize something or let something happen within these locations.

There are tricks to direct the viewers' attention a little bit, for example by movement within an image: if a person who is very present moves in an image, the majority of the viewers will follow that person with their eyes. The moment a scene ends and the next episode begins, I can also guess where the majority of viewers are looking right now. I can also use sound: I'm standing in a prison cell and a door is slammed with a loud noise. I can now be sure that the viewer looks in the direction of the door. For spherical audio I need devices that can record it. And then the viewers also have to able to play the audio.

In addition, as an editor I can also work with speaker text – another way to direct the viewer's attention. But in the end the viewer is given total freedom to look where he wants to look. That's why many people are saying after watching a 360-degree-film that they could re-watch the film right away – there are so many things they haven't seen yet.

What's the role of the reporter in 360-degree-recordings? Is he part of the picture or should he go into hiding?

I already tried to be in the picture and to report as a reporter by speaking directly to the camera. But I don't think that this is the purest form of VR-journalism. Why? In a conventional report the reporter is the viewer's representative on location, gathering impressions and passing them on. In VR, however, we take the viewer on location. So the reporter does not need to play a role, too. My clear advice for almost any situation: the reporters should withdraw to a virtual "hiding place". But there are situations in which the camera cannot be left alone.

Spherical audio is still a considerable challenge, with regard to recording as well as playback. What is your advice regarding audio recording?

I usually hide a small audio recording device in the room or on the set. Why? Because the camera sound is often not good enough. Let's go back to our prison cell example: you could hide the recording device under the bed or behind the toilet. The sound has to be right so that the immersion is not destroyed. The sound does not have to work spatially, though this would be perfect. Sound is not easy. It's a challenge but I think right now we need to work with small audio recording devices that we try to hide.

This book mainly deals with "mobile journalism", i.e. the uncomplicated shoot and material that can be uploaded quickly with the smartphone. So the focus is on smaller cameras such as the Theta S or the Samsung 360. What's your opinion: are these cameras useful?

I wouldn't recommend the Ricoh Theta S as long as it only offers a "Full HD" resolution. With other simple cameras that provide 4K or almost 4K it is possible to create content that works on a website or on a social medium. But you won't win a 360-degree video award with these cameras. I think you can produce 360-degree videos on the side if you have the necessary routine. During the refugee crisis, for example, I sent a reporter to the Balkan region. She mainly created 360-degree videos as well as livestreams and little mobile videos with the smartphone. She delivered high quality material in all disciplines – but only because she didn't do it for the first time. Which means: if you only shoot a 360-degree video as a by-product every 6 months, I usually don't get the quality I expect.

What quality do you expect?

The most important aspect is a high resolution – 4K in the equirectangular panoramic view. The transitions between the different lenses have to be seamless. And the camera has to stand perfectly still, generally mounted to a tripod. Movements might be possible if the viewer understands them: the trip by boat, by car or by scooter, for example. I organise productions in such a way that they allow a good experience on VR-glasses, such as the Samsung Gear VR. At workshops I usually tell my participants: "Imagine that the camera is your viewer's head. This is how careful you have to be with your camera."

In the 80s some of us used cardboard glasses with green and red lenses. Yet this marvellous form of 3D-televison didn't prevail. Why should VR prevail which needs much more elaborate technology in production as well as consumption?

This is a matter of time and not a question of whether VR will prevail or not. The difference to the hype around 3D-television is enormous. Because we are now dealing with a new level of evolution. At first, we saw moving images from a far away distance, surrounded by a lot of other people: in the movie theatre. Then, the moving image entered our homes and our family circle: the TV. Now the TV is in the hands of individuals: the smartphone. The next step of the evolution is that the moving image moves to our eyes. The viewer jumps into the moving image. This elementary level of the evolution is going to happen, no matter what. The only question is whether this will happen in three, five or in ten years. 360-degree is going to be a perfectly normal component of the media mix, as are other forms such as livestreaming. I believe that this is going to be one of many disciplines that we should neither overrate nor underestimate.

Martin Heller's Equipment: light tripod ("as narrow as possible so that the legs don't cover too much of the image" – using a tripod is obligatory"), multiple USB connector ("you need to repeatedly recharge not only your camera when you are on the go"), Freedom360-Mount with six "GoPro Hero 4 Black Edition"-action cameras ("if the setting is not too narrow, I will rely on these; the image quality is amazing – with a screwdriver, of course, so that I can change the batteries"), Kodak SP 360 Mount (also works in narrower spaces). Extra batteries, Sennheiser EW 100 radio path with clip-on microphone, Zoom

H2N audio recorder ("because it is rather small and is easy to hide during a video recording"), back-to-back camera set based on GoPro cameras with "Entaniya 250" extreme wide angle lenses ("the wide viewing angle during filming offers more flexibility, especially during editing. Don't forget the two caps to protect the two attached lenses"), a smartphone ("to review the images in an app or for photos used as thumbnails / preview images"). (Picture © Martin Heller / IntoVR.de)

The Authors

First of all, the authors would like to thank the international mobile journalism community which is evolving around the Facebook group "Mobile Journalism Community". Many of you have inspired us with your ideas, solutions and answers to questions. Glen B. Mulcahy, who gratiously contributed the introduction to this book, founded the "Mobile Journalism Conference" and the mentioned Facebook group. Other mobile journalists whom we are grateful to are Marc B. Settle, Philip Bromwell, Mike Castellucci, Nick Garnett, Philipp Weber, Sumaiya Omar and Martin Heller who agreed to be interviewed for this book. We also thank other mobile journalists like Corinne Podger, Pipo Serrano, Florian Reichert, Bianca-Maria Rathay, John Inge Johansen, Mark Egan, Guillaume Kuster and all the colleagues we have forgotten for their inspiration. This book represents more what we learned from you than what we knew ourselves.

Björn Staschen is a staff reporter with NDR / ARD German Television. He is head of NDR´s „NextNewsLab" and has been leading NDR´s innovation in Mobile Journalism for over three years now. He has trained colleagues at NDR, students, corporate professionals and journalists abroad (in own seminars and with BBC Media Action). He regularly speaks at conferences, including Mojocon, re.publika and others. He wrote the German textbook „Mobiler Journalismus" - the basis for this English edition. Björn is a trained Video Journalists and has worked as foreign correspondent for ARD German TV in London. He lives with his wife and three children in Hamburg, Germany.

http://www.bjoernsta.de

Twitter: @bjoernsta

Wytse Vellinga is an international Video and Multimedia Storytelling trainer from the Netherlands. He works for Dutch broadcasting company Omrop Fryslân as a Mobile journalist making daily news reports with Android, iOS and Windows Phones. He also works as a MoJo expert for Thomson Foundation in London and the European organisation of regional broadcasters Circom-Regional. He also has his own company for teaching people and companies how to tell their story using their Mobile Phones.

http://mobile-storytelling.com/

Twitter:@wytsevellinga

Translation

Tina Busch is a freelance English language expert who earns her living with English training for adults, translating and editing. She graduated from the Technical University of Braunschweig with a PhD in English Linguistics. After living in the United States for 5 years, she now calls Burghausen, Germany her home town.

http://www.tinabusch.com

Twitter:@busch_tina

Printed in Great Britain
by Amazon